TEACHING
1 & 2 THESSALONIANS

The Teaching series is a great resource for Bible study leaders and pastors, indeed for any Christian who wants to understand their Bible better.

Mark Dever
Senior Pastor of Capitol Hill Baptist Church and
President of 9Marks, Washington, DC

The task of moving from the text of Scripture to clear and faithful exposition is challenging. This series of excellent guides aims to help the Bible teacher to observe what is there in the text, and prepare to convey its significance to contemporary hearers. In this way these volumes often do more than the weightier technical commentaries. It is like having the guidance of an experienced coach in the wonderful work of rightly handling the word of truth.

John Woodhouse
Retired Principal,
Moore College, Sydney, Australia

North India desperately needs men and women who will preach and teach the Bible faithfully and PT's Teaching series is of great value in encouraging them to do just that. They are just what we need. We have found the books of great help in English and eagerly anticipate the day when they will be available in Hindi also.

Isaac Shaw
Executive Director,
Delhi Bible Institute

This teaching series, written by skilled and trustworthy students of God's Word, helps us to understand the Bible, believe it and obey it. I commend it to all Bible readers, but especially those whose task it is to teach the inspired Word of God.

Peter Jensen
Former Archbishop of Sydney

TEACHING
1 & 2 THESSALONIANS

From text to message

ANGUS MACLEAY

SERIES EDITORS: DAVID JACKMAN & ADRIAN REYNOLDS

PT RESOURCES
CHRISTIAN
FOCUS

Unless otherwise indicated, all Scripture quotations are taken from the *Holy Bible, New International Version*. Copyright © 1973, 1978, 1984 by International Bible Society. Used by permission of Hodder & Stoughton Publishers, a member of the Hodder Headline Group. All rights reserved. 'NIV' is a registered trademark of International Bible Society. UK trademark number 1448790.

Scripture quotations marked ESV are taken from *The Holy Bible, English Standard Version*. Copyright © 2001 by Crossway Bibles, a publishing ministry of Good News Publishers. Used by permission. All rights reserved.

Copyright © Proclamation Trust Resources 2014

ISBN 978-1-78191-325-3

10 9 8 7 6 5 4 3 2 1

Published in 2014
by
Christian Focus Publications Ltd.,
Geanies House, Fearn, Ross-shire,
IV20 1TW, Scotland, Great Britain
with
Proclamation Trust Resources,
Willcox House, 140-148 Borough High Street,
London, SE1 1LB, England, Great Britain.
www.proctrust.org.uk

www.christianfocus.com

Cover design by DUFI-ART.com

Printed by
Nørhaven, Denmark

All rights reserved. No part of this publication may be reproduced, stored in a retrieval system, or transmitted, in any form, by any means, electronic, mechanical, photocopying, recording or otherwise without the prior permission of the publisher or a licence permitting restricted copying. In the U.K. such licences are issued by the Copyright Licensing Agency, Saffron House, 6-10 Kirby Street, London, EC1 8TS www.cla.co.uk.

Contents

Series Preface... 7
Author's Preface 9
How to Use this Book... 11

Part One: Introducing 1 Thessalonians
1. Getting our bearings in 1 Thessalonians...................... 17
2. Why we should preach and teach 1 Thessalonians..... 25
3. Preaching and Teaching 1 Thessalonians..................... 29

Part Two: Teaching 1 Thessalonians
1. A young church under pressure (1:1-3 and 5:23-28).. 35
2. Genuine Conversion to Christ (1:4-10) 47
3. Genuine Christian ministry (2:1-12)............................ 67
4. The Word and the World (2:13-16) 87
5. The heartbeat of Christian ministry (2:17–3:10) 101
6. A prayer for growth (3:10-13) 121
7. Pleasing God through holy living (4:1-8).................. 135
8. Pleasing God through loving others (4:9-12) 153
9. Rekindling hope (4:13-18).. 167
10. Living in the light of the return of Christ (5:1-11) .. 185
11. Paul's vision for the church (5:12-28) 203

Part Three: Introducing 2 Thessalonians
1. Getting our bearings in 2 Thessalonians..................... 225
2. Why we should preach and teach 2 Thessalonians... 233
3. Ideas for preaching and teaching a series on this book....237

Part Four: Teaching 2 Thessalonians
1. Bringing hope and purpose to God's people – an overview of 2 Thessalonians (1:1, 2; 2:16, 17 and 3:16-18).......... 243
2. The glory of Christ (1:3-12) 257
3. Hold on to the truth! (2:1-15).....................................279
4. The Progress of the Word of the Lord (3:1-5) 305
5. The Application of the Word of the Lord (3:6-15)..321

Further Reading..339
PT Resources 343

Series Preface

Paul's two letters to the Christians in Thessalonica are amongst the shortest of his epistles. Yet their length belies their importance as here we see Paul the loving teacher writing out of concern for a congregation he planted but barely knew. It's not surprising, therefore, to discover warm teaching on fundamental issues – especially to do with growing and living as believers in the Lord Jesus Christ. Thus, these are good books for churches to study whatever their maturity.

The introductory section contains basic 'navigation' material to get you into the text of the letters, covering aspects like structure and planning a preaching series. Each of the epistles (1 and 2 Thessalonians) has a separate introductory section. The 'meat' of the book then works systematically through the major sections of the letters, suggesting preaching and teaching units, including ideas for sermons and questions for Bible studies. These are not there to take the hard work out of preparation, but as a starting point to get you thinking about how to teach the material or prepare a Bible study.

Teaching 1 and 2 Thessalonians brings the number of published volumes in this series to fourteen. We are encouraged at how the series is developing and the positive comments from people that really matter – those working hard in Christian ministry.

Our thanks must go to Celia Reynolds and Crystal Williams for help in proofreading, checking references and making amendments. As ever, our warm gratitude goes to the team at Christian Focus for their committed partnership in this project.

David Jackman & Adrian Reynolds
Series Editors
London 2014

Author's Preface

One of the phrases I remember hearing many years ago at an early Proclamation Trust Preachers' Conference was that we don't need to try to make the Bible relevant – it is relevant! This maxim has been proved true time and time again as I have wrestled with the text of Scripture in preparation for preaching in the local church where I serve. As I have read and pondered over texts written almost two thousand years ago, I have been constantly surprised by their striking relevance to issues facing the twenty-first-century church.

I have found working on 1 and 2 Thessalonians in the last three years to be no exception. In a day when church planting is back in fashion, here is Paul speaking to a newly planted fellowship. In a day when Christians in the West are finding themselves under growing pressure from the surrounding culture, here is Paul encouraging a church facing strong opposition. In a day when we as Christians have not been distinguishing ourselves by our radical holiness, here is Paul encouraging the church not to be complacent. In a day when we as Christians are shaped so much by the norms of society and its values, here is Paul constantly reminding the church of the role of future hope in making an impact on the daily life of each believer.

It is a privilege to serve at St. Nicholas Parish Church in Sevenoaks where I have been able to preach through 1 and 2 Thessalonians, both from the pulpit and in a number of other settings. The opportunity to 'inhabit' a book of the Bible is enormously helpful and has been aided by the generosity of the church family in providing me with space for reading, study and writing.

I am one of a diminishing group of people who write things out in longhand using a pencil and so I am extremely grateful for the skills of Melita Rozario and Lis Lidbetter in our church office in deciphering my handwriting and producing an electronic manuscript. My thanks also go to the team at Proclamation Trust for all their assistance. In particular, I am grateful for the tireless work of Adrian Reynolds and for his personal support, interest and encouragement which have been much valued.

My wife, Sue, has been a constant encourager to me throughout my ministry and she has particularly helped to enable this book to see the light of day. She has given me all the support I have needed, especially when the task has seemed too much amidst all the other competing demands of a busy ministry.

My prayer is that this book would help preachers and all who handle God's Word to see more clearly the treasures within 1 and 2 Thessalonians, so that they can be better equipped to preach God's Word. As a result, my hope is that their hearers will, like the Thessalonians, accept it not as the word of man, but as it actually is, the Word of God (1 Thess. 2:13).

Angus MacLeay
February 2014

How to Use this Book

This book aims to help the preacher or teacher understand the central aim and purpose of the text, in order to preach or teach it to others. Unlike a commentary, therefore, it does not go into great exegetical detail. Instead it helps us to engage with the themes of 1 and 2 Thessalonians, to keep the big picture in mind, and to think about how to present it to our hearers.

Parts One and Three ('Introducing 1 Thessalonians' and 'Introducing 2 Thessalonians') examine the books' themes and structure. This material is crucial to our understanding the books, which in turn will shape the way we preach each section to our congregations. As a preliminary to the rest of the book, these introductory sections divide the letters into manageable units.

Parts Two and Four contain separate chapters on each preaching unit considered in Parts One and Three. The structure of each chapter is the same: it begins with a brief introduction to the unit followed by a section headed 'Listening to the text'. This section outlines the structure and context of the unit and takes the reader through a section-by-section analysis of the text. All good biblical preaching begins with careful, detailed listening to the text and this is true of Paul's letters as much as any other book.

Each chapter then continues with a section called 'From text to message'. This suggests a main theme and aim for each preaching unit (including how the unit relates to the overall theme of the book) and then some possible sermon outlines. These suggestions are nothing more than that – suggestions designed to help the preacher think about his own division of the text and the structure of the sermon. Every preacher should construct his own outlines, because they need to flow from our personal encounter with God in the text. Downloading other people's sermons or trying to breathe life into someone else's outlines are strategies doomed to failure. They may produce a reasonable talk, but in the long term, they are disastrous to the preacher himself since he needs to live in the Word and the Word to live in him, if he is to speak from the heart of God to the hearts of his congregation. However, these sections provide a few very basic ideas about how an outline on some of these passages might shape up. There are also some helpful bullet points on possible lines of application.

Each chapter concludes with some suggested questions for a group Bible Study split into two types: questions to help *understand* the passage and questions to help *apply* the passage. Not all the questions would be needed for a study, but they give some ideas for those who are planning a study series.

How to Use this Book

The aim of good questions is always to drive the group into the text, to explore and understand its meaning more fully. This keeps the focus on Scripture and reduces speculation and the mere exchange of opinions. Remember the key issues are always, 'What does the text say?' and then 'What does it mean?' Avoid the 'What does it mean to you?' type of question. It is much better to discuss the application more generally and personally after everyone understands the intended meaning, so that the Bible really is in the driving-seat of the study, not the participants' opinions, prejudices or experiences! These studies will be especially useful in those churches where Bible Study groups are able to study the book at the same time as it is preached. This allows small groups to drive home understanding, and especially application, in the week after the sermon has been preached, ensuring it is applied to the daily lives of the congregation.

I.

Introducing 1 Thessalonians

I.

GETTING OUR BEARINGS IN
1 THESSALONIANS

Introduction

The story of 1 and 2 Thessalonians begins with Paul's second missionary journey in A.D. 49. The initial purpose of that trip was for Paul and Barnabas to revisit the places where they had originally travelled in modern-day Turkey. However, due to an argument concerning the suitability of taking John Mark with them again (due to his early departure on the previous journey), Barnabas took John Mark to Cyprus whilst Paul chose Silas as his companion to revisit the churches that had been recently planted (Acts 15:36-41). Paul soon added Timothy to this team when he arrived in Lystra (Acts 16:1-5) and it would be this group of Paul, Silas and Timothy who would be involved in establishing the church in due course in Thessalonica (1 Thess. 1:1).

As Paul is gathering his team, he is still in Asia and it is only when he has a vision of a Macedonian pleading with him to come over and help (Acts 16:9) that he responds by setting out to sea in order to arrive in modern-day Greece. The area he arrived in was the long coastal strip which formed part of the region of Macedonia, which included such cities as Philippi (Acts 16:11-40) and Thessalonica (Acts 17:1-9). Following these visits, they then headed south and included the major cities of Athens and Corinth in their itinerary before eventually returning to Caesarea and Antioch to conclude the missionary journey (Acts 18:22).

Returning to Luke's account in Acts of the time spent in Thessalonica, we can immediately see that it corroborates what Paul says in 1 Thessalonians 2:2. The visit to Thessalonica followed a bruising time in Philippi where Paul and Silas had experienced imprisonment, though at the same time the gospel had flourished. On arriving in Thessalonica, despite his previous experiences of persecution, Paul immediately went into the Jewish synagogue and embarked on a process of seeking to explain and prove that the Christ had to suffer and rise from the dead. It was a relatively short visit which included only three Sabbaths – perhaps somewhere between two to four weeks (Acts 17:1-3).

Although a short visit, it was nevertheless a full one. At many points in 1 Thessalonians, Paul can remind them of his teaching during those few weeks by saying 'you know ....' For example, 'you know what instructions we gave you by the authority of the Lord Jesus' (1 Thess. 4:2). Similarly, Paul had obviously found time to teach clearly about the personal return of the Lord Jesus Christ (1 Thess. 5:2), besides much more. Paul had probably intended to stay longer but once again he quickly faced opposition from

Part One: Getting our bearings in 1 Thessalonians

a mob that caused a riot in the city. The lives of Paul and Silas were clearly in danger amidst the turmoil.

Some of the Jews were offended by Paul's preaching that Jesus was in fact the Messiah, whilst many of the Greeks were outraged by Paul's message of the need to give ultimate allegiance not to Caesar but to a different king, called Jesus (Acts 17:5-9). The result was that Paul and Silas were smuggled out of town under cover of darkness (Acts 17:10) in order to continue their journey. Though short, it had been a successful visit. The newly formed church already comprised a number of Jews who had been persuaded by the gospel and a large number of Greeks, including a number of prominent women (Acts 17:4).

Already from Luke's brief account we are able to trace the contours of the resulting situation for the Thessalonian church which will be far more fully developed in Paul's first letter to that church. First, this is a newly planted church which will need to survive its early days without Paul. Second, it is a church which right from the start is facing hostility and persecution. These two factors and the interplay between them will be key features that will guide us in enabling us to understand the way in which Paul writes to them later.

Having now left Thessalonica, they continued their missionary journey but, as we will see from his letter, Paul is uncomfortable about the fact that there has not been any news from Thessalonica. It is, therefore, whilst Paul is in Athens (Acts 17:16) that he can bear this situation no longer and decides to send Timothy back to Thessalonica in order to bring a report to Paul concerning how things are developing (1 Thess. 2:17–3:5). In due course, Timothy returned to Paul with encouraging news (1 Thess. 3:6) and it is probably following this that Paul writes the letter which we know as 1 Thessalonians.

What issues in the church does Paul need to address?

We have already picked up from the narrative in Acts 17:1-9 what are likely to be the main issues facing the church in Thessalonica and this is exactly what we find as we start to dig into the letter itself.

1. It is a church under pressure which needs strengthening

The initial pressure is overt and consists of various forms of opposition and persecution. 'In spite of severe suffering', the Thessalonians welcomed the message with joy (1 Thess. 1:6) but the opposition continued long after the initial reception of the gospel. The hostility of their fellow countrymen continued to be felt (1 Thess. 2:14) and Paul can speak of the danger of trials that could so easily have unsettled them (1 Thess. 3:3).

In addition, however, there is a more subtle pressure at work within Thessalonica and it can be detected by the way Paul needs to defend his own ministry (for example 2:1-5, 18). The allegation is that Paul is not interested in the Thessalonians at all. He is simply a wandering itinerant minister who seeks to make a living out of his rhetoric and who moves on promptly as soon as things get difficult; he is only concerned about himself and the Thessalonians are unlikely ever to see him again. Of course, if such allegations were true, then it would cast doubt on Paul's ministry and, indeed, on Paul's message. Had they been duped by Paul? Certainly the need to consider carefully whether or not they had been tricked would have been a significant additional pressure.

So, in order to bolster their faith, Paul needs to assure them that they are genuine believers (1:4-10) who have received the genuine apostolic message from a genuine apostle (2:1-12) so that they can have confidence in Christ even under pressure. Their experience of suffering is not unusual but normal (2:13-16) and Paul's current concern for them, evidenced in the sending of Timothy, is further evidence of the genuineness of his ministry and longing for them amidst all the pressures that they are facing (2:17–3:13).

2. *It is a newly planted church which needs encouraging*

There have been genuine conversions (Acts 17:4) and even in the earliest days Paul is able to give thanks for their faith, love and hope (1 Thess. 1:2-3). However, all these features need to grow and develop and therefore, following his prayer at the end of the first main part of his letter (1 Thess. 3:10-13), Paul devotes the remainder to encouraging healthy Christian growth. Their faith in Christ needs to be evidenced in a godly lifestyle (4:1-8), their love for others needs to be continually developed (4:9-12) and their hope and confidence in Christ's return need to be strengthened in order to help them to face both death and life (4:13–5:11). Paul rejoices in their conversion but longs for them to grow to maturity as believers so that the newly planted church does not become stunted in its growth.

Understanding the structure of 1 Thessalonians

In order to discern the structure of this epistle, it is essential to pick up on all the various clues that Paul provides. We notice first that, apart from a fairly standard introduction (1:1) and farewells (5:25-28), the letter has two significant prayers to conclude long sections (3:11-13 and 5:23, 24). These act as clear markers signifying the end of a section. This leaves us with two main parts, 1:2–3:13 and 4:1–5:24.

Turning to Part One, we notice that Paul starts with a prayer that features faith, hope and love (1:2, 3) and concludes with a prayer that has similar features (3:10-13). As we then look more closely at this long section, we notice that it is subdivided into four main parts which always begin with the word 'brothers' (see 1:4; 2:1, 14, 17). As the ESV footnote explains, this includes both 'brothers and sisters'. Going further we then notice that sections 1 and 3 relate to the Thessalonians and their faith in receiving God's Word (1:4-10; 2:13-16) whilst sections 2 and 4 relate to Paul and his love for the Thessalonians, both when he was present and now in his absence (2:1-12; 2:17–3:10). One final thing to highlight is that each of these four sections ends by considering an aspect of Christian hope as Paul underlines his convictions and confidence in the future (note 1:10; 2:12; 2:16 and 3:13). So, already, we can see how faith, love and hope not only start and end the whole section but also provide shape and structure to the subsections.

Part One ends with 3:10-13 but these verses also provide the agenda for the rest of Paul's letter. Paul is concerned to supply what is lacking in their faith and prays for their love to increase and for their hearts to be strengthened in readiness for the return of Christ; and each of these themes

Part One: Getting our bearings in 1 Thessalonians

is then developed in Part Two. Their faith in Christ is to be exhibited in godly behaviour (4:1-8), their love for others should continue to increase (4:9-12) and their confidence and hope in Christ needs to be strengthened in order to enable them to cope with the challenges of death as well as how to live in the present (4:13–5:11). Part Two concludes with a prayer that God would sanctify these new believers through and through, so that they grow in maturity (5:23).

A suggested outline of 1 Thessalonians:

1:1 Introduction

- Part One – 1:2-3 Thankfulness for their faith, hope and love
  - 1:4-10 Their experience of the gospel was genuine – faith (and hope 1:10)
  - 2:1-12 Paul's ministry whilst present was genuine – love (and hope 2:12)
  - 2:13-16 Their experience of suffering for the gospel is normal – faith (and hope 2:16)
  - 2:17–3:13 Paul's ministry whilst absent is genuine – love (and hope 3:13)
  - 3:10-13 Prayer for the development of their faith, hope and love

- Part Two – 4:1-2 Pleasing God more and more.
  - 4:3-8 Applying their faith in God's Word to their lives
  - 4:9-12 Increasing their love for others
  - 4:13–5:11 Strengthening their hope and confidence in Christ's return in the face of death 4:13-18 and in the face of life 5:1-11

- 5:12-24 Pleasing God together
- 5:25-28 Concluding farewells

Questions for studying 1 Thessalonians

Each preaching unit of this book includes a set of Bible Study questions which may be of some assistance. In addition, the following questions may also be useful for a group which has read through 1 Thessalonians together in its entirety, as a prelude to the study of individual passages.

- What were the key issues that the church in Thessalonica was facing?

- What sort of things could have caused them to doubt whether they were genuine Christians or not?

- What would the Thessalonians probably have remembered about Paul's ministry when he had been with them?

- How significant was Timothy's visit, described in 3:1-5?

- In what areas could Paul see the need for strengthening and development?

- Why is teaching about the return of Christ so important within this letter and should it receive more attention within the contemporary church?

- In what ways do you see the relevance of the teaching in 1 Thessalonians to your own church?

2.

WHY WE SHOULD PREACH AND TEACH 1 THESSALONIANS

In essence, the reasons for preaching and teaching this letter are likely to flow out of identifying the presenting issues that the church faced then and recognising that they may well also be applicable to the church today.

First, many churches are under considerable pressure, facing various degrees of opposition and persecution. In such situations, it would be easy to conclude that something has gone wrong, either in our understanding of the gospel or in our experience of the gospel; otherwise why would God permit us to suffer? 1 Thessalonians underlines the normality of the experience of suffering within the Christian life. Though in many parts of the world suffering has been a constant experience, nevertheless for those of us in the West we are only just beginning to find out that suffering as a Christian is likely to be a far more common experience. In that context, a letter such as 1 Thessalonians will play its role in encouraging us.

Second, in a day when church planting is back in vogue, there will be many more situations where a preacher needs to address the needs of a young church family, where perhaps relatively few have had substantial experience of living as a Christian. In such situations, the pastor will no doubt be thrilled with the evidence of God's gracious hand at work amongst the Lord's people and yet at the same time be aware of major areas of Christian conduct or doctrine which are missing or misunderstood. In such situations, the practical teaching and wisdom of the Apostle Paul could be invaluable in providing shape and structure to encourage immature believers to get on the road of Christian maturity. Of course, those who are already mature Christians will often need to relearn the same lessons. This is highlighted by the fact that at several points the apostle encourages the believers to grow 'more and more' in holiness and love (4:1, 10).

Third, given that Paul has to defend himself by giving evidence that his ministry was genuinely apostolic, this letter helpfully fleshes out what pastoral ministry should look like. Though Christian leaders today are not apostles, nevertheless pastoral ministry is based on the pattern of apostolic ministry. Rather than being a detached 'professional', Paul reveals his genuine parental concern for the members of the church family in Thessalonica. He describes his sacrificial labours, using images from motherhood and fatherhood. He is able to describe the intensity of his love by speaking about 'being orphaned' when he had to leave. He speaks of being able to 'bear it no longer' when no news from Thessalonica was forthcoming, such that he had to send Timothy. In all these ways, Paul reveals his genuine love for God's people and this stands as a remarkable example to those of us also called to pastoral ministry. Further, Paul's authentic ministry is not just to be observed in his loving relationship towards the Thessalonians, but also in his faithfulness towards the Lord and the gospel (2:1-5). Studying chapters 2 and 3 would be particularly helpful for any who are involved in Christian ministry.

Fourth, there are times when we read Scripture and recognise that we do not share its emphases or concerns. When this happens, it must always be wise for us to wonder why we are out of step with Scripture and whether it matters or not. Perhaps one such area would be our general lack of focus on the personal return of our Lord Jesus Christ. It is a doctrine which we know about and believe, but which may not have the priority that it deserves. Paul is convinced that the return of Christ should motivate and inform everything that we do, as is evident from the way the doctrine punctuates the first part of the letter (1:10; 2:12, 16; 3:13). However it is particularly in the second part that Paul develops the doctrine specifically as a means to strengthen and encourage believers (4:18; 5:11). This is the doctrine which enables the church family to cope with death (4:13-18). This is the doctrine which, rightly understood, should transform the way we live for Christ in the present (5:1-11).

Of course, there are many other reasons why one might wish to tackle 1 Thessalonians, but these reveal, at the very least, how relevant and helpful this letter is for the contemporary church.

3.

Preaching and Teaching 1 Thessalonians

One of the practical issues facing the preacher committed to the expository method concerns the division of a book of the Bible into appropriate sections for preaching. A number of factors must be considered:

Would the congregation benefit more from an overview of the letter taking only a few sermons or by allowing plenty of time to explore all the details of the letter?

How long would the congregation be able to cope with a particular series?

Are there any particular constraints which need to be borne in mind? For example, a time frame such as an academic term, church diary constraints due to special events or holidays, preaching allocations (if there is more than one preacher available)?

There are no right or wrong answers.

A number of series are listed below. In each case, the intention is to work with the structure and flow of the epistle.

Series 1: 5 Sermons

1. Sermon 1   1:1-10
2. Sermon 2   2:1-16
3. Sermon 3   2:17–3:13
4. Sermon 4   4:1-12
5. Sermon 5   4:13–5:28

Clearly, the aim here is to provide an overview of the letter. The basic structure of the letter has been slightly telescoped so that the very short third section in Part One (2:13-16) is included with the preceding material and the first two sections within Part Two (4:1-12) are run together. The drawback is that the final sermon comprises a large amount of material. However, there are times when an overview is particularly helpful – perhaps when a church is covering the material at a slower pace in home groups and would find it helpful to have an overview in order to keep the general discussions on the right track. Of course, this format may also lend itself to a weekend houseparty when there is an opportunity for sustained teaching on one book.

Series 2: 11 Sermons

1. Sermon 1   1:1-3
2. Sermon 2   1:4-10
3. Sermon 3   2:1-12

Part One: Preaching and Teaching 1 Thessalonians   31

4.	Sermon 4	2:13-16
5.	Sermon 5	2:17–3:10
6.	Sermon 6	3:10-13
7.	Sermon 7	4:1-8
8.	Sermon 8	4:9-12
9.	Sermon 9	4:13-18
10.	Sermon 10	5:1-11
11.	Sermon 11	5:12-28

This series corresponds to the selection developed within this book. This is how I chose to preach through 1 Thessalonians myself. It gave me scope for getting into a fair amount of detail whilst not getting too bogged down so that the congregation could still retain a clear idea of the flow of the epistle. Naturally, there were frustrations at not being able to spend as much time in some parts as one would have wished. Using this format, I divided the series into six sermons for Part One (1:1–3:13) and five sermons for Part Two (4:1–5:28). I also had the opportunity in sermons 1 and 6 to give an overview and plan of the whole letter in order to keep the bigger picture in view.

Series 3: 17 Sermons

1.	Sermon 1	1:1-3
2.	Sermon 2	1:4-8
3.	Sermon 3	1:9-10
4.	Sermon 4	2:1-5
5.	Sermon 5	2:6-12
6.	Sermon 6	2:13-16

7.	Sermon 7	2:17–3:5
8.	Sermon 8	3:6-10
9.	Sermon 9	3:11-13
10.	Sermon 10	4:1-2
11.	Sermon 11	4:3-8
12.	Sermon 12	4:9-12
13.	Sermon 13	4:13-18
14.	Sermon 14	5:1-8
15.	Sermon 15	5:9-11
16.	Sermon 16	5:12-22
17.	Sermon 17	5:23-28

The obvious advantage of working slowly through the material is that the details are covered, though there could be the danger of missing the wood for the trees. If undertaking a more sustained exposition, you might wish to consider breaking the series at one or two points. The obvious point to do that using the above scheme would be after sermon 9.

2.

Teaching 1 Thessalonians

1

A YOUNG CHURCH UNDER PRESSURE (1:1-3 AND 5:23-28)

Introduction

At the beginning and end of this letter, the presenting issues concerning the church in Thessalonica are revealed. It is a newly planted church and therefore continuing spiritual growth needs to be encouraged. The spiritual life that is already evident needs to be affirmed. At the same time, there needs to be recognition that further spiritual development is not only possible but required.

It is also a church that from its earliest days has known opposition and persecution and therefore, especially in the absence of those church leaders who planted the church, it will require encouragement and assurance that the Lord is well able to protect and watch over His people. These two presenting issues can easily be detected in both the opening and closing verses of the letter. They therefore provide a natural opportunity to give an overview of the letter whilst embarking on an expository series.

Listening to the text

Context and structure

The context of the letter can be identified by using the material Luke provides for us in Acts 15:36–17:9. Here we see Paul embark on his second missionary journey accompanied by Silas and soon to be joined by Timothy. These three take part in the visit to Thessalonica (Acts 17:1-9) and are involved in the writing of this epistle, though no doubt Paul carried the main responsibility, highlighted by the way in which he refers to one of the others in the text (see 1 Thess. 3:2-6). The material in Acts 17:1-9 supports the view that this is a newly planted church under pressure.

After the usual opening (from…, to…, greetings), Paul turns to God in thanksgiving (1:2-3). Three areas are particularly highlighted relating to their faith, their love and their hope. This triad of faith, love and hope will recur in Paul's prayer at the end of the first section (3:10-13) and will then set the agenda for most of the material in the second section of the letter (4:1–5:11). These opening verses (1:2-3) are highly significant in identifying three different strands of teaching material within the letter which Paul will return to again and again. Indeed, when we arrive at 2 Thessalonians there will be further evidence of their significance [2 Thess. 1:3, 4].

As with all of Paul's letters, he begins and ends with grace (1:1; 5:28). The grace of our Lord Jesus Christ, which was demonstrated at the cross, brings us peace with God the Father which sums up the gospel message in a few brief words. In a sense, everything about the church life which Paul will want to teach is to be bracketed by this understanding of the gospel of grace.

Though at the beginning and end Paul is communicating directly to the Thessalonian believers, nevertheless these verses are also marked by Paul's communication with God. At both start and finish, he is to be found praying for this newly planted church (1:2-3; 5:23). This immediately reminds the church and us that the letter is not a simple two-way communication between writer and recipients, but is set within the broader context of the presence of God and the return of the Lord Jesus Christ.

Working through the text

As we work through the text, attention will be paid to the two main presenting issues and looking at what Paul says both at the beginning and the end of the letter.

1. Encouraging healthy growth

Having planted this church, Paul is excited that already it is showing some signs of life. Therefore, he gives thanks to God continually for this evidence of God's work in their lives. It may well be that the news received from Timothy – which certainly included details about their faith and love (see 3:6) – provided Paul with the information that he needed in order to write directly to them. The shoots and buds that he can see demonstrate that something decisive has happened. Interestingly, the immediate thing he highlights is not their new beliefs but the evidence of changed lives. He focuses on their work, labour and endurance.

Clearly the Thessalonians had not just been hearers of God's Word but had acted upon it. In terms of the parable of the sower, they are like the good soil – those 'who hear the word, retain it, and by persevering produce a crop' (Luke 8:15). Their lives had been changed for all to see as they served and worked for Christ and each other in the church and the world. Later, Paul would speak about the genuine nature of their conviction by pointing to the evidence of their repentance. They had turned to God from idols to serve the living and true God (1:9). Their repentance had been observable.

Beneath the evidence of changed behaviour, Paul can discern three contributing factors to these changes. First, he is aware of their faith in Christ which had resulted in service to God. Their faith was not an intellectual assent but had direct connection with their lifestyle (though not as much as Paul wished, as we shall see later). Further, he is aware of their concern for others that had been prompted by a love for them which had perhaps not been evident before. Not only did their faith result in practical outcomes, but it was particularly seen in their love for others. Their faith in Christ was causing ripples of loving actions within both the church family and the wider society.

Finally, there was evidence that through difficulties and struggles they kept on going in their changed behaviour; this had come about through their confident expectation in the return of the Lord Jesus Christ. This hope had inspired them in the present, knowing that the Jesus who had died for them to rescue them from their sin would one day return. Seeking to be ready for His return encouraged them to keep serving and working for Christ each day. It is worth noticing that these three qualities of faith, love and hope are not to be viewed as abstract qualities. Each one is linked to our relationships with the Lord or with each other and is meant to shape our Christian convictions, character and behaviour.

However, within this opening exposition it is worth giving an overview of the letter because at the end of Part One (3:10-13) we see Paul referring to these three aspects again. Again Paul is praying, but this time he is longing for even more evidence of faith, love and hope. Rather like a gardener who has planted his crop and seen evidence of growth, Paul now returns longing that as time passes there would be further growth. So he tells them that he has been praying for them because he longs to supply what is lacking in their faith (3:10; this is developed at 4:1-8).

He is delighted that they have given evidence of love for one another, but he prays that this love would overflow even further (3:12, see also 4:9-12). He is thrilled that the return of Christ has inspired them but he longs that it would strengthen them even more (3:13; 4:13–5:11). Growth in the spring is wonderful, but Paul longs that it would be sustained into the summer months.

Finally, at the very end of the epistle, Paul is once again praying for them. His prayer is that the Thessalonian believers would be fully transformed (5:23). He doesn't want Christian growth to be compartmentalised, but longs that they would be sanctified 'through and through'. He is concerned for every aspect of their lives and speaks of their 'whole spirit, soul and body'. In terms of the gardening analogy, Paul has sown the seed of God's Word and a church has been planted where there is evidence of growth poking through the ground. Paul is delighted but now longs to see further growth which will result in a rich and fruitful crop of Christians when Jesus returns, completely transformed and living for Christ.

In this light, it is useful to notice Paul's pastoral wisdom. The Thessalonians could not help noticing that Paul is delighted with them. However, neither could they read the letter and drift into complacency due to Paul's clear concern that they keep on growing so that they will be ready when Jesus Christ returns.

2. Coping under pressure

However, though Paul is delighted with the evidence of initial growth, he is also concerned about the environment in which the church is growing. In the same way that the gardener might be concerned that young plants could be adversely affected by frost or drought, so Paul is aware of the vulnerability of this church plant. Returning to Jesus' parable of the sower, we note there are many threats to the growth of the seed from the evil one, persecution and other pressures (see Luke 8:12-14). Knowing that they could easily be unsettled (3:3) by the strong prevailing wind of persecution that had caused Paul himself to flee (see Acts 17:5-10; 1 Thess. 2:2), he realises that he needs to provide assurance and encouragement to them. So, both at the start and end of the letter that is exactly what we find.

In many of his other letters, Paul writes something like 'to the church of God in Corinth' (1 Cor. 1:2). Here Paul uses the same words but in a different order to convey a particularly important theological truth. He writes 'to the church of the Thessalonians in God….' (1:1). Amidst all the storms of persecution that they might face, they are to recognise that they are completely secure within God the Father and the Lord Jesus Christ. They are in His hands.

He will keep them safe for eternity. It is a stunning way to start the letter and surely it would have provided great assurance to the Thessalonians to help prevent them from being unsettled by the events around them.

Similarly, at the end of the letter a note of assurance is sounded at 5:24. After Paul has spent some considerable time challenging the Thessalonians (4:1–5:11) and then has prayed for their entire sanctification (5:23), the believers may have felt understandably unsure about whether they would be ready for Jesus Christ on His return. Rather than leave them in despair, Paul rounds off his prayer with the bold assertion, 'The one who calls you is faithful and he will do it' (5:24). Although Paul is concerned to supply what is lacking in their faith (3:10), nevertheless the really important thing to be persuaded about is God's faithfulness. Not only can the believers have assurance in the present that they are in Christ, but they can also have assurance for the future that in His faithfulness God will get them to their destination. All sorts of pressures may come on the church in the days ahead, but if they understood both verses 1:1 and 5:24 at least they would have confidence of God's protecting hand all the way through to the end.

From text to message

Getting the message clear: the theme
God will protect what has been planted and longs for His people to grow in faith, love and hope.

Getting the message clear: the aim
The aim of this passage is to provide assurance to believers under pressure whilst giving encouragement for them to

keep growing. Preaching or teaching on this passage should help in answering the following questions:

- What is the evidence of genuine Christian conversion?
- To what extent should continuing spiritual growth be expected in the Christian life?
- On what is the ultimate security of a Christian based?

A way in

In recent times, there have been many more new church plants than in previous years. Sometimes new fellowships may be formed largely from an existing nearby fellowship and comprise many mature believers, but in many cases the plant will start with only a small core of Christians. Gradually, as the gospel goes out, the church plant starts to grow but in the latter case there might be many new Christians who have only a limited understanding and experience of what is involved in following the Lord Jesus Christ. In such situations, a letter such as 1 Thessalonians may have particular relevance.

Perhaps the simplest image is to stay with the description of the fellowship in Thessalonica as a church 'plant'. God's Word, the seed, has been sown by Paul, Silas and Timothy and it has immediately germinated (see Acts 17:4). As a result, there are already shoots and buds appearing above ground giving evidence of life. Of course, the gardener wants to see more growth and plenty of fruit even though it will take some time for the plant to mature and fully develop. However, the gardener is also aware of the occasional severe weather conditions that the plant might experience and he is concerned about the possible threat this might pose to it, though ultimately he is confident that through various means the plant will not only survive but also thrive in the future.

Ideas for application

- The preacher will want to use this passage to encourage believers. Though Paul has important things to say to the Thessalonians concerning their behaviour (4:3-8), these are left towards the end of the letter rather than spelt out immediately. Paul's pastoral approach is first to affirm and encourage before correcting them about their lifestyle or thinking.

- The evidence of genuine Christian conversion will primarily be seen in changed behaviour. Such changes reveal that there has been a change in mindset and that there is a new allegiance to the Lord Jesus Christ. Though professions of faith have their appropriate place, actions generally speak louder than words and reveal whether our trust in the Lord Jesus Christ has gripped our whole being.

- The fact that Paul can speak not only of their faith and love but also of their hope is particularly interesting. Teaching about the need for putting our faith in Christ and seeing our Christian life as an outworking of the Great Commandments to love God and each other seems fairly straightforward. Yet clearly Paul had spent time in this initial visit teaching them about the return of the Lord Jesus Christ and the confidence or hope which that brings to our lives as believers.

Perhaps this is an aspect of our teaching which a study of 1 Thessalonians can help us to reclaim.

- It is easy for us to slip into complacency in the Christian life. We may have turned to Christ some time ago and there may be evidence of Christ's work in our lives. However, for Paul this is not enough. He prays for greater and more thorough holiness (5:23). Perhaps this should act as a rebuke to the many of us who exist at a spiritual standstill and who need to be encouraged to keep climbing towards greater Christ-likeness.

- We need to remind our hearers that our security must never lie in our response to Christ or how we have served Him since then. Ultimately, our confidence rests in the fact that we are 'in God the Father and the Lord Jesus Christ'. Though believers or even churches may seem very fragile, nevertheless complete security is found in being placed in Christ. Just as a crash helmet provides some protection to a cyclist or motorcyclist who is in a vulnerable situation, how much more will believers find safety even amidst opposition and persecution if they are in Christ?

- Our faith is certainly important, but it is always God's faithfulness to His people and His promises that are ultimately decisive (see 5:24). Amidst all sorts of difficulties and struggles that we face, it is helpful to remind ourselves that our future lies in God's hands not our own, and that we can trust Him to keep all

His promises. God's faithfulness holds us up and will keep us going right to the end.

Suggestions for preaching

Sermon 1:
- A young church under pressure (1 Thess. 1:1-3; 5:23-28)
- Encouraging healthy spiritual growth (1:2-3; 5:23)
- Coping under pressure (1:1; 5:24)

Other preaching possibilities:
Naturally it would be possible to deal with 1:1-3 alongside the rest of 1 Thessalonians 1. The advantage of dealing with it separately is that there is a lot of material in the rest of the chapter. If the whole chapter were preached in one go, it might prevent the preacher from providing an adequate introduction and overview. That said, there is a case for handling all the material together because verse 1:4 starts 'for we know' which indicates that there is a close link between verses 1:2, 3 and 1:4-10. The evidence of the fact that they are genuine believers rests not just on their changed behaviour (see 1:2, 3) but also on the way in which they responded to the gospel message when they first heard it (also 1:4).

Suggestions for teaching

Introducing the passage
- Consider the fellowship in Thessalonica as a church 'plant'. How was it planted (see Acts 17:1-9 for the background)? How mature is the 'plant' when Paul

writes to the church? What are the dangers that the 'plant' might face?

Understanding the passage
- What is the distinctive point about the identity of the Thessalonian church in verse 1?
- Why does Paul always start and end his letters with references to God's grace? (1:1; 5:28)
- What does the regularity of Paul's prayers for this church tell us about his relationship with them? (1:2)
- What is the evidence in 1:3 that these people in Thessalonica are genuine believers?
- What does Paul ask for in his prayer at 5:23?
- What purpose does 5:24 serve within the letter?

Applying the passage
- Given the context of opposition, why would it have been particularly helpful to refer to the church as 'in God' and 'in Christ' in verse 1?
- In what ways should our faith *in* Christ motivate us to work *for* Christ? (1:3)
- How should 'hope' play more of a part in the way we live our Christian lives? (1:3)
- How should the coming of our Lord Jesus Christ affect us now? (5:23)
- How have these short passages given you greater confidence and security in God's goodness?
- In what ways could the Thessalonians' faith, love and hope be an example to you?

2.

GENUINE CONVERSION TO CHRIST (1:4-10)

Introduction

The Thessalonian church had been newly planted and was under pressure. Fingers were being pointed at Paul and whether he was a genuine apostle, since he had fled the scene so quickly when opposition arose. Given that he had not returned, was he an authentic minister of the gospel and indeed, had the Thessalonian believers really received the gospel at all? Granted, they had received some sort of spiritual experience but was it genuine conversion? If there were doubts flying around about the authenticity of the messenger, it must call into question the authenticity of the message and therefore the genuineness of their conversion experience. From a distance, Paul could see that the first thing that this new church needed was assurance. They needed to know that he was indeed a genuine apostle (2:1-12) and that his message had brought about a genuine conversion to Christ (1:4-10).

Listening to the text

Context and structure

Paul has started his letter by giving thanks to God for the evidence of spiritual life in the church (1:2-3) and he now seeks to bolster these claims by showing that the Thessalonians had been genuinely converted to Christ. It is likely that, though Paul began his ministry in the Thessalonian synagogue amongst Jews, many of the members of the church were from a Gentile background. This is evident from Acts 17:4 where there is a specific reference to a large number of God-fearing Greeks being persuaded to follow Christ and also at 1:9 where Paul speaks of them turning from idols to serve the living and true God. Given this largely Gentile background, Paul cannot rely on knowledge of the Old Testament and needs to find other ways of providing assurance to these believers that they are now part of God's eternal plans for salvation.

The opening word 'for' connects verse 4 to the preceding verses and then 'because' in verse 5 fleshes out the statement within verse 4. So, verse 4 is the headline for the paragraph, indicating that the Thessalonians for whom Paul has been praying are loved and chosen by God. He knows this because of what has happened since he arrived in Thessalonica, and the rest of the chapter highlights the different stages involved which reveal that they truly are loved and chosen by God.

> Stage 1: Paul preached the gospel to the Thessalonians (v. 5).

Part Two: Teaching 1 Thessalonians 1:4-10

Stage 2: *The Thessalonians received this gospel message (v. 6).*

Stage 3: *The converted Thessalonians passed on the gospel message to the Macedonians and many others (vv. 7, 8a).*

Stage 4: *The Macedonians were able to tell Paul what had happened to the Thessalonians (vv. 8b-10).*

The structure of this paragraph reveals a circular pattern. The gospel went from Paul to the Thessalonians, from the Thessalonians to the Macedonians (and others), and then from the Macedonians back to Paul. In this way, Paul has received evidence of the genuine conversion of the Thessalonians.

There is a contrast between the beginning and the end of the paragraph. At the start, in verse 4, the focus is entirely on what God has done (they have been loved and chosen by Him). At the end in verses 9 and 10, the focus is almost entirely on what the Thessalonians have done (they have turned....to serve....and to wait). Genuine conversion must include both dimensions – God's gracious eternal initiative in election and our response to the gospel message when we hear it preached.

There is also a clear pattern seen in the paragraph relating to the coming of the gospel. In verse 5, we see Paul both preaching the gospel and living it out. Similarly, in verse 6, it is not just that the Thessalonians welcomed the message but also became imitators of the apostle. Finally in verse 7 and 8, the Thessalonians became a model to others and the Lord's message also rang out from them. Belief and behaviour are closely linked throughout this passage.

The dominant note in this paragraph relates to the faith of the Thessalonians but, as noted previously, hope in the return of our Lord Jesus Christ features in the final verse. The return of Christ and the other events associated with that event punctuate the whole letter until the more detailed exposition at 4:13–5:11. This is a reminder of the fact that this doctrine is not a 'bolt-on' feature to the gospel message, but is inextricably linked to the whole gospel of our Lord Jesus Christ.

Working through the text

As we work through the text, use is made of the structure of the paragraph identified above. The fact that the gospel is dependent upon God's initiative (1:4) and human response (1:9-10) provides us with a framework for looking at the whole passage in a way which respects its flow and emphases.

1. God's initiative in the gospel (1:4)

Paul's praying ('we always thank God for all of you' 1:2) is based on his knowledge about the Thessalonians: 'We know' that certain things are true about all of you. Though they may be experiencing opposition and persecution (3:3), Paul is convinced that they are loved and chosen by God. Though rejected by others within their community (2:14), they have been completely accepted by God Himself. Amazingly, though it was the Jews who were chosen out of love in the Old Testament (Deut. 7:7, 8), these privileges are now also to be experienced by Gentiles who had previously been worshipping idols!

Evidence of God's love is to be found in His choice and selection of the Thessalonians, which we learn elsewhere happened 'from the beginning' (2 Thess. 2:13) and 'before the creation of the world' (Eph. 1:4). They are to recognise that their conversion to follow Christ was not simply about a decision made when they heard Paul preach at the local synagogue, but was part of God's eternal plans of grace that were being worked out in history. Their assurance is ultimately rooted not in their choice of God but in God's choice of them. It is perhaps worth adding that, though God's election involves individuals, it is also corporate – He has chosen a people to serve Him. Further, it must not be thought that such a choice made by God in eternity was an impersonal, cold decision. Rather, it was a choice that flowed out of His love, though that love was completely undeserved.

As so often in the Scriptures, the doctrine of election is introduced not as a polemical subject but as a means of providing solid assurance for believers going through difficult times. Such is certainly the case here.

2. *The advance of the gospel (1:5-8)*

Having identified that the Thessalonian church members have been loved and chosen by God, Paul now seeks to show how that has been worked out in their own experience. To show that they really have been chosen, Paul looks at the evidence of what has happened since he arrived in Thessalonica. The very fact that the gospel has been preached, received and then proclaimed by the Thessalonians themselves (such that others could testify about their conversion) reveals that they have been genuinely converted and were therefore chosen by God and part of His eternal purposes of grace.

Stage 1:   Paul preached the gospel to the Thessalonians (v. 5)
As already noted, there were two aspects to Paul's communication of the gospel amongst them. It involved his message but also his Christian lifestyle and behaviour.

In terms of his message, Paul states that the gospel came to them 'not simply with words'. He is partly defending himself from the charge that he was a mere professional speaker who used flattering words to persuade people to accept his message (2:5). Indeed, the gospel did come to them in words but these words were accompanied by God's power demonstrated in the work of the Holy Spirit, and the 'deep conviction' evidenced by Paul in his own preaching. The Word of God and the Spirit of God are seen working together as the message went out – there is certainly no division between Word and Spirit. It is possible that 'deep conviction' could refer to the effect on the Thessalonians of the preaching of the gospel. However, their response to the preaching comes later in the passage at verse 6 and therefore it is more likely that it relates to Paul's convictions rather than those of his hearers. Paul's message did not come across as a cold lecture full of information which people were open to accept or reject. Instead, the picture being painted is of the apostle on fire for God, deeply convinced of the truths of the gospel that have been burned into his own soul and urgently, earnestly calling out to people to repent and believe whilst they have opportunity. Genuine gospel preaching will do far more than convey words and information, but will convey them with warmth, urgency and passion coming from a heart set on fire for God.

In addition, Paul did not merely preach the gospel but he also lived it out. This will be further expanded at 2:7-12 where Paul goes into detail about his conduct whilst amongst them. The important point is that the Thessalonians were not simply hearing a message about God's love from a powerful preacher but they also saw the message of God's love being enacted through the behaviour of the apostle. Of course, Paul is not claiming that his behaviour was perfect, but it highlights the importance of the preacher watching both his life and doctrine closely – exactly the advice that Paul would later give to Timothy (1 Tim. 4:16) and which Timothy would have witnessed during this missionary journey.

So the gospel message came to the Thessalonians through a preacher on fire for Christ who preached the gospel with great zeal and sought to live out the gospel in his behaviour. How had the Thessalonians responded?

Stage 2: The Thessalonians received the gospel message (v. 6)
The response of the Thessalonians is similarly divided into two aspects that are totally complementary. First, in their behaviour and lifestyle they began to imitate the Apostle Paul and the Lord Jesus Christ. The sign that convinced Paul that the gospel had taken root was not listening to their words but looking at their actions. Something had happened which was taking their lives in a very different direction from before (see 1:9). In particular, it would appear that their imitation of Christ related to their willingness to follow Him in enduring suffering with joy, which was also evident in Paul's life. A willingness to suffer for the sake of Christ and the gospel is a great indication that a genuine conversion to Christ has taken place.

Second, Paul reports the fact that they had welcomed the message with the joy given by the Holy Spirit. They had clearly understood the heart of the message of the gospel. They knew that they were now forgiven and adopted into God's family with a glorious eternal future. As a result, even though others might persecute them, they were full of joy. Such joy amidst suffering was evidence that the Holy Spirit was indeed at work in their lives. Again it is helpful to notice how Paul keeps things together. The Holy Spirit had been at work in Paul's preaching and had also been at work in the response of the Thessalonians. The Thessalonians had received the Word and had also received the Holy Spirit.

So, the gospel had been preached and the Thessalonians had responded, but was there any further evidence that Paul could produce which would enable the Thessalonians to have greater assurance that they had indeed been chosen by God?

Stage 3: The Thessalonians passed on the message to the Macedonians (and many others) (vv. 7, 8)

The response of the Thessalonians was personal but not private. Their faith in Christ was not hidden from view and Paul now refers to the way in which the Thessalonians had been used to spread the gospel further. He identifies two areas. Macedonia was a region which included the cities of Philippi and Thessalonica. Achaia was further south, stretching down from Macedonia towards Athens and beyond. Together these regions correspond to a significant portion of modern-day Greece. It is in this area that Paul himself travelled after his short visit to Thessalonica as he stopped at Berea, Athens and then Corinth (Acts 17, 18). The advance of the gospel did not depend, humanly speaking, on his direct ministry alone because, as we see here, the gospel was quickly being communicated through the witness of the Thessalonian believers.

Their witness, once again, combined their change of behaviour and their proclamation of the message that they had embraced – not one without the other. As a result, the believers in Macedonia and Achaia could testify to the change in their lifestyle as the Thessalonians modelled what they had seen in Paul and heard about Christ. Their behaviour was consistent with a profession of faith in Christ. However, it was not just their reputation that spread, as Paul was also aware of the gospel message spreading through their witness. Like bells ringing out and being heard across the town, so the Word of the Lord rang out across these regions. Not only could people see the effect of the gospel on their lives, but they could hear the message of the gospel themselves through the Thessalonians.

So, not only had the gospel come to the Thessalonians but they had received it, been changed by it and were able to articulate the message to others so that the gospel was now bearing fruit across the world. Surely no greater evidence is available to convince them that they have been chosen by God?

Stage 4: The Macedonians (and others) were able to tell Paul how the Thessalonians had received the gospel (vv. 8, 9)

It would have been perfectly possible for Paul to have stopped in the middle of verse 8. At that point, he would already have given convincing proof of a genuine work of the gospel in the lives of the Thessalonians by showing how they had received the gospel and then gone on to proclaim it to others. However, Paul proceeds to a fourth stage. Not only had the Macedonians and Achaians heard the gospel through the Thessalonians, but they themselves were able to articulate the gospel and the response required. In other words, not only were the Thessalonian believers converted and witnessing but their testimony revealed their profound grasp of the gospel of our Lord Jesus Christ. Hearing and seeing their response to the gospel first-hand must have delighted Paul, but for others to have come to a living faith in Christ and to report what had happened to them must have given him further assurance that their faith was not superficial or temporary but was absolutely genuine and permanent.

3. An authentic response to the gospel (1:9, 10)

Paul concludes the chapter by reporting what the Macedonians were saying about the Thessalonians' faith in Christ. Though this belongs to the previous point, it has such significance in its own right that it deserves to stand on its own within the exposition. It mirrors the opening verse 4 which focused on God's initiative by looking in these closing verses at an authentic response to the gospel. Also, it continues the thought of the previous few verses by demonstrating once again that receiving the gospel involves both trust in the gospel message and an appropriate change of behaviour. Both are demonstrated here in this report of the repentance and faith exhibited by the Thessalonians.

Repentance (v. 9)

Repentance signifies a change of mind leading to a change of behaviour. This is stated in a very straightforward way. The Thessalonians had turned to God from idols. There had been a clear change of direction in their lives. Whereas

Part Two: Teaching 1 Thessalonians 1:4-10   57

their previous focus had been on the religious idols that were prevalent in these days (see Acts 17:16), they had now turned away from them. However it involved not simply a renunciation of past patterns of behaviour and worship, but a positive turning towards God. Nor was this an intellectual exercise only, since it specifically states that they had turned to God from idols in order to serve the living and true God. In other words, it involved action. They had turned in order to serve.

Their new faith was therefore intensely practical. The God whom they now knew to be both the living God (in contrast to their idols) and the true God (in contrast to the many false gods that they had previously worshipped) was not a 'bolt-on' extra to their lives. Now their lives were to be characterised as being in the service of God. He had become their Lord, and it was now their privilege and responsibility to serve Him and please Him (4:1) through discovering His will in the instructions given by the apostle through the authority of the Lord Jesus Christ (4:2). Their goal now was to serve God through obedience to His Word.

Faith (v. 10)
Their actions were based on specific knowledge about this living and true God. Though they could not see Him, they had heard about Him and put their trust and confidence in Him. In particular, in receiving the gospel they had heard about His Son, the Lord Jesus Christ. In passing, it can be seen that this would naturally mean that God reveals Himself as Father (1:1; 3:11) and it also highlights Jesus' position both as Jewish Messiah and the eternal Son. More particularly, the verse reveals three aspects of Jesus' life and ministry:

- He has been raised from the dead. This statement implies Jesus' death on the cross, which is later stated to be 'for us' (5:10). However the focus, as with Paul's sermon at Athens in the same part of this missionary journey (Acts 17:22-31), is on the resurrection. This is the decisive moment which gives evidence that Jesus is who He claimed to be. He is alive and reigning as the victorious Son of God.

- He will one day return from heaven. Jesus is not a remote figure whom people can simply dismiss. One day He will return and everyone will meet Him. Viewing Jesus as the Son of God, they know that He will judge with justice. That day will be a day of wrath (2:16 as well as 5:1ff; 5:9) because it will be a day when all sins will be punished. Everyone who has not obeyed the gospel and put their trust in the Lord Jesus Christ will one day face God's judgment (2 Thess. 1:5-10).

- When the risen One returns, He will rescue believers. Though believers know and experience God's goodness, their full salvation awaits the day when they are rescued from God's final judgment and ushered into glory. We experience a foretaste of that now through our relationship with Christ, but it is only then that we shall be fully rescued and saved. Christian 'hope' is simply our confidence that Jesus will rescue us on that last day on the basis of His sin-bearing sacrifice 'for us' on the cross (5:10). Only then will we know what it is to be rescued from sin, Satan, death, and God's wrath, and only then will we know the blessedness of being with the Lord Jesus in glory.

From this we can see that their knowledge of Jesus was not in the slightest bit rudimentary. Against the backdrop of final judgment, it is precisely this knowledge of Jesus' ministry which is required. Therefore, the characteristic aspect of their faith described by Paul was that they were 'waiting for....Jesus'. Though they had already put their trust in Christ and sought to be obedient to His Word, their main orientation was fixed on that day when they would meet and see the Lord at His return (4:16, 17). Therefore they waited for that great day. Of course, such waiting was not passive, since each day was a day to serve the living and true God. Nevertheless, their faith was directed towards the future and towards personally meeting the Lord Jesus Christ, and this theme is constantly repeated within the epistle (1:10; 2:19; 3:13; 4:17; 5:23).

An authentic response to the gospel must therefore include repentance and faith. There needs to be a genuine turning of our lives from our old idols to the living and true God and this needs to be accompanied by trust in the Lord Jesus Christ who will one day return and bring us full salvation. Such a response would have brought assurance to the Thessalonians that they were indeed loved and chosen by God. Chosen by God before the creation of the world for rescue on the last day by the Lord Jesus Christ, these Thessalonians, though only just established in this newly planted church, were in fact right at the heart of God's eternal plans of grace!

From text to teaching

Getting the message clear: the theme
Responding to the gospel shows that you are loved and chosen by God.

Getting the message clear: the aim
The aim of this passage is to show what genuine conversion looks like. Preaching or teaching on this passage should help in answering the following questions:

- What is the evidence that you are loved and chosen by God?

- To what extent is behaviour as important an indicator as belief within the Christian life?

- What are the signs of genuine conversion?

A way in
Being selected or chosen can be a great honour. For example, being selected to represent your country at a particular sport at the Olympics must be an enormous privilege. Similarly, being selected for a job out of many candidates is also something to be excited about. Obviously in both these examples the choice is based on abilities or skills which have been observed or can be detected within the individual, whereas God's choice is based purely on His love (Deut. 7:7, 8). However, the similarity still stands that even though we cannot point to any specific reasons why God should have chosen us (and indeed we are able to point to many good reasons why He should definitely not have chosen us!), nevertheless it is an enormous privilege that He has welcomed us into His family.

Part Two: Teaching 1 Thessalonians 1:4-10

One of the compelling images from the text is the picture of the Word of God ringing out from the Thessalonians (v. 8). Just like a peal of bells is heard throughout the surrounding area despite the sounds of traffic, so the Word of God rippled out from the Thessalonians. God's Word had been sounded originally through Paul's preaching and the effects now spread out so that many hear that same gospel word. It is a picture full of joy and enthusiasm which probably represents a contrast to what we see in our own churches. Another important image relates to the way that the conversion is explained. It was based on the idea of turning around (v. 9). They had turned from idols to serve the living and true God. Having proceeded in one direction all their lives, they had now changed direction. As a result of that they were now walking away from their idols and were now seeking to serve God. It is a simple and powerful image which also demonstrates that conversion includes both a change of mind and a change of behaviour.

Ideas for application

Everything is based on God's initiative in the gospel. The Thessalonians did not volunteer for conversion – it all flowed from God's election and sovereign grace. God is the One who turns Paul's life around when he was intent on persecuting Christians (Acts 9). God is the One who provides Paul with a vision of a Macedonian calling out 'come over and help us' (Acts 16:9). God is the One who sends His Holy Spirit to enable Paul's preaching to be more than mere words. God is the One who enables the Thessalonians to respond with joy in the Holy Spirit even in the midst of considerable suffering. We will certainly want to recognise that God's eternal purposes of grace are worked out through the preaching of the gospel and the considered response to that message, but all such actions must be viewed from within the perspective of God's divine initiative to choose a people for Himself.

It is vital that God's Word and God's Spirit are kept together rather than being separated. So often we hear about the ministry of the Word needing to be augmented by a separate and additional ministry of the Spirit. Yet in 1 Thessalonians 1 we are given two striking examples which highlight that the ministry of the Word was equally a ministry of the Spirit. When Paul preached the gospel word, it was not simply a word since it came through the powerful work of the Spirit (v. 5). Similarly, when the Thessalonians received the gospel, it states that they welcomed the Word with the joy given by the Holy Spirit (v. 6). Again the experience of hearing, receiving and welcoming the gospel word is not divorced from the experience of the work of the Spirit in their lives. In both examples, the ministry of the Word is a ministry of the Spirit and vice versa.

It is also vital that belief and behaviour are kept together. For Paul evangelism was not simply about delivering a message with great conviction – important though that was. It was a message that was backed up and flowed out from his life (v. 5). Life and lip were held together. The message of Christ's sacrificial love for others could readily be seen in Paul's sacrificial love for them (2:7-9). Equally Paul is convinced about the genuineness of their conversion when he sees both a change in belief as they welcome God's Word and also a change in behaviour and lifestyle as they start to imitate both Paul and the Lord Jesus Christ (v. 6). Paul clearly wasn't the sort of preacher or evangelist who would quickly count 'decisions for Christ'. Rather he wanted to see lives that demonstrated a decision to follow Christ.

Whilst considering the importance of holding Word and Spirit and then belief and behaviour together, it is also worth reflecting on the significance of keeping joy and suffering together. It is possible for any of us, but perhaps particularly younger Christians, to think that joy is a mark of God's blessing and that suffering is probably a sign of God's displeasure. As a result, an unrealistic view of living the Christian life can be adopted which is likely sooner or later to lead to trouble when the believer starts to experience suffering and opposition to their faith in Christ. Once again however in 1 Thessalonians 1, we see Paul holding things together. Suffering and joy ran along together in the experience of these new Christians (v. 6) without any question being raised that the two were incompatible. Helping new Christians to recognise that genuine Christian experience will constantly embrace both joy and suffering (and often at the same time) is vital to help them to grow to Christian maturity.

The Thessalonian believers also model for us that a genuine profession of faith should be accompanied by a desire for that faith to be passed on to others. Having received the gospel, they passed it on to others. Though their faith in our Lord Jesus Christ was clearly personal, it was not private. Rather than seeing themselves as the terminus of the gospel, they acted as one stop along the route that the gospel would take across the region. We are not specifically told how it happened, so we should be careful about laying down any rules, but there should be the prayerful expectation that others would hear of the good news of Jesus Christ through the lives of those who have come to faith in Him.

An authentic response to the gospel involves repentance and faith. Repentance will involve a decisive turning from the idols of our age and a consequent turning to God. Our idols are those things which we most treasure or value and which hide or cloud our view of the living God. So often our idols may be good things – family, job, wealth, sport, holidays – but as soon as they take their place between us and God they have become idols. To turn from the gifts to the Giver is a vital first step within the whole process of conversion as we begin to recognise God for who He truly is.

Compared to the knowledge of the Lord Jesus that the Thessalonians possessed, our faith seems very weak. They had confidence in the return of Christ as the final guarantee of their salvation. Through the Word of the Lord they realised that everyone would one day stand before God Almighty to be judged. Therefore the most important thing about being saved was not just salvation from sin, death and Satan, but being delivered from God's wrath. In that context, no wonder they particularly looked forward to the return of Christ – the One who through His death and resurrection would be able to rescue them on that last day. This should at the very least make us pause to think whether our understanding of judgment or salvation is as profound and deep as these young Thessalonian believers.

Suggestions for preaching

Sermon 1:
- Genuine conversion to Christ (1 Thess. 1:4-10)
- God's initiative in the gospel (v. 4)

Part Two: Teaching 1 Thessalonians 1:4-10   65

- The advance of the gospel (v. 5-8)
- An authentic response to the gospel (v. 9-10)
- Other preaching possibilities

There are several different possibilities that could be considered. For those wishing to travel quickly through the text, the first few verses could be incorporated so that the exposition covers the whole of the chapter. Having given thanks for their conversion (1:1-3), Paul shows how they had received the gospel (1:4-8) and then the significance of repentance and faith in their response (1:9, 10).

Alternatively for those wishing to take a bit longer savouring the material, the text could be divided into 1:4-8 and 1:9, 10. The former sermon would focus on the progress of the gospel from God's purpose in election through the preaching of Paul, the response of the Thessalonians and then their own preaching. The latter sermon would then focus on the marks of genuine conversion and the nature of repentance and faith.

Dealing with 1:9, 10 would be particularly appropriate in an evangelistic setting either within the expository series or as an independent sermon. If we focus on these verses there is the opportunity to look at repentance and faith, and focus especially on the person of the Lord Jesus Christ – risen, returning, rescuing!

Suggestions for teaching

Introducing the passage
What do you think are the signs that someone is genuinely converted to Christ? What sort of things would you look for and what aspects are particularly significant?

Understanding the passage
- What are the important features described by Paul about how the gospel came to the Thessalonians? (1:4, 5)
- How is their response to the gospel described and is there anything striking about it? (1:6)
- What happened after the Thessalonians became Christians? (1:7-9a)
- How is repentance described in verse 9 and what might this have looked like in practice? (1:9)
- What is surprising about the description of their faith in 1:10?
- What does 1:10 tell us about their understanding of the Lord Jesus Christ?

Applying the passage
- In contrast to 1:5, 6, in what ways are we tempted to separate the ministries of Word and Spirit? Why is that a mistake?
- In contrast to 1:5, 6, in what ways are we tempted to separate belief and behaviour? Why is that a mistake?
- In what ways should evangelistic witness be a natural outworking of genuine conversion as at 1:7-9a? Why is this often not the case?
- Do you think waiting for the return of Jesus should be part of our outlook as Christians? Are there any reasons why it is not particularly evident? (1:10)
- Are there areas of your life where turning from idols to serve the living and true God is required? (1:9)
- In what ways should the experience of the Thessalonians described in chapter 1 be an example to you?

3.

Genuine Christian ministry (2:1-12)

Introduction

The Thessalonian church had been planted during Paul's brief visit described in Acts 17:1. However, he had left under the cover of darkness (Acts 17:10) and, as far as most people were concerned, had not been heard of since. Perhaps he was simply a professional speaker who made his money where he could, deceiving people with all sorts of promises and moving on when it became clear that he was no longer welcome. It is easy to imagine non-Christians in Thessalonica taunting their Christian neighbours by indicating to them that they had simply been deceived by a charlatan who was only interested in lining his own pocket. The longer the period that they had not heard from Paul, the more their fears would be growing – perhaps he isn't an apostle at all? In this passage, therefore, Paul needs to answer these concerns by showing that the ministry that he exercised amongst them was genuine apostolic ministry.

Listening to the text

Context and structure

Paul has provided assurance to this young church that they have been chosen by God and are genuinely converted. However, he is also aware that doubts have been circulating about his own ministry and whether he is a genuine apostle. If such doubts were not dealt with, then they would not only undermine the Thessalonians' faith but also cast doubts on every aspect of Paul's ministry. So Paul launches into this apologia for his ministry. He needs to explain that he has not in any sense deceived them with his message. Further, he wants to remind them of the sort of loving, sacrificial ministry he exercised whilst among them in order to dispel any thoughts that he was an uncaring professional speaker simply thinking about his own needs.

The reference to 'brothers' (2:1) strongly suggests that this is a new section of the letter which runs from 2:1 to 2:12 before Paul resumes his thanksgiving prayer for the Thessalonians at 2:13. It seems fairly clear from the context of this passage that there are two main themes. First, he wants to show that he has not been deceitful but has carefully delivered them the truth. Second, his aim is to remind them of his loving concern while he was with them when he acted as both mother and father to them. It is not completely clear where the transition between these two themes comes because different translations divide up the sentences in varying ways (compare verse 6 in the ESV, where it is all one sentence, and the NIV, where there is a paragraph break). The sentence structure of the NIV translation seems to make most sense with the division in the middle of verse 6 (though this seems to correspond with the start of verse 7 in the Greek text).

Despite these uncertainties, the basic structure seems to be as follows:

- 2:1-6a Pleasing God's people – faithfully serving the gospel.
- 2:6b-12 Loving God's people – sacrificially caring for the church.
  - ..as a mother (6b-9)
  - ..as a father (10-12)

In contrast to 'we know' (1:4), this passage is dominated by 'you know' (see vv. 1, 2, 5, 11). This reflects the fact that Paul is reminding them of his previous ministry amongst them so that they can see how he had conducted himself. If chapter 1 is all about Paul knowing of their faith and joy, then chapter 2 is all about the Thessalonians knowing of his faithfulness and love. There is also a verbal link between the two chapters. The words translated 'reception' (1:9) and 'visit' (2:1) are the same (*eisodos*), which helps us to see that both chapters refer to the same events.

The reference to Philippi (2:2) and Paul's suffering there fits exactly with what we learn from the narrative of Acts 16 and 17, and corroborates what has happened. The reference to Paul's teaching (2:1-5) and then his lifestyle (2:6-12) also links with his previous description of his ministry (1:5) and underlines that ministry based on the apostolic pattern should reveal both aspects.

As already noted, once again Paul ends the section with a reference to hope (2:12). The gospel is a message of salvation that will only be fully realised and experienced when believers enter God's glory.

Working through the text

The structure identified above will shape the exposition and assist us in seeing the flow of Paul's argument as he defends himself against various charges. Though Paul is an apostle (2:6), the principles which he outlines apply to all pastoral ministry since he reveals how he has endeavoured to preach the gospel and plant a church in Thessalonica. This section, therefore, has particular application to those involved in church leadership because church leaders should be involved in exactly the same sorts of activities.

1. Pleasing God (2:1-6a)

One of the most striking things about this paragraph is the large number of denials. These negative references reveal the allegations that the apostle was facing from individuals who were intent on damaging Paul's reputation. If we gather all these points together, it is possible to reconstruct the charges. 'Paul, your motives were impure (I guess you were probably trying to get a good amount of money and at the very least enhance your reputation as a travelling speaker – in other words, your visit to Thessalonica was all about what you could get out of us) and you were attempting to trick us (see 2:3), perhaps by your eloquence or empty promises, into believing your message. You used all the techniques you could to please the crowds (see 2:4) and get a good following. You flattered us (see 2:5) in order to get our appreciation and applause (see 2:6) but it was all a mask for your financial greed (see 2:5). However, though you used all the tricks in the book you were eventually forced to get out of town and your mission here was essentially a failure (see 2:1).'

For new Christians to be told that they had been tricked and exploited by a fraudulent speaker would, of course, be enormously unsettling, especially if combined with a degree of persecution (see 2:14). So Paul feels compelled to mount a defence in order to show that his ministry was not motivated by greed (money) or pride (reputation).

What are the signs that Paul's ministry was authentic? Merely issuing denials is insufficient and so in this paragraph he makes a few key assertions:

We suffered for the gospel (2:1, 2)
Paul starts by showing that his ministry was not linked with a life of ease and prosperity. Wherever he went, he and his fellow workers experienced suffering, insults and shameful treatment. This was certainly the case in Philippi and was also their experience in Thessalonica (see 2:2). If they had simply been out to feather their nest and establish a reputation across Macedonia, they would not have embraced a ministry that almost inevitably involved real suffering and difficulty. It wasn't a simple thing to come to Thessalonica and preach the gospel, maintains Paul – he needed God's help to have the courage to come, as he knew it would inevitably involve him and his colleagues in suffering (2:2).

This underlines the first mark of an authentic gospel minister – a willingness to suffer for the gospel. Suffering itself is not a sign of failure (see 2:1). On the contrary, it is likely to be an indication of the genuine nature of the ministry being exercised.

We were entrusted with the gospel (2:3-6)
Rather than handling a message that they could change and shape according to their circumstances and desires (see 2:3), Paul and his colleagues felt no such freedom at all. Instead, they knew that they had been entrusted with the gospel message by God and they had no liberty to change it in any way and certainly not to make it more palatable. The fact that God had entrusted them with this task indicated His approval of them for this role, though they knew that how they had fulfilled such a task would be assessed by God.

It is a little bit like being entrusted with someone's money, car or house. There is no liberty to act how we wish according to our own desires. Instead, we have been entrusted with them in order to look after or use them in ways intended by the owner, and at some point in the future how we have acted will be assessed. To that extent we are acting as stewards or trustees. Similarly, Paul saw himself in that sort of role as he came to Thessalonica.

Given this understanding of gospel ministry, Paul's underlying aim was to please God rather than himself or other people (see 2:4-6). If you were entrusted with someone else's money for a particular purpose, it would be possible to use it for oneself or to spend it on others in order to impress friends, but neither of these uses would be in line with the intention of the person who has entrusted you with their money. Paul knows that he is accountable to God and therefore he pleads that God is his witness (see 2:5) to underline that he has acted faithfully according to God's desire when the gospel was entrusted to him.

All this underlines the second mark of an authentic gospel minister – a desire to be faithful to God and the gospel message. Trustworthiness is the key ingredient. Pleasing God is essential. Obtaining the applause of others is not a sign of success. On the contrary, it may be an indication of seeking to please others rather than God. The gospel is His gospel (see 2:2 – the gospel of God). It belongs to Him and therefore we have no liberty to change it, whether by watering it down or omitting certain aspects.

So the two marks of an authentic gospel ministry which are highlighted here are a willingness to suffer for the gospel and a determination to be faithful in presenting the gospel message. Paul maintains that this is how he has acted and that all this is known already by the Thessalonians.

2. Loving God's people (2:6b-12)

The striking thing about this passage is Paul's use of parental imagery and particularly the focus on the maternal aspect of his ministry. Just as Paul is able to plead that God is a witness to his faithfulness to the truth (see 2:5), so he is also able to call on God as a witness to his sacrificial love for the Thessalonians (see 2:10). Though an apostle of Christ with authority from God, Paul's behaviour reveals the Christ-like pattern of authority being extended by means of selfless love and care. Again, Paul is revealing the marks of an authentic gospel ministry applicable not just to apostles but to all involved in pastoral ministry.

How does Paul describe his ministry among them?

As a mother (2:6b-9)

At the beginning and end of this short paragraph, Paul issues yet another denial. Though he could have been a burden to them (see 2:6), he worked in such a way as not to be a burden (see 2:9). In other words, as an apostle he could have exercised a degree of authority requesting financial support or requiring the Thessalonians to serve him in various ways. Yet though he could have 'milked' them for what he could have obtained from them, in fact he provided milk for them (see 2:7)! He uses the image of a mother but particularly focuses on the role of a nursing mother who is gently caring for her own children. She provides milk from her own breast to strengthen the baby and cares for its every need. It is the opposite of someone wielding authority – it is a picture of tenderness and love.

In terms of discipleship, it links in with 1 Peter 2:2 and the need for new Christians to be fed on spiritual milk or 'the milk of the word'. Paul is aware that new Christians, whatever their age, will require a careful diet of teaching from God's Word in order to strengthen them and enable them to start the process of growing to maturity in our Lord Jesus Christ.

Not only does Paul utilise the picture of the nursing mother but he also develops it in two complementary ways in the following verses. First, he points to his genuine affection and love for the Thessalonian Christians (see 2:8). A nursing mother would not see the role of looking after and feeding her children as merely a job to perform. Her natural affection and love for her children will mean that her life is bound up with theirs. She is not interested simply in providing them with some food. She is a mother and so her whole life is shared with her children.

Similarly, Paul saw himself as performing the role of a nursing mother, such that his relationship with his spiritual children was marked by deep affection and concern. Rather than taking from them, he had given them all that he had. He had given them the gospel in his teaching and preaching but he had also given himself in seeking to meet their needs, such was his love for them.

Second, he points to his hard work and labour on their behalf (see 2:9). A mother with young children knows all about hard work. There are constant demands throughout the day revolving around their care: feeding, changing, washing clothes, cleaning, comforting, etc. However, such care also extends through the night in feeding or comforting a crying infant. Paul describes this commitment to a child as involving toil and hardship. Indeed, many new parents would agree. Though they deeply love their young children, it is hard work to provide round-the-clock care.

Yet that is how Paul had sought to care for the new Thessalonian believers. Though Acts 17 informs us that he preached for three Sabbaths in the synagogue, his commitment to them amounted to far more than a weekly sermon. Day by day, Paul gave himself to them, seeking to strengthen and build them up.

Paul's use of the nursing mother as an image for his own ministry points to the sacrificial love that is the mark of an authentic gospel ministry. It is not a job with confined tasks or hours but a vocation that brings about a strong bond of affection and commitment.

As a father (2:10-12)

In this next paragraph, Paul now uses the image of a father. He introduces this new angle by reminding them of his holy, righteous and blameless behaviour (see 2:10). These words all have a similar feel in indicating, Paul's observable behaviour was above reproach, though not that he was sinless. As a father he wanted to set a good example for his spiritual children that they could follow and emulate. Later he prays that they would be blameless and holy (see 3:13) and be kept blameless (see 5:23). He saw his role as a father as a means of modelling appropriate Christian behaviour for new believers.

Yet more than providing an example, he also uses the image of the father to show how he was constantly encouraging them (see 2:11, 12). Though delighted that they had come to a living faith in the Lord Jesus Christ, Paul doesn't want them to drift or become complacent. Similar to his use of 'more and more' later in this letter (see 4:1, 10), Paul wanted to see them grow and make progress towards greater Christian maturity. Whereas it might have been quite possible for him to have simply used the word 'encourage', he actually uses three words of growing intensity to reveal his great desire for them to live in a manner worthy of God. So, as a father he exhorted, encouraged and charged or urged them to keep going forward in their Christian life, understanding and experience. Just as a father might encourage his child to swim or to complete some difficult homework, so Paul was alongside the Thessalonians giving every encouragement for them to progress.

Perhaps we could imagine a father seeking to encourage a young child to climb a steep hill. Much encouragement and cries of 'come on!', 'well done!' and 'keep going!' might be heard. We can also imagine the father pointing to the summit and describing the impressive view that can be experienced. So with Paul as he ministered alongside the Thessalonian Christians as a father, encouraging them forward and pointing to the summit. Their destination is to experience the glory of God as members of God's everlasting kingdom (see 2:12) and Paul is determined to assist them on their way.

Paul's use of the image of the father corrects our own observations and experiences of fatherhood. Though many fathers might adopt the practice of 'do as I say, not do as I do', Paul is burdened with a concern to set them an example. Though many fathers might have a laissez-faire attitude, adopting the line of least resistance in order to have a quiet life, Paul is thoroughly involved in wanting to encourage his children onwards to Christian maturity. Ultimately Paul's vision of fatherhood is modelled on his vision of God as Father (see 1:1, 3; 3:11) which he has sought to reflect in his relationship with the church family at Thessalonica.

An authentic gospel ministry is marked by this sort of maternal and paternal care. In a sense, authentic pastoral ministry as described by the apostle is parental ministry. Far from practising a ministry which sought to grab and get, Paul's ministry – whether described as mother or father – was all about giving. Rather than it being a job that can be stopped and started at will, the use of these images by Paul suggests the all-consuming nature of sacrificial love and care which should flow within every Christian ministry.

In summary, Paul has provided a striking portrait of authentic Christian ministry. Alongside a willingness to suffer for the gospel, there must be a faithfulness to the gospel and a desire to please God rather than anyone else. Alongside a concern to preach God's Word, there must be a sacrificial commitment to love, care and work amongst God's people in order to encourage them to greater spiritual maturity. In describing ministry in this way, he has defended himself against the various slanderous accusations that have been levelled against him, but he has also provided a wonderful template to shape and inspire all future Christian ministry which is to be based on this apostolic pattern.

From text to teaching

Getting the message clear: the theme
- Authentic Christian ministry involves pleasing God and loving God's people.

Getting the message clear: the aim
- The aim of this passage is to show how Christian leaders are to act as they plant and then lead a church. Preaching or teaching on this passage should help in answering the following questions:
    - What is the evidence that someone is exercising an authentic gospel ministry?
    - How should the idea of being entrusted with the gospel shape the practice of gospel ministry?
    - In what ways do motherhood and fatherhood inform our approach to Christian ministry?

A way in
Full-time, salaried pastors face many pressures. Above all, there is the temptation to please others and to please ourselves. When the world is shouting insistently that the church must move with the times and be willing to adopt the values and practices of the age, it is tempting to seek to change the message of God's Word ever so slightly, such that

Part Two: Teaching 1 Thessalonians 2:1-12

we gain the approval of people around us (and also avoid any suffering for continuing to preach an unpopular message). Similarly, it is very tempting for the busy pastor to please himself and neglect the needs of the flock because such care is demanding and energy-sapping. They can rationalise this by stating that through their preaching ministry all are cared for, and as a result remain detached and aloof. Both these scenarios reveal the value of Paul's description of authentic gospel ministry? It should give us courage to be faithful to the gospel once and for all delivered to us and should lead us to a greater sacrificial love for the flock of God bought with the blood of the Lord Jesus Christ.

The main instructions used within the passage relate to the picture of the pastor as both mother and father. The image of a mother nursing her tiny baby, coping with sleepless nights and developing an incredibly strong bond of love and affection, is a powerful one in helping us to see the sacrificial love and willingness to serve which should be evident in pastoral ministry. The image of the father encouraging a seven-year-old (too heavy to carry!) on a family walk to keep going in order to get all the way home is also a striking picture of the need for those in pastoral ministry to be engaged with, walking alongside and encouraging believers to keep going in their Christian lives, despite all the obstacles and difficulties that they face.

Ideas for application

- The many denials that Paul has to issue highlight the opposition and persecution that he received as a matter of course in his ministry. Though no one would choose to suffer and face misunderstanding and slander, nevertheless within the New Testament it appears to come with the territory. It may be that in the West we have been preserved from suffering due to the fact that the fabric of our society has been woven, partly at least, out of a rich heritage of Christian traditions. Yet as that fabric unravels, it is likely that Christians and pastors will find themselves more and more in situations where, like Paul, they face hostility, misunderstanding and slander. In such situations, we should recognise that such suffering forms part of the normal Christian experience and to retreat from suffering at all costs is almost a guarantee of a retreat from the biblical gospel.

- Boldness in Christian witness in the face of suffering is not an automatic reaction. Often we are frightened or cowed into silence. It is only with the help of God that Paul was able to dare to tell them the gospel. Similarly, it is only with the help of God that we will be able to share the gospel in our own day. Not only do we need to be persuaded of the importance of the gospel for eternal salvation but we need to be prayerfully dependent on the Lord to give us the courage and boldness required to speak for Christ in a hostile environment.

- Every believer and particularly every Christian leader has been entrusted with the gospel. We have no liberty to change the gospel to suit the desires of those who listen. Though others may pronounce their own judgments upon us, ultimately it is God's approval that matters and which should shape the way in which our ministry is discharged. Having been entrusted with the gospel, the crucial issue is whether we will have been found trustworthy or not. Imagine a situation where a doctor prescribes a particular medicine with a specific dosage to treat a member of your family. You go to the chemist and are entrusted with this medicine. Even though it may be unpleasant, it is vital that you are found to be trustworthy in administering it in order to bring healing and restoration.

- Those called to be involved in church leadership are given a powerful encouragement to exercise their ministries in ways which reveal sacrificial love and care. There can be an imbalance such that it is possible to focus so much on preaching God's Word that we forget about the people to whom we are speaking. As a result, the preacher can easily become detached and distant from the congregation. It is also possible to develop the wrong mindset where we begin to think that the main purpose of the congregation is to support the church leader and forget that the role of the leader is to serve the church family. Paul was careful not to be a burden on anyone.

- Reflecting on the use of the image of acting as a mother should remind church leaders of the enormous commitment, sacrificial love and sheer hard work which should be expected to be part and parcel of all pastoral ministry. The church leader may find it easy to resent intrusions into their time, and indeed sensible precautions often do need to be taken in order to cope and certain boundaries may need to be established. However, a mother is a full-time role with round-the-clock demands and therefore church leaders should not expect everything to run according to their own timetable. Pastoral needs and emergencies can and do occur at any point. The wise leader will seek to ensure that they are acting as part of a team but he will recognise that he can never be completely insulated from the demands of loving and caring for the church family as particular situations arise.

Indeed a wise pastor will also ensure that they are pastored by members of their own church family, so that they do not become aloof and unaccountable. That said, it is clear from the passage that Paul loved them and worked hard amongst them 'while he preached the gospel'. His focus, therefore, was on using every opportunity to teach the gospel. Pastoral ministry should not be thought of as something separate from preaching and teaching. Rather, it is the loving application of God's Word to God's people through the lives of God's servants.

- Paul's use of the image of a father encouraging and urging his children onwards also needs to be applied to those involved at all levels of church leadership, whether leading a home group or pastoring a large congregation. Amidst the busyness of life it is easy to focus on preparing for a particular meeting or event and the responsibility of helping people to understand God's Word. However, the work of the leader is not done when they have led their Bible Study or explained the text. All Bible teaching needs to be applied as personally as possible. The aim is not simply to impart information or enable someone to understand how a portion of Scripture 'works', important though these things might be. The aim is to see Christians growing in maturity and advancing in faith and goodness. Those in leadership will, like Paul, need to lead by example as they seek to encourage each member of the flock that the Lord has placed under their care.

Suggestions for preaching

Sermon: *The marks of Genuine Christian Ministry*
(1 Thess. 2:1-12)

- Pleasing God (2:1-6a)
  - Suffering for the gospel (1, 2)
  - Entrusted with the gospel (3-6a)

- Loving God's people (2:6b-12)
  - As a mother (6b-9)
  - As a father (10-12)

Other preaching possibilities
The most obvious alternative for the preacher wishing to go at a slightly slower pace would be to divide this passage into two sections in order to look first at the relationship with God and His Word and then to consider the relationship with God's people. Both subjects are extremely important and highlight the value of being able to work slowly through the text.

Another possibility for the church leader to consider is whether it might be beneficial to run a short series of four talks which could be the basis for a training course for leaders or small groups or for others within the church family who have leadership responsibilities or who might be invited to consider serving in this way. Such a short series might have the following titles:

- Suffering for the gospel (2:1, 2)
- Faithfulness to the gospel (2:3-6a)
- Loving God's people (2:6b-9)
- Encouraging God's people (2:10-12)

Suggestions for teaching

Introducing the passage

- What are the sorts of things that you look for in a Christian leader? Which do you consider to be the most important?

Understanding the passage

- Why might people have thought Paul's visit had been a failure? (see Acts 17:1-10 and 1 Thess. 2:1, 2)
- How had the thought of being 'entrusted with the gospel' shaped Paul's ministry? (2:3-6a)
- What is the danger if a preacher is primarily seeking to please men and women? (2:3-6a)
- How could Paul's ministry have been a burden on the Thessalonians? (2:6b-9)
- What aspects of the role of a mother are highlighted by Paul in his ministry? (2:6b-9)
- What aspects of the role of a father are highlighted by Paul in his ministry? (2:10-12)

Part Two: Teaching 1 Thessalonians 2:1-12

Applying the passage
- Why is it so important that church leaders are prepared to suffer for the gospel?
- What are the pressures that can cause a church leader not to be faithful to the gospel?
- How should the image of a mother help us to understand the role of a Christian leader?
- How should the image of a father help us to understand the role of a Christian leader?
- Having studied this passage, how should you pray for your own leaders within your church family?
- If you have leadership responsibilities, how has this passage challenged the way that you exercise your ministry?

4.

THE WORD AND THE WORLD (2:13-16)

Introduction
Paul has already given evidence that the Thessalonians have been genuinely converted (1:2-10) and that his own ministry was genuinely apostolic (2:1-12). He now follows this up in this next short paragraph by anticipating the response: so if this is the case, why are we experiencing suffering? Could it be that suffering is a sign of God's displeasure? What should the normal Christian life look like? Having spent some time reflecting on his own ministry, Paul once again returns to the Thessalonians. At the outset in 1:2-10, he had spoken about how they had started in the Christian life. Now at 2:13-16, he reflects on how they were continuing in their Christian life.

Listening to the text

Context and structure
Having looked back to his initial ministry amongst the Thessalonians (2:1-12), Paul returns to his theme of

thanksgiving (2:13). This links in with how he had started his letter to them (1:2, 3). However, now Paul wants to move on from their initial reception of God's Word whilst he was with them to their ongoing and current experience, which included a fair degree of suffering. Perhaps that is why he had needed to underline his ministry of encouraging and urging them forward in the Christian life (2:11, 12), because as these new believers had gone forward they had experienced even more suffering (2:14). Could this be normal or had something gone wrong with God's plan? This is the issue which he now needs to address.

The most noticeable thing about this short paragraph is the way that it repeats some of the key elements of 1:2-10.

+ We thank God continually (1:2, 3; 2:13)

+ Brothers (1:4; 2:14)

+ You became imitators (1:6; 2:14)

+ Suffering (1:6; 2:14)

+ The wrath of God (1:10; 2:16)

Although the content is very different, there is an interesting parallel between 1:2-10 and 2:13-16; in terms of the basic shape, the two sections are the same. In more detail it can be seen that this passage divides into two parts.

First, there is the thanksgiving offered by Paul. This is then connected with what follows by 'for' (2:14) which introduces the theme of suffering, just like the churches in Judea. At 2:13, we see the Word of God at work in them. In 2:14-16, we see the world at work against them.

It is worth observing the links between 2:4-6a and 2:13 and the contrast between God and men. Paul preached the Word of God in such a way as to please God and not men. As a result, the Thessalonians received it from Paul as the Word of God not as the word of men. If Paul had tried to advance the gospel through pleasing men, the Thessalonians would simply have received it as the word of men and given it no greater significance!

The theme of imitation continues into this passage. The Thessalonians imitated Christ (1:6), the Apostle Paul (1:6) and God's churches in Judea (2:14). It all amounted to the same thing. They had not simply taken on a new set of beliefs but had changed their lifestyle and behaviour. They were being shaped by what they saw in Christ's obedience, suffering and joy – which were evident in Paul's ministry as he shared his own life with them (see 1:5, 6 and 2:8) and in the testimony of the churches in Judea.

Working through the text

As we work through the text, attention is given to the two main themes identified in the structure of the passage.

1. The Word at work within you (2:13)

Paul gives thanks that when the Thessalonians heard him preach during this brief visit, they received his message not as the word of a gifted speaker but as the Word of God. In the act of preaching, the words faithfully entrusted to him by God (see 2:4) – the words used by Paul – became the Word of God. As the Second Helvetic Confession memorably states: 'the preaching of the word of God is the word of God.' In forwarding an email to someone, you are the one who is doing the communicating. Yet, as you forward the message, you are enabling someone to receive first-hand the words of the original sender. Though merely an illustration, it shows how important it is for the preacher to be faithful to the gospel with which they have been entrusted. It also highlights that the ultimate recipient of the gospel is actually hearing a message from God Himself. What an awesome experience it is that, through the preaching of the gospel, people are able to hear directly from God the Father and the Lord Jesus Christ through the working of the Holy Spirit (see 1:5 for the role of the Spirit)!

The Word of God had clearly done its work as the Thessalonians welcomed it with joy (1:6) and the effect was a turning from idols to serve the living and true God (1:9). However, now Paul reminds them that God's Word is still doing its work since it is at work within them (present tense). God's Word is an active agent reshaping and rebuilding their lives. From Jesus' parables of the kingdom in Mark 4:1-34, God's Word is like a seed growing and producing a harvest. Though it would have been perfectly acceptable for Paul to speak of the Spirit being at work within them, he can speak of exactly the same experience as the Word of God being at work (e.g. Ephesians 5:18-20 and Colossians 3:16, 17 where the work of the Spirit and the Word are referred to in identical contexts). Imagine someone ill being prescribed medicine. They take the medicine, receiving it into their body and there may well be immediate beneficial results. However, the medicine may continue to do its work many hours after it has been received as it fights infection and restores health. So it is with the Word of God which actively works within the life of the believer to resist sin and bring spiritual health.

Such is the normal Christian experience according to Paul. Believers are those who initially hear God's voice as God's Word is preached and, having received that Word, find that it is actively working away within them fulfilling God's intended purposes.

2. The world at work against you (2:14-16)

Given that God's Word is at work in the lives of all believers it is not surprising that it produces a family likeness. God's Word within is doing the same sort of work and forming people into the same basic pattern – to enable believers to imitate the Lord Jesus Christ. Therefore, if God's Word is at work within, making you more like Christ, then it will not be surprising if we experience what happened to Him. Paul therefore moves naturally from the Word at work within the Christian to the world at work against the believer.

Opposition from the world (2:14, 15a)

The sign that God's Word is at work within them is the fact that their current experience is identical to many other believers, including those in Judea, where the church had first been established following the death and resurrection of Christ. The fact that they are suffering like other Christians is therefore not a surprise at all – it is part of the normal Christian experience. Jesus Christ Himself suffered at the hands of the Jews, as did prophets in the Old Testament, apostles like Paul in the New Testament and the churches of God in Judea. Given that pattern, Paul is not surprised that the Thessalonians have suffered from their fellow countrymen. The experience of the Word at work within will often go alongside the experience of the world at work against the Christian. The two go together.

The rejection of the Word of God (2:15b, 16)
Why is such hostility a normal experience for Christians both then and now? The answer is that when the Word of God is preached, it must either be received or rejected. If it is received, it does its work within the believer. If it is rejected, it will lead to people rejecting both the message and those who have brought the message (see 15a), though there are inevitable consequences for rejecting the God who has spoken through His Word and for rejecting His servants who have faithfully conveyed it.

What are the results of rejecting God's Word and persecuting believers who preach it? First, it displeases God since it is a personal rejection. If you refuse to listen to someone when they are talking to you, it is a clear sign of personal antagonism. Second, such opposition is to be interpreted as a hostile act not just against God but all mankind, since it is calculated to prevent others hearing the lifesaving gospel of our Lord Jesus Christ. Ultimately all those whom God chooses (see 1:4) will be gathered into His Kingdom but nevertheless that does not excuse the calculated attempt to prevent people from entering. Our sinfulness is serious enough but opposing the preaching of God's Word by God's servants has the effect, says Paul, of heaping it up even further so that it can be even more clearly seen. It is like building up a stockpile of illegal weapons and then finding the storeroom overflowing, so that the illegal activity becomes completely obvious to the police with the evidence of what you have obtained illegally.

Yet the Thessalonian believers need not be anxious or worried despite enduring such opposition. Though it might appear that their own future as persecuted Christians seemed bleak and uncertain, Paul again wants them to take the long view and remind them that one day Jesus Christ, though rejected by men, will return. At His return, He will rescue believers from God's wrath (1:10). Therefore, though it might appear that those who persecute Christians hold all the reins of power and are able to live in luxury and ease, believers can be confident that one day they will face the full weight of God's wrath for their rejection of His Word and His servants. The really striking thing is that Paul can even speak of this eventuality in the past tense (see v. 16). It is possible that this could be a prophetic announcement of something that was certain to happen to the Jews in Judea in the near future, such as the fall of Jerusalem twenty years later in A.D 70, or it could simply refer to the fact that God's wrath is absolutely certain. This is a very difficult verse but, whatever the precise interpretation, it highlights the danger of rejecting God's Word and opposing His people.

In summary, this brief interlude, before Paul resumes speaking about his ongoing relationship with the Thessalonians, highlights what is involved in normal Christian experience. God's Word will be at work but so will the world, bringing suffering. However, persecution by the world is not the last word.

From text to message

Getting the message clear: the theme
The normal Christian life involves God's Word working in you whilst the world works against you.

Getting the message clear: the aim
The aim of this passage is to provide assurance of the reality of God's work even amidst times of persecution. Preaching or teaching on this passage should help in answering the following questions:

- How is it possible for the word of men to be the Word of God?

- To what extent is the experience of suffering part of the normal Christian life?

- How can Christians be confident that ultimately God is in control and will hold everyone to account for their opposition to Him and His people?

A way in
Since Paul left Thessalonica he was probably aware that the new believers were going to face difficulties from Jewish (and pagan) opposition. How could he have any degree of confidence that his work would survive and continue? The answer lies in the effectiveness of the Word of God. The Word of the Lord came to the Thessalonians and it was still at work amongst them performing God's work. Similarly, what is the main thing which will enable believers today to continue, especially in times of growing opposition and hostility? The answer lies in the effectiveness of God's Word to continue to do His work in the lives of each believer. A thoroughgoing ministry of God's Word is absolutely essential to enable God's people to stand firm.

Most people probably have played the game of 'Chinese whispers' where a message is relayed from person to person along a line. Usually when it gets to the last person it has been

Part Two: Teaching 1 Thessalonians 2:13-16

distorted considerably in meaning during transmission. However, if each link in the chain hears the message clearly and passes it on faithfully, then the message heard at the end will not simply be from the last person who whispered it on but from its originator. Similarly, in our passage, given Paul's commitment to the faithful transmission of the gospel (see 2:4), he is able to reflect on the fact that the message which the Thessalonians heard wasn't merely a message from his lips but originated from God Himself. Therefore it was the Word of God which they had heard and it needed to be treated in that light.

Ideas for application

- One of the key points to stress to those who have the privilege and responsibility of teaching is the importance of faithfulness in handling God's Word so that it is conveyed accurately. The result is that God's voice is heard. It highlights the need for great care and attention in preparing talks, sermons and Bible studies, so that the original meaning is properly understood before conveying and applying it to a particular situation. From the other angle, in those who hear the Bible taught there needs to be a sense of awe that as the Scriptures are faithfully unpacked so we have the incredible experience of hearing God speak to us. It is easy for those of us who regularly attend church gatherings to become blasé about what is happening when we come to the sermon, but if God's Word is being handled faithfully then it means we are hearing God's voice.

- The spiritual growth of Christians is primarily dependent upon God's Word working within them. It continues to teach, rebuke, correct and train in righteousness (see 2 Tim. 3:16) long after it has been preached as the Spirit of God applies the Word of God to the individual's life. It dwells within the Christian (see Col. 3:16) and actively does the job of rebuilding the pattern of Christ from within. It is therefore important for believers to make the most of the available opportunities to hear God's Word so that it is planted into their lives. Without God's Word our Christian life will soon drift and we will start listening to many other voices.

- We should not be surprised by suffering in the Christian life and particularly by opposition and even persecution. In the passage it was noted that the Lord Jesus, the prophets, the churches in Judea and the church in Thessalonica all experienced suffering and persecution. Therefore, if we are being conformed to the pattern of Christ, it can be expected that at some point each Christian will have to face a degree of opposition. Imitating Christ is not about calm meditative techniques but is forged in the heat of difficulties and opposition.

- We should not be surprised by the hatred of non-Christians and especially that which is directed at those who preach and teach God's Word. They won't want people to hear God's message and therefore they will often do all that they can to hinder people from doing so. However, Christians should not get discouraged as the Lord has many ways to enable His Word to be heard, and even those words which were sown many years ago and have lain dormant for all that period can easily germinate and bring about a harvest. A modern-day example of what has happened in China over the last sixty years reminds us that though hostility comes and threatens to silence the Word of God, it has continued 'to spread rapidly and be honoured' (see 2 Thess. 3:1).

+ Even amidst times of great suffering and persecution, believers need not despair. Though it may be tempting to think that God is not in control, Paul reaffirms in this letter that everyone, including those who persecute Christians, will face judgment. Everyone will be held accountable for their actions and treated accordingly with justice. The teaching about the wrath of God is therefore a doctrine which should bring great encouragement to believers and especially those who are in the midst of persecution. They need to know that it is always God who will have the last word.

Suggestions for preaching

Sermon 1: The Word and the world (1 Thess. 2:13-16)

+ The Word at work within you (2:13)
+ The world at work against you (2:14-16)

Other preaching possibilities

For those moving at a faster pace through the letter, it would be possible to include this short paragraph with 2:1-12 as there are a number of links. For example, 2:4 and

2:13 need to be understood together since it is only through faithfulness to God's Word that preaching can convey God's Word. A possible outline in tackling this longer passage could be as follows, which seeks to draw out the parallels within it:

- Faithfully teaching God's Word (1-6a)
- Suffering in serving God's people (6b-12)
- Faithfully receiving God's Word (13)
- Suffering in living as God's people (14-16)

Alternatively, it may be worth moving at a slower pace than the suggested exposition and concentrate on preaching simply on a single verse – 2:13. It would provide a good opportunity for the preacher to explain what should be going on in any sermon in order to help the congregation to recognise the privilege of hearing God's voice and also to help them see the great importance of praying for the preacher so that God's voice is truly heard.

Suggestions for teaching

Introducing the passage

- Consider together where the church is facing persecution. Why is there so much hostility to the Christian faith? What are our own experiences of opposition or hostility if any?

Understanding the passage

- What is it that Paul is particularly thankful to God for in verse 13?

Part Two: Teaching 1 Thessalonians 2:13-16

- In what ways was the Word of God continuing to be at work in their lives? (see 2:13)
- In what ways had the Thessalonian church imitated other churches? (see 2:14, 15)
- What was especially displeasing to God about the actions of those who persecuted the church? (see 2:15, 16)
- What are the consequences of the actions of those who persecute the church? (see 2:16)
- To what extent would these verses have provided encouragement to these new Thessalonian believers?

Applying the passage

- How is it possible to ensure that God's Word is heard? (consider 2:13 in the light of 2:4)
- What part should hearing God's Word play in our lives as believers and in what ways could this be developed or strengthened?
- What positive role does suffering play in the Christian life?
- To what extent is Paul describing normal Christian experience in this paragraph?
- How could you encourage those who preach at your church so that God's voice is heard?
- How could you encourage those who are persecuted for their faith in Christ?

5.

The heartbeat of Christian ministry (2:17–3:10)

Introduction

Paul may have had to leave the Thessalonians rather hastily but he had certainly not left them behind in his heart. This next section opens a window into Paul's love for this new church and his ongoing concern for them. Rather than viewing himself as a professional apostle who had important new ministries to pioneer and an exhausting schedule ahead of him, Paul wants them to realise how much he genuinely loves them in his absence. He viewed them as part of his family and in this section he exhibits all the natural concerns that parents tend to have for their children. We also need to recognise that in this passage we see mutual encouragement. Paul certainly wants to encourage these new believers, but on hearing the latest news from Timothy we shall see that the great apostle himself is encouraged by them. So, in this passage we have some rich material to inform our own pastoral relationships.

Listening to the text

Context and structure

It is important to understand that almost certainly Paul has been facing criticism for his sudden departure from Thessalonica (see Acts 17:10). Was he only in it for what he could get out of the Thessalonians in terms of prestige, reputation and perhaps money? To answer such criticisms and provide assurance to the Thessalonians, he has already reminded them of the quality of his pastoral ministry while he was present with them (2:1-12). Now he develops this by assuring them of his great concern whilst he is absent from them. In some ways, therefore, this section naturally follows on from 2:1-12. Paul's other concern is that he is aware of the persecution of this young church (see 1:6 and 2:14) and therefore he wants to encourage and strengthen them in their sufferings, which is how he came to the decision to send Timothy to them (see 3:1-5). His assistant would not only find out how things were going in Thessalonica but also help them to stand firm as they faced hostility to the church. Seen in this light, this section naturally follows on from 2:13-16.

There is a fairly obvious structure to this section which focuses on Paul's concern for them and how it led to the decision to send Timothy, based around his desire (mentioned at the beginning and end) to see them again (2:17; 3:10):

- Paul's desire to visit in person out of a concern for the church family. (2:17-20)

- Paul's decision to send Timothy to encourage them and find out how they were coping. (3:1-5)

- Paul's reaction to the news about them brought back by Timothy. (3:6-10)

In part, therefore, this section has a narrative structure focusing on the visit by Timothy to see them.

There is also a clear structure to the central portion. It begins and ends with the phrase 'when I could stand it no longer' (3:1, 5). This identifies this short paragraph as a subsection of his narrative whilst also highlighting his pastoral love and concern for them.

As usual, these paragraphs begin with 'brothers', which characteristically introduces a new section within the letter. The reference to being brothers and sisters within the same family is intensified by a whole series of words which reveal the depth of love and concern Paul has for them. He describes his intense longing to see them (2:17) which is repeated (see 3:6) and he is delighted to learn that they long to see him (also 3:6). Twice he says that he 'can stand it no longer' not having news about them. As we shall see, he also uses a term in describing being torn away from them which could literally be translated as 'being orphaned' (see 2:17). These references all link in with his self-description that he had acted like a mother and like a father when he had been with them (see 2:7-12). They all reveal the depth of love evident within his pastoral ministry whether present or absent.

Paul has already described something of the struggle that the believers were facing from those hostile to the Christian faith (see 1:6; 2:14f). In our current passage, he now specifically informs them that both he and they are involved in a spiritual battle. He refers to the activity of

Satan (2:18) and then describes him as 'the tempter' (3:5). Though they face hostility from their fellow countrymen (2:14), it can equally be described as the activity of the evil one since the two go together.

Key words in this part of the letter are the cluster 'strengthen', 'encourage', 'standing firm', 'established' (see 3:2, 7, 8, and 13). This lies at the very heart of Paul's concern for them. Though they are only new to the faith and blown around by many trials, his great desire is that they should be encouraged, strengthened and established in their faith so that they are able to stand firm.

Once again we see Paul praying. In almost every part of 1:1–3:13 we see Paul praying for the believers in Thessalonica, either giving thanks (1:2, 3; 2:13; 3:9) or praying for their strengthening (3:10-13).

Working through the text

In working through the text, use is made of the structure already identified above. This seeks to let the narrative flow of Paul's experiences shape the way in which it is preached.

1. The depth of Paul's love (2:17-20)

'Out of sight' can often mean 'out of mind'. Though the Thessalonians may have been tempted to think like that, in this passage Paul emphatically reveals that this had never been the case for him. Whether present with them (2:1-12) or absent (2:17–3:10), he wants them to be fully aware of the depth of his love. If anything, perhaps another proverbial saying would be more appropriate: 'absence makes the heart grow fonder.'

What is the evidence of Paul's continuing love for the Thessalonians? He is able to point to the past, present and

Part Two: Teaching 1 Thessalonians 2:17–3:10 105

future within this narrative about his ongoing relationship with them.

Past (2:17a)
Paul describes his departure with considerable depth of emotion. Rather than speaking in a cool, detached 'professional' manner, he speaks of being 'torn away' from them. He felt that he had been clinging to them in love, such that his fingers had to be prised open so that he could let them go when he left. The same phrase could also be translated as 'being orphaned'. From his point of view, his departure had felt like bereavement and he felt lost without them. This figure of speech reinforces the mutuality of their relationship (see also 3:6, 7). Though he had described himself as their father and mother, he now speaks of himself as an orphan ripped away from his parents (the Thessalonians?). The emotional intensity of this figure of speech provides the first strand of evidence of his depth of love for them.

Present (2:17b, 18)
Having been ripped from their grasp, Paul is quick to say that he has longed to see them again (see 2:17 and 3:10). So he speaks of his intense longing and says he had made every effort to see them. However, he constantly found his plans thwarted, which he attributes to the malign influence of Satan (2:18). It may be that this links in with the persecution of Paul and the church in Thessalonica to which he has just made reference (see 2:14-16), since later, at 3:3-5, he refers to the tempter seeking to unsettle people through various trials. Satan had been active, stirring up trouble so that the Gentiles would be prevented from hearing the gospel

message which could bring them salvation (see 2:16) and part of that strategy involved disrupting Paul's plans to return to Thessalonica. Paul is aware of the spiritual battle and wants the Thessalonians to be aware of it also. Even though prevented from seeing them, he still wants them to know of his great efforts to get to them and of his continued, intense longing to see them again. Such words and phrases could describe a couple in love and again serve to show the evidence of Paul's affection for them.

Future (2:19, 20)
As usual, Paul sees everything in the light of the personal return of the Lord Jesus Christ. The coming of Jesus determines salvation and judgment (1:10) but it also gives a perspective on all relationships. The real surprise is that we might expect Paul to link glory (or 'boasting', ESV) and joy with the person of Christ. However Paul applies each of these terms to the new Christian believers in Thessalonica. Though it is clear from 2 Thess. 1:10 that all believers will glory in Jesus, nevertheless in our current passage Paul's hope and joy are focused on seeing the Thessalonians in glory! Again, such is the intensity of his love for them that he tells them that he is longing for the day when he will see them alongside Christ.

In narrating his depth of love for the Thessalonians, Paul is modelling what pastoral ministry is all about. It involved a burning passion for those entrusted to him. For Paul pastoral ministry could be renamed parental ministry. Just as parents have a great longing to see their children and take pride in them, so Paul has a similar concern for those amongst whom he had ministered.

2. The extent of Paul's concern (3:1-5)

Of course it would be easy to criticise Paul if he had finished the section at 2:20 by stating that his concern only amounted to words. By themselves, words may not mean very much at all. So in the following paragraph the apostle reveals that his love also was evidenced in a particular action also, which may have been quite costly for Paul – he sent Timothy to them. Clearly, Timothy was regarded by Paul as a very valuable Christian worker (see 3:2) and to be without him for any lengthy period would have added to the strain and workload that Paul already faced in his ministry. The narrative nature of this paragraph is very clear. Perhaps the easiest way to unpack what it contains is to ask some simple questions which enable us to evaluate what Paul had done and for what reasons.

Why did Paul act? (3:1, 5)

The paragraph begins and ends with a reference to the fact that he couldn't stand the situation any longer (3:1, 5). He simply could not cope with the fact that since he had left he had received no news at all about how they were faring. Clearly he had expected to return (2:17, 18) but that was simply not working out. Perhaps he had hoped to receive a message from them, but would they realise that by now Paul had moved on from Berea and was now in Athens (see Acts 17:10-34)? Paul felt like a parent who had expected to hear from his daughter but no news had come through. Eventually Paul states that he could stand it no longer. He simply had to find out how they were doing! Again it reveals his genuine concern. Though perhaps busy with all sorts of things, his mind is constantly drawn back to them. A pile of letters arrive for him but none from the Thessalonians and he knows that he simply must act in order to find out how they are faring. He acted simply because he had to; such was his love for them.

What was his main concern? (3:3-5)
Paul knew that they had faced hostility whilst he was with them (see 1:6) and he himself had been driven out of Thessalonica in a wave of persecution (Acts 17:5-10). He remembered warning them during his brief visit that such trials and difficulties would come (see 3:4). This was not because God was unable to prevent them from happening. They would come not because God was not in control of all things but as part of God's sovereign plans (see 3:3b). Somehow these trials would be woven into God's eternal purposes which God had ordered and destined. So they will turn out for their good even though at the time the believers in this life may not have seen how that could have been possible. The question that perplexed Paul, however, was whether these new Christians would be sufficiently strong in their faith to cope with the assault that he expected them to be facing.

So Paul was concerned for their safety, as any parents are concerned when their child is facing danger. Would they be unsettled by their trials and be blown off course by the sheer strength of the forces against them (3:3)? Had they been tempted by Satan in some way such that Paul's efforts amongst them would have been rendered useless (3:5)? Perhaps some of the Jews were seeking to persuade them not to abandon all their old Jewish rituals – a temptation which Paul had needed to counter in Galatia and at the Council of Jerusalem (see Galatians and Acts 15). Perhaps the pagan authorities were tempting them by stating that there would be no persecution if they only acknowledged Caesar as Lord (see Acts 17:7). The temptations were likely to be insidious and subtle. If they provided a route which would remove all opposition and persecution, then it might be very appealing. For established believers these temptations might prove challenging enough, but for a new church plant they might prove irresistible. One can imagine Paul giving thanks to the Lord for the Thessalonians (1:2, 3; 2:13) and yet at the same time crying out for their safety. He simply must act.

What was Paul to do? (3:2)
Though it might mean being left alone in Athens (see 3:1 and Acts 17:16), Paul is more concerned about them than his own needs. So he selects Timothy and gives him a particular commission, which is described twice ('we sent' verse 2….'I sent' verse 5). Timothy is described as a brother and God's fellow worker in spreading the gospel of Christ. The Thessalonians would have known Timothy from the first visit and no doubt had enjoyed his subsequent time with them. Perhaps they would have been struck by this description of him. He could have been accurately described simply as 'Paul's fellow worker' (see 1:1) and yet Paul wants both the Thessalonians and Timothy to view his helper in a different light as 'God's fellow worker'. Though Timothy's task is to provide encouragement, Paul wants to ensure that Timothy himself is also encouraged…..and what an encouragement to be described in this way! Of course, Paul also knows that he himself needed encouragement and as we shall see that is soon provided through the news which Timothy brings to Paul from the Thessalonians (see 3:7). Mutual encouragement between Paul, Timothy and the

Thessalonians is at the heart of this glimpse of Christian ministry.

Specifically there are two aspects to Timothy's role. On the one hand, verse 5 indicates that part of his responsibility was to learn or find out about their faith and how they were coping under pressure. Paul wanted an update on their news and what had happened over the intervening period since his hasty departure. However, the task extended further (see v. 2) and it was also 'to strengthen and encourage you in your faith so that no-one would be unsettled.....' His role was, therefore, to continue the role which Paul had faithfully performed amongst them as described at 2:7-12.

A nursing mother feeds her baby to give it strength. In the same way, Paul had ministered amongst them and so Timothy was charged to continue this ministry. A father encourages and urges his children on; in the same way Paul had ministered amongst them and Timothy was charged to continue that same ministry. What Timothy had observed first-hand under the leadership of Paul was now to be worked out within his own ministry. It highlights the significant strategic role of working in teams and mentoring younger Christians. If Paul had gone to Thessalonica by himself, he could not have modelled pastoral ministry to Timothy and, as a result, the church would not have been able to receive a continuation of this kind of pastoral care through Timothy at a later date when it was particularly required.

Paul's aim, as we shall see at verse 8, is that through this ministry of strengthening and encouraging they would be able to stand firm in the Lord. Though the trials around them might briefly shake and disturb them, he wants them to be sufficiently strong so that as a result of his initial ministry and Timothy's follow-up visit they would be able to stand firm. Like a lighthouse shining strongly in the midst of the storm, with waves crashing all around and sending up a spray which briefly obscures it from view, so Paul's purpose is that, even when plunged into experiences of severe persecution, the Thessalonians would be sufficiently strengthened and encouraged to stand firm.

In narrating his own thought processes once again, we see Paul's pastoral heart and concern for these new Christians. He is not naïve about the situation; he knows the very real danger posed by the attacks of Satan and therefore he takes decisive action. Onlookers might consider it quaint and unworldly that to counter Satan's attacks and vicious persecution involving swords and suffering, Paul sends a preacher. Yet Paul knows that as the Word of God is sown it is able to do God's work and build His kingdom. Though sending Timothy may seem so weak and insufficient, Paul is fully convinced that it is only through the ongoing ministry of the Word that God's church is established.

3. *The heights of Paul's joy (3:6-10)*
Having sent Timothy off, he must have had a period of anxious waiting in Athens (even though as usual Paul immediately got involved in further gospel ministry – see Acts 17:16 ff). What news would Timothy return with and how had the Thessalonians fared without him?

What news did Timothy bring? (6-8)
It was good news! In terms of their relationship with God, they were continuing to stand firm in the Lord (v. 8). Their faith was holding firm despite all the pressures they

were facing. True, Paul is aware that their faith in Christ evidenced in their behaviour – is still not mature – He recognises that at some point he will need to supply what is still lacking (see v. 10), but this should not obscure the fact that as young Christians they are showing all the important signs of genuine Christian life and vitality. In the same way we might look at a plant which has still some way to go in terms of mature growth and fruitfulness and yet still be delighted with the progress that has been made since the seed was originally sown – so it was in this situation.

Further, Paul also received news of their love which clearly included their pleasant memories of Paul's earlier visit (see v. 6). Paul has made no secret of the fact that he longed to see them but it must have been tremendous to hear the news that they longed to see him.

What effect did this have on Paul? (7, 8)
The effect of hearing this news is that Paul himself is encouraged (v. 7). Though he is still facing seasons of difficulty and persecution, Timothy's report brings him tremendous encouragement. Even though the primary purpose of sending Timothy was to encourage them, the result was that Paul received encouragement. The effect of Paul's pastoral ministry was therefore to open up a two-way street of mutual encouragement. Though Paul was the experienced apostle, he also at times needed encouragement from them. This is developed in verse 8, since having heard that they are standing firm in the Lord he is able to say that he is now really able to live. Perhaps it's like a situation where you are awaiting news from the hospital following an operation on a dear friend. Whilst there is no news, your life in some ways is 'on hold'. When eventually news comes through that

everything is all right, you breathe a sigh of relief and joy, and you can then get on with life with renewed zest.

What is the result? (9, 10)
Paul concludes by describing how the news had drawn him back to God in thankfulness and joy. Thanking God for the faith, love and hope of the Thessalonians had been his initial impulse at the start of the letter (see 1:2, 3) and this had been enriched by Timothy's report which had provided even more reasons for thankfulness. Paul is full of joy for the Thessalonians – both for their conversion (see 2:19, 20) and for their continued faithfulness (see v. 9) – and as a result pours his heart out in thankfulness to God, aware that both he and they stand in God's presence. Every transaction between Paul and the Thessalonians on a horizontal dimension is also given a vertical dimension through Paul's insistence on continual prayer night and day (1:2, 3; 3:10) for them.

So, from a situation where Paul has no news and is anxious about them and sends Timothy because he 'could stand it no longer', we now end the passage with Paul overflowing with joy and thankfulness. It reveals the richness of Christian fellowship which is able to provide mutual encouragement in the faith.

In summary, we return to our main theme which helps to put everything into context. The Thessalonian church is newly planted and under pressure. Part of the pressure is from persecution but it also comes from the doubts being expressed by some within the community about Paul's ministry and his apparent lack of interest and concern for them now that he has left. This passage from 2:17 to 3:10 deals with all these issues. It acknowledges the strains and pressures that the young church is facing and shows how Paul seeks to build up these young believers through sending Timothy to them. It reveals Paul's ongoing love for them by showing his anguish at not being able to visit and his subsequent joy on receiving good news about them from Timothy. In this autobiographical manner, Paul is rebutting any lingering doubts arising from his detractors that he might not be interested in them. Instead the passage brims over with his ongoing love, concern and joy about them. At the end of the passage at 3:9, 10, we picture the apostle on his knees before God focusing entirely on the Thessalonian church, giving joyful thanks for them and praying for further growth and ministry. How could anyone say that Paul is not interested in them?

From text to teaching

Getting the message clear: the theme
Pastoral ministry involves a depth of love and concern which should lead to mutual encouragement and joy.

Getting the message clear: the aim
The aim of this passage is to reveal rich relationships which should provide encouragement and support to each other within the church. Preaching or teaching on this passage should help in answering the following questions:

- What sort of relationship should those involved in pastoral leadership have with their church family?

- How important is the ministry of encouragement within the Christian life?

Part Two: Teaching 1 Thessalonians 2:17–3:10

* What are the dangers that particularly younger Christians might face?

A way in

When you have been out of touch with someone for a length of time, it would be easy to wonder whether they are not at all bothered about you. Why haven't they been in contact? Do they know what a tough time you've been having? Have they simply moved on and quietly 'dropped' you? These are all very understandable thoughts and provide a helpful point of contact when we consider the relationship between Paul and the Thessalonians. Given Paul's absence, is he at all interested in how they are faring? Is he bothered about the fact that they are facing persecution for their faith in Christ? These concerns and the emotions which spring from them provide a helpful background to teaching on this passage.

Some areas of the world are subject to violent earthquakes which can devastate an entire region. In such places, it is vital that adequate means are used to strengthen buildings in order to survive the next dose of seismic activity. Paul uses terminology which can be linked to life in an earthquake zone. He is aware that there are trials or afflictions which could easily 'unsettle' these new Christians with the result that Paul's previous building efforts would be rendered useless (see 3:3, 5). As a result, he sends Timothy to 'strengthen' the new church family/building so that even after all the destructive activity of the earthquake/Satan/persecution, they are still to be found 'standing firm' (see 3:8). It paints a picture of the real threat that such destructive forces bring but also of the security provided through a ministry of the Word which brings strengthening and encouragement (see 3:2).

Pointers to application

- Throughout this portion of Scripture there is evidence of the deepest love between Paul and the Thessalonian Christians. Rather than being emotionally detached, he is completely engaged with them even though physically absent. Rather than focusing completely on his work in hand in Athens which might have involved preparing talks, networking with other believers, church planting and a whole range of other activities, he is also still eager to strengthen his relationship with the Thessalonians. His focus is on people and their need for the gospel and being built up in Christ, rather than on specific projects from which he can move on. For Paul it is all about relationships – with Christ, with new Christians, with fellow gospel workers, with non-Christians. For those of us in pastoral ministry it is easy to forget this amid the welter of meetings, commitments and sermons to prepare. People matter to Paul and should do to us.

- Paul has a balanced view when it comes to thinking about Satan. He doesn't ignore the role of the evil one who tempts and seeks to knock believers off course with all sorts of strategies. However, neither does he think Satan deserves a mention concerning every problem that the Christian faces. Paul clearly recognises that he is involved in a spiritual battle (see 2:18; 3:3-5) but equally clearly he recognises that the weapons with which he can fight are simply the Word

Part Two: Teaching 1 Thessalonians 2:17–3:10

of God (applied to believers in order to strengthen and encourage) and prayer.

- Paul does not want the Thessalonians to be surprised by suffering and particularly by the trials and afflictions which come from the active persecution of Christians. Paul had warned them in his brief visit that such things would come (see 3:3, 4). In other words, in his original visit he had carefully spelt out the cost of following our Lord Jesus Christ so that they were completely prepared for what might happen. Often today we can be surprised by opposition or be unprepared for it when it arrives. Perhaps we need to be clearer about recognising it as part of the normal Christian life and also see that through it God's purposes are not derailed but furthered in ways which we often cannot imagine.

- Paul sent Timothy with a clear agenda. Through the ministry of the Word, he was to strengthen and encourage them. His teaching was to be carefully and thoughtfully applied in order to enable young believers to stand firm in the storm. Our teaching must also be seen not as an end in itself ('I've explained the passage') but as the means to build up believers by applying God's Word to their lives. Application of God's Word must therefore be a key component whether within a sermon or Bible Study.

- Within the passage we see the importance of mutual encouragement. Paul does not present himself as self-sufficient without any needs at all. Instead, we see him valuing the encouragement provided by the

Thessalonians through their obedience to God's Word. Similarly, we should not expect ministers or Bible Study group leaders to remain aloof, dispensing encouragement themselves but not requiring or receiving it in return. Those involved in using their gifts in leadership must ensure that they do not cut themselves off from those they lead, and everyone within the church family should use every opportunity to encourage each other, including those with leadership responsibilities.

- Within this passage, and also often at the end of Paul's letters, we notice the richness of fellowship in the gospel. There is an inter-connectedness about the network of relationships within the wider church family. The Thessalonians both receive and give encouragement, as do Timothy and Paul in their different ways. Paul thanks God for Thessalonians and we can be sure that they are thanking God for the ministries of Paul and Timothy. Nobody stands alone. Though Paul is Jewish and the Thessalonians are mainly from a pagan background, they are knitted together in a growing fabric as God's gospel purposes are worked out. We need to recognise the privilege of being in God's worldwide church and the rich network which it provides to undergird and strengthen us.

Suggestions for preaching

Sermon 1: The heartbeat of Christian ministry (1 Thess. 2:17–3:10)
- The depth of Paul's love (2:17-20)
- The extent of Paul's concern (3:1-5)
- The heights of Paul's joy (3:6-10)

Part Two: Teaching 1 Thessalonians 2:17–3:10

Other preaching possibilities

Many preachers might want to include 3:11-13 within this sermon. Paul's report of praying night and day for the Thessalonians naturally leads into 3:11-13 and it can be noted that he prays for a further strengthening work within them (see 3:13 and back to 3:2). Within this suggested programme, however, the decision has been taken to deal with 3:11-13 in a separate sermon simply because of its importance as a hinge in summing up 1:2–3:10 and providing a launching pad into 4:1–5:11.

The other likely possibility is to split this section into its three constituent paragraphs. There is a risk of duplicating material because Paul's great concern for the Thessalonians is evident in each passage, but nevertheless adopting a slower journey through this part of 1 Thessalonians does give the preacher more time to develop the themes found. This is particularly true with 3:1-5 where the themes of Paul's concern, the reality of satanic opposition and the need for a ministry of encouragement are more than sufficient for covering in a single sermon, rather than as part of a much larger passage.

Suggestions for teaching

Introducing the passage

+ Imagine a situation where parents have not heard from their child away at university for a lengthy period of time and for some reason is not able to get through to them on a mobile phone. How might they feel? What might they do?

Understanding the passage
- What is the evidence within 2:17-20 of Paul's depth of love for the Thessalonians?
- What activity is attributed to Satan at 2:18 and 3:5 and why does he seek to do such things?
- What is Paul's purpose behind sending Timothy and how do you think Timothy would fulfil this commission? (3:1-5)
- What had Paul taught the Thessalonians right at the start and why? (see 3:3, 4)
- What was the news that particularly encouraged Paul? (see 3:6-8)
- How did the Thessalonians feature in Paul's prayer life? (see 3:9, 10)

Applying the passage
- What do Paul's feelings for the Thessalonians show us about his view of pastoral ministry?
- To what extent do we prepare young Christians for times of opposition and persecution?
- What are the things which have particularly strengthened and encouraged you in the Christian life?
- To what extent does your group or church foster mutual encouragement and how could this be developed?
- In what ways could the example of Paul's depth of love for other believers shape your own life and ministry?
- How could you encourage others within your church family, your church leaders or your mission partners this week?

6.

A PRAYER FOR GROWTH
(3:10-13)

Introduction

It is very easy to become complacent in the Christian life. Since Christ has achieved forgiveness for us and granted us new life with the prospect of glory to come, whatever we now do as Christians may seem fairly irrelevant. The really important thing is that we have come to know Christ. Now though that may all be true, the danger is complacency – since Christ has done it all, then I don't need to do anything. With that mindset, it is easily possible to drift and then find ourselves living our lives at some distance from Christ. Paul is alert to this danger at Thessalonica. He has spent time in this letter giving them assurance that they have been genuinely converted through the gospel.

He has also tried to provide assurance that his own ministry was a genuine gospel ministry so that they could have confidence in the message preached. However, having now received news that they are continuing in the Christian faith, the last thing he wants is for complacency to set in. They are a newly planted church and healthy plants should grow. So from this point onwards in his letter Paul changes his focus and urges these young Christians to keep growing – and he starts by taking the matter directly to God and praying for the Thessalonians.

Listening to the text

Context and structure

These verses form a vital 'hinge' within the letter. They face both backwards and forwards. On the one hand, they form an 'inclusio' with the thanksgiving prayer at the beginning of the letter (see 1:2, 3), and on the other hand they set the agenda for the rest of the epistle. In his opening prayer of thanksgiving, faith, love and hope are all mentioned and these words or themes are all evident at 3:10-13. Further, these themes all appear to be developed in the second half of the letter (faith 4:1-8, love 4:9-12 and hope 4:13–5:11). It seems therefore that these verses hold a particularly significant place within the letter and warrant particular attention. The immediate context is that having received news from Timothy about how well the Thessalonians were doing, Paul has turned to God in prayer (see 3:9, 10). This report of his prayer includes both thanksgiving (3:9) and a petition that he would be able to see them in order to supply what is lacking in their faith (3:10). It is out of this reported petition that Paul's prayer at 3:11-13 flows.

The prayer itself features three petitions. The first is connected with the previous verse (3:10) – the reason Paul wishes to be able to come to them is in order to supply what is lacking in their faith. The second and third petitions are slightly longer.

A key thought in Paul's prayer is the need for the Thessalonians to be strengthened (see 3:2, 3:13 and also 2 Thess. 2:17; 3:3). This fits with the observations already made that this is a young church facing considerable opposition and persecution. Another point to observe is to compare Paul's prayers at 3:11-13 and 2 Thessalonians 2:16, 17. Both have the aim of strengthening the Thessalonians and in both the petition is made to God the Father and the Lord Jesus Christ. However in 2 Thessalonians 2:16 the order is reversed. Considering these two prayers together, coming as they do amongst Paul's earliest writings, it is possible to observe right from the outset an extremely high Christology. The Lord Jesus is viewed as fully part of the Godhead.

Further, we can see that though the prayer is to God the Father and the Lord Jesus Christ, the verb indicating what Paul longs for them to do is in the singular, highlighting the unity of the Godhead. In addition it is also clear that although the prayer is initially addressed to God the Father, most of the content relates to requests to the Lord (i.e. the Lord Jesus Christ). All this helpfully shows how the doctrines of the deity of Christ and the Trinity were right at the centre of Christian understanding and prayer from the earliest years of the mission of the church.

Working through the text

As we work through the text, attention is given to the clear threefold structure of the prayer already identified.

1. Consistent Faith (3:10, 11)

The first petition is extremely straightforward. He prays that our God and Father and our Lord Jesus would enable him and his companions to be able to return to Thessalonica. Having already told them that he had been prevented from returning due to the activity of Satan (see 2:18), he has reiterated on a number of occasions his desire to see them again (see 2:17; 3:6, 10). This prayer is the culmination of such desires. Was it answered? Insufficient detail is given but certainly during Paul's third missionary journey (Acts 19:21; 20:1, 2) he passed through Macedonia 'speaking many words of encouragement to the people', and it is highly likely that during this time he visited Thessalonica.

However, the main reason for his prayer to be able to visit is contained in the previous verse (3:10). He longs to visit in order to supply what is lacking in their faith. Though Paul has already given thanks to God for their faith which was already being evidenced in various ways (1:3), nevertheless he is aware that there were some obvious gaps which needed filling. As will shortly be seen, these gaps did not relate so much to any deficiency in their knowledge of the Christian faith but rather in the application of their faith to every part of life (see 4:1-8). In the area of sexual relationships there was little evidence, certainly amongst some of the church members, that their faith in Christ had any impact at all. So Paul prays that he will be able to visit specifically so that this sort of issue can be dealt with. He longs for a consistent faith which is worked out across the whole of these new believers' lives.

2. Overflowing love (3:12)

Having mentioned their faith (3:10, 11) Paul turns to their relationships with each other and those around them. He has already given thanks for their labour prompted by love (1:3). Yet he has also detected that there is something deficient. Again this probably only relates to a minority within the fellowship, but it is a matter which he will raise at 4:9-12 and then again in 2 Thessalonians 3:6-15 and seems to relate to a group who were refusing to work and serve others. His prayer is therefore a desire that their love for others around them would increase and overflow, and that this would be evident amongst both the Christian family and the wider Thessalonian community ('everyone else').

Within this prayer, Paul again points to his own example. He has certainly modelled such love, having given ample demonstration of his love towards them, both whilst present (2:7ff) and now whilst absent (2:17; 3:1). This picture of love increasing and overflowing is ultimately modelled on God's love for the Thessalonians (see 1:4) which has led to the death of the Lord Jesus Christ for them. It is a dynamic picture of abundance, life and activity which should be the hallmark of the Christian community.

3. Sustaining hope (3:13)

Having mentioned faith (by implication from 3:10) and love, we would expect to see the final petition relate to Christian hope. Though the word is not actually used, the theme of Christian confidence concerning the future is very evident in this final petition. Once again Paul has already given thanks for their endurance which had been inspired by their hope in our Lord Jesus Christ (see 1:3) but it would appear that amongst some such confidence had been shaken. For some it may have been the bereavement of a Christian brother or sister (see 4:13-18) and for others it may have been a degree of puzzlement about how and when the Lord Jesus would return (see 5:1-11), but in both cases some members of the church had been unsettled and perhaps some doubts had crept in concerning whether Christ would return or not.

As a result, Paul prays for the strengthening of their hope. He had sent Timothy to them with the express intention of strengthening them (see 3:2) and now he prays for the same thing so that they would keep going, amidst persecution and bereavements, until the day when the Lord Jesus Christ would return. It is a prayer that they would keep going and not be discouraged (which is why Paul ends both his subsequent 'hope' sections with the instruction to encourage each other through imbibing this teaching – 4:18; 5:11).

Once they are strengthened, he longs for them to be ready for Christ's return when they would stand in the very presence of God. His prayer is that on that day it would be evident that they had been set apart (holy) and had lived for Christ. Though it would not be possible for them to avoid all sin, his longing is that in their outward visible conduct they would be blameless (a prayer which is repeated near the end of the letter at 5:23). Therefore, this is a prayer that they would live a godly life pleasing to Christ.

Yet the main focus of the prayer relates to the emphasis on the return of the Lord Jesus accompanied by all His holy ones. On the basis of Zechariah 14:5 (and see also 2 Thessalonians 1:7, 10), this is probably a reference to

Jesus being accompanied by angels and brings to mind a very vivid picture of the nature of His glorious return. With such an accompaniment, there is no way that such a return could be overlooked or missed! Paul is therefore reinforcing the fact that everything that the believer does should be done in the light of the certain, personal, public return of the Lord Jesus Christ.

In ending his prayer for the Thessalonians on this note, Paul completes the pattern that has already been identified. Each passage within the first main section of the epistle ends on a note which links in with the future and the return of Christ. Those who do not follow Christ but persecute believers will experience God's wrath (2:16), whilst believers will experience Jesus' rescue (1:10). They will then experience fully what it is to be called into God's kingdom and glory (2:12). Aware of all these future developments associated with the return of Christ, he prays that these Thessalonian believers would be strengthened so that they can keep going until that great final day, even whilst they endure persecution and opposition in the present (3:13).

In summary, this prayer forms a crucial link at the very centre of the epistle linking both halves together. It completes the first half whilst also preparing for the second half. It highlights the fact that these are young Christians with much still to learn who need strengthening, whilst also acknowledging Paul's love for them and delight that they are still standing amidst the persecution they have suffered. This is Paul's prayer for a young church under pressure so that it may grow in maturity and be able to withstand all other assaults that may come.

From text to message

Getting the message clear: the theme
Growth and development should be a normal feature of the Christian life.

Getting the message clear: the aim
The aim of this passage is to show Paul's priorities in prayer for these believers. Preaching or teaching on this passage should help in answering the following questions:

- How is it possible to help believers to avoid complacency and drifting in the Christian life?

- What are the key areas where believers may need to be challenged in their Christian life?

- How should the future return of the Lord Jesus affect how Christians live today?

A way in
Imagine a situation where you are wishing to purchase a house and as part of the process you need to obtain a surveyor's report. Hopefully it is as accurate as possible and reveals that the house is in good condition, but nevertheless there may be particular problems highlighted in the report which require attention. Some may be more pressing than others but it is helpful to be able to get the report in order to assess what needs to be done. In Paul's 'survey' of the Thessalonian church family, he has found that there is much that is in very good working order (see 1:2, 3). Nevertheless, there are a number of key things which do require attention and, returning to our illustration, these are the things that the surveyor now needs to bring to your attention so that

Part Two: Teaching / 1 Thessalonians 3:10-13

they can be remedied. It is these areas where there are shortcomings that are now highlighted by Paul as he prays to the Lord in this short passage (see 3:10-13) which then leads into the second half of his letter.

Paul's desire to 'supply what is lacking in your faith' (3:10) uses language which immediately suggests a variety of images which the preacher may find useful in pressing home the point. A football manager lamenting over his side's latest heavy defeat might say to the press that he needs a decent striker who can score goals and a new centre-half who can shore up the defence. Those are the things he is 'lacking' and which need sorting out if the team is going to thrive. Or imagine someone cooking a meal and discovering that they have run out of one or two key ingredients. Those are the things which are 'lacking' and which might require a trip to the shops to remedy. As so often, paying attention to the verbs which are used in the passage can be helpful in providing illustrations which may then bring the passage to life for the person listening. As they consider an everyday situation where 'something is lacking', so they may more easily be able to see the importance of remedying the deficiencies within their own Christian life.

Pointers to application

- Paul is always alert to the dangers of complacency in the Christian life. Though there is plenty for him to give thanks for concerning the Thessalonians, nevertheless he recognises the need to provide continual encouragement for them to push on in their Christian lives. Paul seems to strike exactly the right balance of providing assurance (chs. 1–3) whilst at the same time encouraging them forwards in key areas (chs. 4, 5). The way that he blends thanksgiving (1:2, 3) and prayer (3:11-13), assurance and encouragement, reveals his pastoral wisdom and concern for the Thessalonians and is a great example to us.

- If the apostle were to conduct a survey of our Christian life, where would he find gaps and deficiencies? Where would he feel that he needed to supply things that were lacking? It may be that there are gaps in our understanding of the Scriptures or the message of salvation which need to be remedied. If so, they need to be attended to through a careful study of the Bible, perhaps with the assistance of others or through good Christian literature. Yet it may well be that the gaps relate more to a patchy application of God's Word to our lives, as appears to be the case with the Thessalonians. Often through the preacher observing his own deficiencies and through his pastoral contact with the church family he will know fairly accurately where correction is required.

- Paul's vision is for the believers in Thessalonica to be modelling their love for each other on God's love for His church and also Paul's love for them. He longs to see their love, which undoubtedly exists, increase and overflow so that many others both within and outside the church community are affected. It is relatively easy to show love to those around us or to those who are like us, but Paul longs for their love to be much more indiscriminate. The challenge for us is that we should take every opportunity to show love within our church

Part Two: Teaching 1 Thessalonians 3:10-13

and the surrounding community. Paul's prayer should be a spur for us to be far more proactive so that through us many others would experience a taste of the love of the Lord Jesus Christ which has overflowed to us and which, like a cascading fountain, now overflows to others.

- Going on a long journey to reach a holiday destination can be a gruelling experience. There may be traffic problems with roadworks and lane closures on the motorway due to accidents. There may be problems with the car which requires roadside assistance. There may also be problems with the passengers as the children express their frustration with being cooped up in a hot car for endless hours. The journey with all its trials only makes sense in light of the destination. Having a clear picture of the joys awaiting you at the destination helps to give fortitude for the journey. Within 1 Thessalonians, Paul is constantly pointing to the Christians' destination, reminding them of the day when the Lord Jesus will return in glory. We also need to remind ourselves of our destination – not so much a place but a person. This will surely help to strengthen us in seeking to please Christ in readiness for the day when we will meet Him.

- Paul's basic concern behind this prayer is to encourage the Thessalonians to go forward in their Christian life. Just as the crowd at a sports venue are cheering on their team, so Paul is also saying 'come on!' as he prays for God to be at work in their lives. This is the focus of his prayer and his letter. No doubt it would be his message when he finally managed to see them face to face. So it should be with us as we use every means to encourage each other forwards in the Christian life to greater Christ-likeness. In particular, however, the means by which Paul seeks to encourage them is through praying for them, and this is something that is open for each of us to do as we long for Christians around us to grow to full maturity as believers. Before writing to them he has been praying for them and this should be an encouragement for us also to make prayer a priority.

Suggestions for preaching

Sermon 1: A prayer for growth (1 Thess. 3:10-13)

- Consistent faith (10, 11)
- Overflowing love (12)
- Sustaining hope (13)

Other preaching possibilities

The advantage of taking such a short passage is that the preacher can attend to most of the details of the text. Since this passage dovetails very neatly with the start of the letter (1:2, 3) and also acts as a hinge setting out the agenda for the rest of the letter, it may also provide a valuable opportunity for a further overview of 1 Thessalonians. If the preacher needs to find a natural break within his series, then this might be the most natural place either to finish the first series or to start the second one because of its location within the letter.

Part Two: Teaching 1 Thessalonians 3:10-13

Alternatively, it would be easy to include these verses within an exposition of 2:17 – 3:13, especially since Paul's reaction to hearing the good news from Thessalonica drives him to prayer (3:9, 10). His prayer in 3:11-13 simply flows out of his earnest prayer for them which he has been praying night and day (3:10).

Suggestions for teaching

Introducing the passage
Imagine receiving the results of a survey on your home which highlights the deficiencies along with the good points. What might a survey by the Apostle Paul reveal in your life? What might be his response on seeing the results of such a survey?

Understanding the passage
- What do we learn from the way Paul prays? (3:9, 10)
- What are the features in common between 1:2, 3 and 3:10-13?
- Why is Paul so keen to see the Thessalonians again according to 3:10? (see 4:3-8 for the background).
- In what ways does he want the Thessalonians to grow at 3:12? (see 4:11, 12 for the background).
- Given the context of suffering (e.g. 2:14, 3:3), why does Paul pray as he does at 3:13?
- What does Paul tell us at the end of each section in the first half of 1 Thessalonians? (study 1:10; 2:12; 2:16 and 3:13).

Applying the passage
- What might be the things that are lacking in the outworking of our faith?

- In what ways may our lack of overflowing love be exposed (both within the church family and the wider community)?
- Do we neglect the teaching about the personal return of the Lord Jesus and, if so, how do we explain this deficiency?
- How might a clearer understanding and application of the truth of the return of the Lord Jesus Christ affect our Christian lives for the better?
- In what ways could you use this prayer for any Christians you know and what impact might that have on your own Christian life?
- With God's help, how could you seek to see this prayer answered in your own life?

7.

Pleasing God through holy living (4:1-8)

Introduction

Our culture and our media are dominated by stories relating to sex. Week by week various sexual scandals are unveiled. Sadly a number of these stories relate to the church. Though as Christians we might expect the standard of behaviour to be considerably better within the church and especially within church leadership, sadly it is not always the case. As a result, the church has had its reputation tarnished through stories of sexual abuse or adultery by Christian leaders. The teaching contained in this next portion of 1 Thessalonians is therefore of particular significance. It seeks to deal with an issue prevalent in the church in Thessalonica, at least amongst some of its members. Yet in doing so, as so often happens, we find that God's Word speaks to our contemporary situation. It is powerful and relevant and may be exactly the word which our churches need to hear today.

Listening to the text

Context and structure

With these verses we start the second main section of this epistle. The first section has finished with a prayer (3:11-13) which echoed the opening thanksgiving (1:2, 3). Paul has now achieved his first main aim in providing assurance to a church under pressure. He has presented convincing proof that they are genuine believers, that his ministry was genuine and that he still had enormous affection and concern for them amidst all the suffering they were experiencing. Having wrapped things up with a prayer, Paul now attends to his second main aim. Since this church is only newly planted, he is aware that there are several areas which require attention so that there is appropriate growth in godliness and understanding. He therefore turns his attention at this point in the letter to this second key area of encouraging the Thessalonian believers in living for Christ. The word 'finally' is probably better translated as 'concerning what remains to be said' and is used by Paul both here and at 2 Thessalonians 3:1 as a means of signalling a change in topic within the letter.

Paul's concluding prayer (3:10-13) in the previous section has also set the agenda for the rest of the letter. This is particularly clear with the reference to 'love' (see 3:12 and 4:9-12). It is also easy to see the link between the reference to the return of Christ (3:13) and Paul's further explanation (4:13 – 5:11) designed to strengthen their hope and confidence in what Christ will do. However, is there a link between the reference to what is lacking in their faith and the material before us in 4:1-8? It depends upon how 'faith' is defined. If it is narrowly defined as knowledge of Christ and His work leading to trust in Him, then it is not easy to see any connection between 3:10, 11 and 4:1-8. However, at the outset Paul has spoken of their 'work produced by faith' (1:3) which perhaps indicates that he sees 'faith' in a slightly broader way. Genuine trust in Christ should initially be linked to trust in His Word and trust in Christ's Word given through the apostles should inevitably lead to a different lifestyle which is pleasing to God. This is exactly the sort of material that is found in 4:1-8. The presenting issue is that at least some of the Thessalonian Christians have put their faith in Christ but are not expressing such trust through obedience to Christ's Word in the area of sexual control. Paul writes to supply what is lacking in their faith in order for them to lead lives where they trust and follow Christ's Word rather than betray such trust by following the ways of the surrounding culture.

This passage falls into two parts. The opening verses (4:1, 2) provide a headline for the whole of this section up to 5:11, but also give a natural introduction to the specific issues developed in the following paragraph (4:3-8). In providing this introduction, it may be possible to see a chiasm in this passage. It is important that this is expressed tentatively as a number of respected commentators would take a different view. However, there is certainly some evidence for viewing the passage in this way, and if this approach is correct, it will provide a very helpful structure for the preacher.

  A 4:1, 2 Instructions to please God given by man (Paul) by authority of God.

    B 4:3a God's will = holiness

    C 4:3b avoid sexual immorality

       D 4:4, 5 contrast between self-control for Christians and lack of control amongst others.

   C1 4:6 avoid sexual immorality

  B1 4:7 God's call = holiness

 A1 4:8 Rejecting these instructions involves rejecting God, not man

At the outside of the chiasm (A, A1) is the reference to the instructions which Paul passed on to the Thessalonians whilst he was with them. These are to be followed because they come with the authority of God (see also 2:13 on this theme). If they are rejected, it is ultimately God who is being rejected. In the next step (B, B1), these instructions are specified and relate to God's desire for Christians to live holy lives. This is developed (C, C1) by explaining that the call to holy living will necessarily include avoiding certain sorts of behaviour. Finally at the heart of the chiasm (D), which is often the focus of the teaching, there is a call to believers to be self-controlled.

If this structure is correct, then the preacher will probably want to give particular attention to the centre (D) and the outer sections (A, A1) as, within the logic of Paul's argument, these are the key lessons which he is seeking to drive home.

As so often in this letter, the use of 'brothers' (4:1) signals a new subsection which is clearly the case here. Paul also refers in this passage to what he had previously said to them. This has already been indicated by his references to the fact that the Thessalonians already knew how he had acted when he was with them (e.g. 2:1ff) and that they had received certain teachings during that first visit (e.g. 3:4). This theme is now developed considerably, and at a number of places Paul continues to make reference to his earlier teaching from his initial visit – see 4:1, 2, 6 (and then later at 4:9; 5:1, 2). His teaching in much of this second main section of the epistle is therefore by way of reminder. He is simply applying truths which had already been previously taught.

Another key theme to observe is the fact that Paul is continually seeking to encourage them forwards in the Christian life. Whilst with them, he acted like a father, encouraging and urging them on to live lives worthy of God (2:12). Whilst absent from them, he was so concerned that he sent Timothy to them with the particular remit of strengthening and encouraging them (3:2). The word variously translated as 'urge' or 'encourage' comes repeatedly at 4:1, 10, 18; 5:11, 14. Paul's ministry is to urge them forwards in order that they would grow to live lives worthy of God in every area.

Working through the text

In working through the text rather than considering the verses consecutively, use is made of the chiastic structure of the passage in order to pick out the main thrust of the apostle's teaching.

1. How can I please God? (4:1, 2, 8)

Paul's starting point is to remind the Thessalonians that they had received teaching from him (both by word and also by example – see 2:4) that the primary aspect of living the Christian life was all about seeking to please God. The information that he had already received, perhaps from Timothy, was that many of them were doing this and so his simple instruction is that they continue to do this 'more and more'. This is also his request at 4:10 where his desire is that they continue to love each other 'more and more'. The apostle does not want them to drift or stagnate in the Christian life but is passionately committed to their continued growth and development. As it is a new 'church plant', he is expecting further growth in this plant in terms of spiritual maturity. Continuing to please God is the main thing Paul is looking for in the Thessalonian church and which he is seeking to encourage through his ongoing ministry. Pleasing God and not men had shaped his own ministry (2:4) and pleasing God not men would be the key to the outworking of their Christian faith.

The question then arises: if pleasing God is so important, how can I please Him? The answer which Paul gives is that the Thessalonians Christians will please God not by rejecting His teaching (since that would involve rejecting God – see 4:8) but by following it (since that would involve living under the authority of the Lord Jesus who had given the teaching to Paul – see 4:2). Pleasing God is therefore intimately linked with accepting God's Word. Rejecting God's Word will involve rejecting God. The extent to which Christians please God, therefore, can be assessed by their desire to follow Christ's Word given through the apostle.

A key step in this argument which Paul is making is the link between the word he had passed on to them and the Word of God. Earlier Paul had commended them as he thanked God that they had received his word as the

Word of God (see 2:13). Now he makes a similar point by referring to the instructions which he gave them as having come by the authority of the Lord Jesus (4:2). Christ had delivered an authoritative word through the apostle about how to live in a way which pleased God.

The final point to make is that once again we see that Paul does not make a division between Word and Spirit. This was evident at 1:5, 6 where it could be seen that in both Paul's preaching of the Word of God and the Thessalonian reception of that Word, the Holy Spirit was at work. God's Word and God's Spirit were inseparable. So it is in this passage. God gives His Holy Spirit to believers (4:8), that is, to those who have received Paul's word as God's Word (see 2:13; 4:1, 2). To please God I therefore need to receive and follow this Word and the Holy Spirit is given to enable me to do so.

In other words, the only way I can please God (4:1) is through obeying Christ's Word (4:2) through the power of the Holy Spirit (4:8). In this way the work of the Trinity is brought together. Rejecting Paul's word will involve rejecting God's Word, which entails rejecting God, which ultimately means rejecting God's Spirit. So it is that rejecting the apostolic word we have been given in the Scriptures will involve rejecting God's Word and God's Spirit. So Paul starts by seeking to encourage them and urge them on in the Christian life through seeking to please God more and more. This can only be done as they obey God's Word. However, the question then arises concerning the content of God's Word.

2. *What does God's Word say about pleasing God?* (4:3, 6, 7)

Paul's basic point is that God's Word instructs us to live a life of holiness. Both God's will, which expresses His purpose and desire, and God's call, which expresses His invitation and instruction, are united in focusing on holiness for every believer (see 4:3, 7). At 4:3 the word 'sanctification' (ESV) is the same word translated elsewhere as 'holy'. To be sanctified is to be set apart for a particular purpose. A holy life is one which is set apart for God and His use. To be sanctified is to be set apart so that we belong to God. This happens primarily at conversion and our growth in holiness is simply an outworking of our new relationship with the living and true God. The call to holiness also points to our final glorification since it links to God's call to bring each believer into His kingdom and glory (2:12). So in very positive terms Paul reveals that God's Word calls and instructs us into a holy lifestyle.

However the positive instruction can often be made clearer when it is adjacent to the corresponding negative instruction, and this is evident within the chiastic structure at 4:3 and 4:6, 7. God's Word gives clear boundary markers to enable believers to see where it is no longer possible to please God. So both sexual immorality (4:3) and impurity (4:7) are to be avoided. It may be that though sexual immorality identifies the particular area of concern, Paul also refers to impurity as it probably has a wider range of meaning. Paul is not just concerned about whether a Thessalonian believer has acted in a sexually immoral manner, for he is just as concerned about other aspects of behaviour or thoughts which might betray impurity and which might also then lead to sexually immoral acts. He wants to guard against the Christian legalist who might feel that, because he had not actually committed an act of sexual immorality, he was living a life pleasing to God.

Part Two: Teaching 1 Thessalonians 4:1-8

The warnings against immorality or impurity are then backed up at 4:6 by reference to the punishment that comes from the Lord Jesus to all who follow a sexually immoral lifestyle. Paul's teaching had come with the authority of the Lord Jesus (4:2) and this is no empty authority. The Lord will not tolerate such wilful disobedience and He will act accordingly. Paul stresses that the Thessalonians should not be surprised by such a severe warning since this was something that he had already told them about in his initial visit. Holiness had clearly been on the agenda even on such a short trip. The call to follow Christ included the call to live for Him.

The reference within 4:6 to wronging his brother or taking advantage of him is likely to relate to adultery, though it may have a wider application. Within a new Christian community which was under intense pressure from the surrounding culture, particularly through persecution, one could readily imagine the Thessalonian church becoming a close-knit gathering where believers are encouraging and supporting one another. Within such a setting, Paul is concerned that some of the men might take advantage of others through forming relationships outside marriage. It may be that the natural reference would be to adultery but it could relate to sexual relationships with a male or female slave. Either way, it is a specific application of the general warning to avoid sexual immorality and impurity.

So the Christian who wishes to please God must listen to and obey God's Word. This Word encourages believers to embrace holiness and also warns about the consequences of embracing sexual immorality (such as adultery) or impurity. These are things which are to be deliberately and consciously avoided. Seeking holiness and avoiding immorality are to go together in shaping the lives of believers.

3. *What is the practical route to holiness? (4:4, 5)*
However, having recognised that God's Word points to holiness, Paul is concerned to give as much practical help as possible to the Thessalonian believers so that they can see the key issue which relates to holiness. It is the importance of exercising self-control (4:4). The contrast is with the surrounding Gentile culture (4:5). The hallmark of this culture was a sexually immoral lifestyle featuring very little self-control. Instead, people were driven along by their lusts without any particular restraints. This is how many of the Thessalonian believers may have acted in their pre-conversion years when they did not know God and therefore it would not be surprising if, despite their new allegiance to Christ, they found it difficult to disentangle themselves from their previous lifestyle. They had turned from such behaviour to the living and true God (see 1:9) but perhaps their repentance had been inconsistent or patchy. Perhaps the pressure of conforming to the world around had been so considerable that they had permitted themselves to go along with what everybody else was doing. Then, as now, swimming against the tide is not particularly easy.

Given this context, Paul seeks to give clear practical assistance by encouraging self-control in the specific area of sexual behaviour. At this point it is worth recognising that there are a number of different possibilities in translating and understanding 4:4. The main problem is how to handle the word which is usually translated elsewhere as 'vessels'. It could be a metaphor for a wife, which is how the NIV footnote deals with it, but there would have been simpler ways to have expressed it if that was the case. Both the ESV and NIV speak of controlling 'his own body', which seems to be a slightly better translation. It points the way, however, to the most likely solution which is that the word is being used by Paul as a euphemism for the male sexual organ.

Paul is being directive and wants to give clear guidance within the bounds of decency about how holiness could be achieved. Avoiding sexual immorality and pursuing holiness would for men entail self-control of their sexual organs. Believers are not simply to follow where their desires might lead them. Instead, they are to learn or to know how to exercise sexual self-control in such situations. Such a course of action is described by Paul as both holy and honourable. The holy life, which others recognise as honourable, is a self-controlled life.

If it is claimed that Paul is resorting to legalism, it needs to be recognised that self-control is part of the fruit of the Spirit (see Gal 5:22, 23). If we recognise, as 4:8 does, that God gives His Holy Spirit to believers, it can be seen that self-control is only possible with the help of God. This is a clear indicator of the presence of God's Spirit within the life of a believer and within the Christian community. Believers who are seeking to live a holy life in conformity to God's Word will be those who seek to learn and practise self-control in all their relationships.

In summary, the apostle recognises that he needs to address a particular issue within the young Thessalonian church. Some of them are not as distinctive as they should be in their sexual behaviour and relationships as they follow the pattern set by their surrounding culture. Into this situation Paul provides a glorious, uplifting vision for the Christian life as a life which brings pleasure to God. In order to please God, attention must be paid to His Word through the apostle. That Word gives clear boundaries concerning what to avoid as well as guidance about God's desire that believers should live holy lives. In practice, holiness is gained through self-control, which is the fruit of the Holy Spirit. In this way Paul's argument addresses the presenting issue in order to encourage believers to grow in their new-found faith as they trust and follow Christ's teaching through Paul in this contentious area.

From text to teaching

Getting the message clear: the theme

- We please God through obeying God's Word with its call to holiness by exercising self-control.

Getting the message clear: the aim

- The aim of this passage is to persuade Christians to be self-controlled, especially in the area of handling sexual desires. Preaching or teaching on this passage should help in answering the following questions:

- How can believers find out the ways they can go about pleasing God?

- How does God's Word inform how believers are to act in the area of their sexual behaviour?

- What is one of the main practical ingredients required in responding to the call to holy living?

A way in

Too often the church simply mirrors the values and behaviour of the world around us. We recognise that as Christians we have been called to a distinctive, holy lifestyle but there are many occasions when we conspicuously fail to be different. Whether it is the uncovering of patterns of sexual abuse perpetrated by church leaders or comparable divorce statistics to the general population, it is important to recognise that in many situations we are not as distinctive as we should be. Seen in this light, this passage in 1 Thessalonians has a particular resonance with our own times when following your own desires appears to be the main consideration for so many people. We need to embrace Paul's counter-cultural teaching, recognising that it was just as hard then as it is now to exercise restraint in order to live a holy life pleasing to God.

Self-control is vital in all sorts of areas of everyday life. For example, most people learn to drive a car at some point in their life. Driving fast and ignoring all the rules within the Highway Code may be great fun at the time but the consequences are likely to be serious both for other road users as well as yourself. Though it may be frustrating at times to drive within the lane markings and at a particular speed, it is of course far safer for you and for everyone else and is likely to get you to your destination in one piece. This illustration can help us understand the significance of learning self-control and not being driven by our desires (4:4, 5). If we give free rein to our passionate lusts, then we are likely to be a danger to ourselves and others. We won't be surprised if we end up in a relationship crash where others, perhaps even innocent parties, are caught up in the damage. How many wives and children become collateral damage to the actions of a man driven by his own lusts? This image helps us to see the significance of self-control over one's own body whilst recognising the danger of letting our own fallen desires take over in the driving seat.

Pointers to application

- Paul's great desire is that the Thessalonians should seek to please God more and more. It is important to review in what terms we describe our relationship with God. Is it just obedience? Would it make a difference within our Christian life if we viewed each activity as the opportunity to bring pleasure to God? Is this something we are urging and encouraging others to do? Our relationship with Christ should be a joy, not a burden and seeing things in this light should lighten the load considerably.

- Pleasing God is intimately linked in to our response to the Word of God. If someone has told us very clearly that they do not like milk or sugar in their coffee, then ignoring their requests is unlikely to be the means of pleasing them. So it is with the Lord. He has revealed the way in which He can be pleased. We are deluded if, for whatever reason, we feel that we can ignore God's Word and enjoy His pleasure at the same time.

- Sometimes we may come across people who do not like what the apostle has written on a particular issue. They may think that they can reject the apostle whilst being loyal to Christ. However in this passage (and also 2:4, 13), we see how Paul is very conscious that he is writing by the authority of the Lord Jesus. Hence to reject the Apostle Paul's word is to reject God's word. This should, therefore, encourage us to pay greater respect to what has been revealed to us through the apostles by the Lord Jesus Christ.

- Every Christian has been called to a holy life, set apart for God. There can be no distinction between ordinary Christians and those who are seeking to be holy. Each of us has been called to live in a way which pleases God and such a life is characterised by holiness. We may often struggle in areas of guidance to know what God's will is for us. Should I marry this person? Should I pursue this job? Should I move house or not? There are times when we can be unsure of the details of what God's will might be. Yet in every situation and wherever we are, we can know one thing for sure, God's will is for us to live a holy life.

- In the Christian life there are some things which we must avoid if we want to navigate our way safely through life in a way that pleases God. Just as there are warning signs on our roads to protect us and others, so God in His wisdom has given us clear instructions and guidelines for our safety and spiritual well-being. Of course, we may feel that we can break some road signs with impunity but that is certainly not the case with God's Word. Aware of the consequences, therefore, we should make every effort to avoid behaviour which is contrary to God's good purposes for His children whom He loves.

- The prevailing culture in Thessalonica was far removed from a life pleasing to God. People were quite content with following their desires wherever that took them. The pressures on the Christians to conform to such a culture must have been intense, and especially for those who were new Christians, as many of them must have been. However, all of this resonates with our own culture where following your desires is the most natural and obvious thing to do and no longer warrants disapproval from wider society. Yet Paul is convinced that Christians must be distinctive and such is still the case now as we seek to please the Lord.

- Many of us may need reminding that self-control is an authentic fruit of the Spirit. Learning to exercise self-control, especially in the area of sexual conduct, is a clear mark of the work of the Spirit in the life of a believer. Failure to exercise self-control is a sign that God's Spirit is not as active as we might think in our lives, even if we are exercising all sorts of spiritual gifts and have many spiritual responsibilities in our church. In encouraging self-control we will want to avoid any legalism and we will do this best by setting the teaching on self-control (4:4) within the wider context of the call to please God (4:1) and the assistance of the Holy Spirit (4:8).

Suggestions for preaching
Sermon 1: Pleasing God through holy living (1 Thess. 4:1-8)

- How can I please God? (4:1, 2, 8)

Part Two: Teaching 1 Thessalonians 4:1-8

- What is God's will for every believer? What does God's Word say about pleasing God? (4:3, 6, 7)

- What is the practical route to holiness? (4:4, 5)

Other preaching possibilities

The advantage of looking at 4:1-8 in one sermon is that it gives an opportunity for the structure of the passage to shape the exposition. If, for example, 4:1, 2 were taken separately, it would break up the flow of the structure and would decouple the important link between sexual self-control and pleasing God.

That said, an argument for dealing with 4:1, 2 in a separate sermon is that it would give the preacher an opportunity to provide an overview of the second main section of the epistle (4:1–5:11) through the lens of the call to please God more and more.

The preacher wishing to move at a faster pace could easily incorporate the material at 4:9-12 into their sermon. Perhaps it would be simplest to divide the material into two parts:

- Honouring God (4:1-8)

- Loving others (4:9-12)

Suggestions for teaching

Introducing the passage

- What are the principles that appear to govern the conduct of relationships in our culture and what are the differences between them and the view of the Bible? How different do you think the pressures to conform to the prevailing culture would have been in Thessalonica compared with our own day?

Understanding the passage
- What is Paul's main purpose in 4:1, 2? Why does he feel the need to write like this?
- How is pleasing God linked with accepting God's Word? (see 4:1, 2, and 8) Might it be possible to please God at the same time as rejecting God's Word?
- What reasons does Paul give for believers to live a holy life? (4:3, 7)
- What should be our response to temptations towards sexual immorality and what might this mean in practice?
- What contrast does Paul draw between 4:4 and 4:5?
- How does the inclusion of 4:6 strengthen Paul's argument in this passage?

Applying the passage
- To what extent is the idea of 'pleasing God' something that we naturally consider or not?
- What misconceptions do we often have about what a holy life involves?
- Are there any helpful strategies that can be suggested to help us avoid sexual immorality?
- In our culture why is self-control so difficult?
- Consider what it might mean for you to please God more and more?
- Pray for grace to avoid sexual immorality and to practise self-control in this coming week.

8.

Pleasing God through loving others (4:9-12)

Introduction

In the prosperous West we live in a consumer culture. There are all sorts of products and choices out there. When this is married to rampant individualism, selfishness and greed, we then arrive at a situation where people are constantly thinking and asking 'what's in it for me? What do I get out of it?' We shop around for a better deal. It's all about the choices I make and my lifestyle. Yet if this is the general culture, it is easy to see how such thinking can infiltrate the church. Once this happens, then 'getting' rather than 'giving' becomes more important as we mirror the surrounding society. It would appear that very early on Paul had spotted similar traits amongst some of the members of the Thessalonian church family. Rather than being productive church members giving to others, there were some who were disruptive and gave little. It is with this group in mind that Paul now continues his teaching.

Listening to the Text

Context and structure

Paul's prayer at the end of the first part of the letter (3:11-13) has not only provided a conclusion but has also set the agenda for the second part. Having dealt with issues that related to their faith, trust and obedience to God, especially in the area of sexual ethics (4:1-8), he now turns to the second topic. This relates to the issue of their love for each other. At 3:12, he has prayed that their love, which is already evident (see 1:3) and for which he is profoundly thankful, should increase and overflow both within and beyond the boundaries of the church family. Further, Paul has introduced the whole of the second half of this epistle with a strong encouragement for the church family to please God more and more on the basis of the teaching that he had already given (4:1, 2). So as Paul picks up his prayer request at 3:12, he continues with his general exhortation at 4:1, 2 in order to tackle a particular presenting problem within the church family at 4:9-12.

This short passage would appear to divide naturally into two brief sections. In the first part (4:9, 10), Paul gives general advice which directly flows from the links already observed with 3:12 and 4:1, 2. Although there is a seamless transition, nevertheless the next two verses (4:11, 12) give particular advice which is applied to the Thessalonian situation. So the movement within these verses is from the general, addressed to all, to the particular, which though addressed to all has a particular group of church members in mind.

Part Two: Teaching 1 Thessalonians 4:9-12

There are a number of very strong links in this passage, both with this letter and also with 2 Thessalonians. Within 1 Thessalonians we can note again that Paul is simply reinforcing the teaching that he had already delivered at his brief first visit. Paul had already taught them to love each other (4:9) and he had also spelt out how that could be applied through not disturbing others and working with their own hands (4:11). Further, it can also be seen how Paul continues with his basic theme of encouragement. In his initial visit, he had spent time as a father encouraging and urging them on in their Christian life (2:12). Whilst absent it had been one of his main concerns which had led to the sending of Timothy to encourage them further (3:2). Now in writing to this young church plant, he continues to encourage and urge them on (see 4:1, 10, 18; 5:11, 14). He wants to see more growth within this plant and so the call is for 'more and more' (4:1, 10).

Paul himself continues to be a model to them through the way in which he had acted amongst them from the outset (see 1:5b). He had worked and toiled night and day in order not to be a burden to them (see 2:9) and this provides the model for the Thessalonian believers at 4:11, 12.

Finally, it should be noted that this section links in with 5:14 where there is a reference to those who are 'idle', which almost certainly refers obliquely to the same group at 4:11, 12. Furthermore, it seems clear that Paul's teaching in 1 Thessalonians to this group was not as effective as he would have hoped since he returns to the same theme, which he develops in a more extended way at 2 Thessalonians 3:6-15.

Working through the text

As we work through the text, attention should be paid to the structure already identified. However in order to earth this teaching it may be appropriate at the outset to consider why Paul needed to include this brief section. What was the presenting problem which needed to be addressed? In other words, the first point seeks to answer the question 'why is this text here?'

1. Getting without giving?

It is not always easy to be accurate about an issue when only one side of a conversation is heard. However in this case we have a little bit of extra assistance provided through the other material at 5:14 and 2 Thessalonians 3:6-15. This helps to flesh out the presenting problem. Something was clearly not right, though it probably only applied to a small group within the church family. The likelihood was that there were some who were being disruptive whilst also refusing to work with their hands. Obviously things were very different then in economic terms, but it is unlikely that Paul is referring to those who had been made redundant. For some reason which needs to be explored, these people had chosen not to work, and as a result, with time on their hands, they had become a disruptive influence within the church community (4:11).

As a consequence of this stance two things flowed. First, it was likely to lead to a loss of respect for the church (and therefore for the gospel) amongst the surrounding non-Christian community. Second, it had led to a situation where individuals within this group had become economically dependent on others within the church and had become a burden (4:12). A culture was developing which involved getting without giving and this was profoundly unhelpful both for the witness of the church and the functioning of the church family.

The difficulty is to know why this had happened. Why should certain individuals within the church who had heard the gospel and started to follow Jesus have acted in this manner? What could have caused them to think that it was no longer necessary for them to be involved in manual work? There are a couple of possibilities which both link in to the fact that these people were all new believers and therefore may have misunderstood key truths, and so given evidence of immaturity in their faith. So one option is that the implications of the teaching about the return of the Lord Jesus had not been worked out properly. As has been noted, the second coming of Christ is a key theme within the letter.

It is possible that some had concluded that since Jesus was returning there was no point in continuing to work. Perhaps this was from an understanding that His return was imminent – why work today if Jesus is returning tonight? Or perhaps their misunderstanding of the return of Jesus had convinced them that work was of comparatively little consequence compared with the need for everyone to be ready for Christ – why work if we should be getting everyone ready for the return of Jesus? Alternatively, some may have revelled in being part of a loving church family modelled in Paul's love for them (see 2:8) which had the effect of causing some to be so captivated by their enjoyment of being part of the church family and recipients of such overflowing love that they neglected to contribute in any meaningful way.

It is not an easy task to make an assessment between these and many other possible views, though in general terms it is probably wiser to lean towards views which do not turn this group of church members into unthinking idiots! Granted that Paul needs to correct them, but there must have been reasons which seemed to them as believers to be entirely valid for their actions (or lack of actions!).

Perhaps we are on safer ground in terms of analysing the results of their practice. Whatever the reasons for their refusal to work with their hands, and recognising that they could have come from godly, though misguided, motives, the result was that they failed to contribute to the church family or to the mission of the church within the wider society. In fact their actions hindered the church and the gospel. This is what Paul had seen and this is why he included this section.

2. Loving without stopping (4:9, 10)

As we have considered the presenting problem, it is now possible to proceed with the exposition of the passage. Though Paul needs to correct a group within the church family, he does not wish to discourage the majority. Therefore, he begins by reinforcing the fact that, on the whole, the church does have a wonderful reputation for loving one another both in the immediate Christian community in Thessalonica and the wider fellowship of God's people in the surrounding district of Macedonia. They had followed Paul's initial teaching (which had been received not as a word of a man but as the Word of God – see 2:13) and there was already plenty of evidence of the fruit of God's Spirit (see 1:3; 3:6, 12).

However Paul's great desire, especially given the presence of a group who were deficient in love for other believers, is that the church should overflow even more with love for one another and for everyone else (see 3:12). He therefore encourages and urges them to demonstrate even greater love (4:10). Just as God's love had overflowed to them (1:4) and as Paul's heart overflowed in deep concern whether present or absent (e.g. 2:8, 17), he urges them to overflow in love so that many others both within and outside the church family benefit. Paul does not regard love for one another as an achievement that has been attained once and for all time but as a fountain which should continually be overflowing.

3. Contributing without hindering (4:11, 12)

How is overflowing love to be best expressed within the Thessalonian situation? Paul's aim is that their actions should contribute to the church and its mission, rather than hinder it. He wants their daily life or walk not to be a burden on the church family and he also wants it to enhance the reputation of the church and the gospel in the world (4:12). This represents Paul's heartbeat. He wants the church to mature and grow and for the gospel to make further progress.

As a result of these concerns, his advice directed to all, but no doubt aimed in particular at a certain group within the church family, is spelt out at 4:11. He wants them to have an aspiration (ESV) or ambition (NIV) to get on with their affairs in a way which doesn't disrupt other people's lives by preventing them from working or distracting them. Perhaps some Christians were idle and spent a good amount of their time chattering to other members of the church during the working day and so Paul simply has to ask them 'to mind their own business'. Instead they are to work with their hands. Getting on with ordinary work would then have the effect of enabling them to support themselves and their family without being a burden on other members of the church family, whilst it would also serve as a good example to those outside the Christian community.

The apostle sees no divide between the practical and the spiritual. Perhaps through some members of the church becoming super-spiritual and as a result neglecting their practical work, the spiritual work of the fellowship was actually being hindered! Paul's remedy is to hold creation and new creation together. Through ordinary manual labour and toil, to which Paul himself was no stranger (see 2:9), God's church would be strengthened with resources which could be lovingly shared in order to contribute to the needs of the whole church family and to the work of the gospel. Through such work an example would be given to the wider community which might open a way for the gospel. In giving these instructions, Paul undercuts any thoughts of super-spirituality and sets out a vision of human life and community transformed by the gospel.

From text to message

Getting the message clear: the theme
We must consider the extent to which our actions may hinder the development of the church and the growth of the gospel.

Getting the message clear: the aim

The aim of this passage is to encourage church members to show practical love towards each other. Preaching or teaching on this passage should help in answering the following questions:

- How is it possible for our actions to hinder the church and the gospel?

- How can we be encouraged to show greater love within the church family and beyond?

- How can we hold the doctrines of creation and new creation together?

A way in

In many relationships there is both giving and receiving. In normal circumstances, if this balance is not maintained it is possible for the relationship to become one-sided, draining and perhaps even toxic. Compare two lakes and the differences between them. One is the Dead Sea which has water from the River Jordan flowing in but has no outlet. The result is that the Dead Sea is full of salt and is highly toxic. The other is the Sea of Galilee where water both flows in and out. The result is a freshwater lake in which fish can thrive. Constantly receiving from others can become toxic – the normal pattern should be a constant interplay of giving and receiving. Obviously there are many exceptions to this, especially where somebody is ill, infirm or has particular needs, but in the normal course of church life Paul is spelling out an important principle to us.

Paul speaks of loving each other more and more, and two illustrations immediately spring to mind. An elastic band may be used to hold together some papers and it does the jon comfortably. More papers arrive and yet the elastic band can easily be stretched further to accommodate them. Although in the illustration there are limits to how far the elastic band will stretch without snapping, nevertheless it reminds us helpfully that there are many situations where our love for each other within a fellowship could stretch further as we seek to care and provide for each other. The other illustration of 'more and more' could be a fountain. The normal function of a fountain is not to pump out water for a bit and then stop. Instead, it is constantly pushing out water so that it is constantly overflowing. In a similar way, Paul is longing for such overflowing love which will continually refresh others.

Pointers to application

+ What effect does my behaviour have on the health of the church family? In Thessalonica the behaviour of this group was becoming a burden on the rest of the church which could easily have been avoided if they had been willing to work. There are times when we are a burden to others and we can do nothing about it. In such cases, it is the privilege of church members to care, serve and provide. However, where the burden has been imposed wilfully through the deliberate behaviour and actions of an individual or group, then something is not right and the call for people to show overflowing love needs to be heard.

+ What effect does my behaviour have on the reputation of the church and the gospel to those outside the Christian community? The church in Thessalonica was in danger of losing respect through the behaviour of this group. Those who are not Christians will always be offended by some aspects of our faith and especially the offence of the cross, but we are to avoid giving unnecessary offence through poor decisions or lifestyle choices we have made, which detract from the gospel and adversely affect the reputation of the church.

- To what extent do we need to be encouraged to exercise more and more love towards one another? It is easy to reach a plateau in our Christian life in various ways. We can become comfortable in our friendships where we might show consistent love, kindness and hospitality and yet be poor at welcoming the newcomer or supporting a believer we hardly know through a time of crisis. The Thessalonians were a loving church family but they needed to be encouraged to widen and deepen their love, and that may be exactly the same challenge which many of us need.

- There is nothing wrong with work, especially manual work, in the Bible. God is a worker who created the heavens and the earth. There is therefore great dignity in working hard. God has designed things in creation such that work and service are part of our humanity. Granted that, following the Fall in Genesis 3, there are many frustrations attached to our labour. At times it may not be particularly purposeful or productive. Nevertheless in our work, which may or not be salaried, there is the opportunity to contribute to the needs of ourselves, our family, the church family and the world.

- Linked to the previous point, it needs to be stressed that there should be no sacred/secular divide. As believers, we are part of God's creation and His new creation. Seeking to focus entirely on the new creation will entail us losing aspects of our humanity and denigrating God's goodness to us in creation. If some of the Thessalonians were indeed focusing on the new creation with the result that they wanted nothing to do with creation and work, then, as Paul recognised, it would actually be a hindrance to the gospel. We have bodies and bodily needs and in our theology we must remember that God will create not just new heavens but a new earth as well. God's work in creation and redemption must be held together.

- Paul's teaching in this passage is driven by a concern for the health of the church and the reputation of the gospel. We can be extremely concerned about our own health and our own reputation but the apostle wants us to be zealous for the church and the gospel. How would things be different if our individual choices were shaped by these concerns, as opposed to our own selfish desires?

Suggestions for preaching

Sermon 1: Pleasing God through loving others (1 Thess. 4:9-12)

- Getting without giving
- Loving without stopping (4:9, 10)
- Contributing without hindering (4:11, 12)

Other preaching possibilities

The advantage of devoting a whole sermon to this short passage is that it gives a good opportunity to explore the material at some depth. Not only does the passage connect to other themes within 1 Thessalonians (e.g. Paul's previous teaching, encouragement, love) but it gives the opportunity to focus on how our choices may affect the health and reputation of the church.

As highlighted in the previous chapter, it would be relatively straightforward to include this passage alongside 4:1-8 since the material after 4:13 takes us into rather different territory.

Suggestions for teaching

Introducing the passage

To what extent do you think that a 'consumer' mindset has infected the church? Is it evident that even Christians are more concerned about 'getting' rather than 'giving'?

Understanding the passage

- How does Paul's teaching in 4:9, 10 flow out of his thanksgiving and prayer at 1:2, 3 and 3:11-13?
- What sort of things had Paul already taught them about in his initial visit according to 4:1, 2, 9, 11?
- What does Paul want to see within the Thessalonian church according to 4:10? What might this mean in practice?
- Why does Paul give these particular instructions in 4:11?
- What twin aims did Paul's teaching have according to 4:12?

- How might the behaviour of some of the members of this church have affected the church's reputation?

Applying the passage
- Try to reconstruct what was happening in part of the Thessalonian church which caused Paul to address the issue here.
- What can we learn from Paul's frequent use of the word 'encourage'/'urge'? (see 2:12; 3:2; 4:1, 10, 18; 5:11, 14)
- To what extent might the instructions in 4:11 still be useful for us today?
- How does Paul show that there should be no secular/sacred divide within this passage?
- In what ways could you show more and more love within your church family this week?
- Consider how your behaviour could win the respect of outsiders in the coming week?

9.

Rekindling hope
(4:13-18)

Introduction

It is very easy for hope to evaporate extremely quickly. Exam results arrive in the post and suddenly all those hopes for the future that have been nurtured for years are suddenly dashed. An athlete focuses for four long years on gaining entry into the Olympics and winning a medal, and following one loss of concentration at a particularly crucial part of a race all hopes have evaporated. In this passage we see the Apostle Paul dealing with some people within the church whose hope had evaporated. They had confidently embraced the teaching that the Lord Jesus Christ would return. Indeed that had been at the heart of their understanding of the gospel message (see 1:9, 10). Yet now the church family was faced with the death of some of their members before Jesus had returned (4:13). It left huge unanswered questions. What happens to those believers who have already died? When the Lord Jesus does ultimately return would they be included in God's ongoing purposes or not? The Thessalonian Christians had been left stunned by these developments. Paul's aim is to rekindle their hope and confidence in the Lord.

Listening to the text

Context and structure

Paul is picking up the third of three areas which he has highlighted in both his thanksgiving (see 1:2, 3) and prayer (see 3:13) which relates to the issue of hope. In this context, hope is a future-orientated faith or trust based on the return of the Lord Jesus Christ. Therefore, having tackled issues relating to the outworking of faith in God, evidenced in obedience to His Word (see 4:1-8) and the development of practical love within the Christian community (see 4:9-12), Paul now turns to this remaining item. Once again a new section is introduced by 'brothers', which appears to be Paul's regular device in this epistle to signal a new subject. Within the broader argument of the letter it is also worth recognising once again the key role played by issues relating to the return of Christ and its associated events. Each section within the first main part of the letter has made reference to the future hope at the end (see 1:10; 2:12; 2:16 and 3:13). Seen in this light, we can tell what a significant dimension this area is within Paul's understanding and preaching of the gospel.

Paul has a straightforward structure to his argument which is based on the two key doctrines of the resurrection of Christ and the return of Christ:

- The problem identified – the absence of hope (13)

Part Two: Teaching 1 Thessalonians 4:13-18

- The basis of our hope – the resurrection of the Lord Jesus (14)
- The focus of our hope – the return of the Lord Jesus (15-17)
- The response – the restoration of hope (18)

One of the main things to notice in Paul's teaching about the future is how it is completely focused on the person of Jesus. We would need to look elsewhere if we wanted to discover more about the resurrection body or the nature of the new heavens and the new earth. Paul's focus is not so much on heaven but on Jesus and His interaction with believers, both those who are still alive at His return and those who had died previously.

We should also notice that though Paul is aware of the reality of death when he speaks of the dead in Christ (see 4:16), he characteristically reinterprets death for the believer. It has now become 'falling asleep' (see 4:13, 15) which in itself holds out the promise of a new day in which to rise from sleep and continue serving the Lord.

On a number of occasions we have seen that Paul's main aim is to encourage and urge them on in the Christian life. This theme surfaces at 2:12; 3:2; 4:1 and 4:10. It now reappears at the end of both sections which relate to the return of Christ (see 4:18 and 5:11) and will recur on one final occasion at 5:14. It reminds us of our overall theme. Paul is writing to a very young church under great pressure. Having given assurance to help them withstand all those pressures, his aim is to encourage these new believers in faith, love and hope so that they can grow to maturity.

Working through the text

As we work through the text, attention will be paid to the structure already identified. The first and last points introduce and conclude. The main part of the exposition focuses, therefore, on the middle two points and the attention that Paul pays to the person and work of the Lord Jesus.

1. The problem identified – the absence of hope (4:13)

Two related issues are identified by Paul – ignorance and grief. Even though it is only a comparatively short time since Paul visited Thessalonica, there appears to have been at least one bereavement within the church family. It is likely that due to their ignorance about what would happen to a believer who had died, they had exhibited unrestrained grief. Paul compares it to the grief commonly shown by others who are not Christians whose grief is fuelled by the fact that they have no hope or confidence about what will happen to the dead person in the future. The lack of understanding amongst the believers had led to behaviour which was not distinctively Christian at all. For their behaviour to change, Paul will need to teach them and provide understanding. Even in the terms that he uses we can see that he is eager to do this. So death is now reinterpreted as 'falling asleep' to help them to change their mindset about the significance of death for the believer.

It is interesting to note in this practical part of the letter how Paul wants believers to live a distinctive life against the backdrop of a pagan world. They are not to act in passionate lust like others (4:5). They are not to grieve like others (4:13), though Paul is not saying that they should show no grief or sadness whatsoever. They are not to act complacently like others (5:3). Their lifestyle is meant to win the respect of outsiders (4:12). Paul is therefore writing with one eye on the impact that the believers will have on the surrounding culture. They are to be distinctive in every area, including how they cope with the raw reality of bereavement. In this way they will commend the gospel and cause people to consider the person of Christ. So Paul identifies the main issue as being that, in the face of death, for all their recognition of the return of Christ (1:10), in practice they have 'no hope'. They have no secure confidence concerning the future for those who have died. In order to rekindle hope, Paul needs to dispel ignorance and this is what he now proceeds to do.

2. The basis of our hope – the resurrection of the Lord Jesus (4:14)

Paul begins with a reference to the resurrection. Hope in the face of death must start with the recognition that Jesus died and rose again. This is the foundation for all that Paul subsequently says. He has already made reference to Jesus' resurrection (see 1:10) as a prelude to His return, but here it is referred to as the basis of all that follows. In what ways, then, does the resurrection of Jesus help in the particular situation of a believer grieving over the loss of a member of the church family?

First, the resurrection of Jesus is the model for the resurrection of believers. In the same way that Jesus genuinely died but rose to new life, so believers can expect to follow the same path. We also will die or fall asleep (4:14) with the prospect of rising to new life in Christ (4:16). Through the resurrection of Jesus, death has now been redefined as 'falling asleep' because, as with Christ, we know that it is no longer the end. Death has now become merely the prelude to a resurrected, physical life beyond the grave for all believers. What has happened to Jesus will happen to every believer who has died. This undergirds all of Paul's teaching in this passage.

Second, the resurrection of Jesus is the means of the resurrection of believers. Right at the beginning of his letter, Paul has reminded the whole church that they are 'in God the Father and the Lord Jesus Christ' (1:1) and he has further reminded them of God's churches in Judea which are 'in Christ Jesus' (2:14). This terminology has also been used at 3:8 and 4:1 and there will be a further reference at 5:18. Each believer is already in Christ, united with Him. Therefore if Jesus has been raised and is now alive, then it means that all those who are in Him have a secure future. So when the resurrected Jesus returns, all those who have fallen asleep in Him will be raised to new life. Given our location as believers in Christ, the resurrection of Jesus means that no believer can ultimately be forgotten or lost.

Paul starts, therefore, with the historical foundation of the death and resurrection of the Lord Jesus. Christian hope is not free-floating, dependent upon feelings and experiences, but is anchored firmly through solid events that happened in history. The resurrection of Jesus is both the model and means, the pattern and the pathway, for our own resurrection as believers.

3. *The focus of our hope – the return of the Lord Jesus (4:15-17)*
Having already spoken about God bringing with Jesus those who have fallen asleep in Him, Paul now expands this point by revealing what will happen when Jesus returns. As he looks to the future, his teaching is not at all speculative since

it is based on the teaching of the Lord Jesus Himself (4:15). It may be that this is a reference to the teaching contained at Matthew 24:31 which refers to angels arriving with a trumpet call as God's people are gathered together at the end. Certainly all these features are mentioned at 4:16, 17. The underlying point, however, is that in each of those three teaching sections (4:1-18), Paul has laid the emphasis on the fact that his teaching comes by the authority of the Lord Jesus and is therefore not just a word of a man but the Word of the Lord (see 4:1, 9 and 15 as well as 2:13).

To start with, it is worth noticing what Paul says directly about Jesus in these verses. The Lord will return (4:15). This will happen when He comes down from heaven (4:16). At that point believers will meet Him, with the result that believers will be with Him forever (4:17). Very little attention is given to the resurrection body of the believers. Nothing is said about the new heavens and the new earth. Instead the focus is on the personal return of the Lord Jesus. He Himself has promised that He will return and this is the focus for the believer's hope. As was mentioned near the beginning of the letter, one of the characteristics of Christians is that they are waiting for the Son to come from heaven (see 1:10) and look forward to His coming (see 2:19; 3:13). Believers can be confident that Jesus will not break His word and that He will indeed return in all His glory.

So, if that is the case, what will happen to believers? At this point Paul knows that, for the pastoral reasons already mentioned at 4:13, he needs to deal specifically with the situation of those who have already died before His return. As a result, he divides believers into two groups at 4:15 –

those who will still be alive at His return and those who will have already died as Christians. He deals first with those who have already died, and addresses the issue of whether they will in any way miss out on things. So, at 4:15, he reinforces this point by saying that the people still alive at that point will certainly not precede those who have already died. How will that happen since their bodies are dead and buried? In answering this at 4:16, Paul now proceeds to give the order of events at the return of Christ. The Lord Jesus Himself will come down from heaven and will be accompanied by three phenomena. There will be a loud command, the voice of an Archangel and a trumpet call. It is analogous to the entry of the Queen at a special occasion, where there is a command to stand for her entrance, accompanied by a trumpet fanfare. The voice of the Archangel links back to 3:13 and the reference to the fact that Jesus will return with all His holy ones, which seems to be a reference to angelic beings. The command may actually be the voice of the Lord Jesus Christ Himself to the dead in Christ. As He arrives, He speaks to the graves and calls out believers, with the result that the dead in Christ rise.

When Lazarus had been in the grave for several days, Jesus called out in a loud voice, 'Lazarus, come out' (John 11:43). Similarly, with the dead twelve-year-old girl in Mark 5:41, Jesus took her by the hand and said, 'Little girl, I say to you, get up'. At Luke 7:14, Jesus says the same words, addressed this time to a dead young man. As Jesus speaks to the dead in the gospel narratives, they respond and receive life. How much more when Jesus returns in all His glory. So, through the power of the Word of the Lord, those who have died in Christ are raised to new life

Part Two: Teaching I Thessalonians 4:13-18

beyond the grave and this all happens before the effects of Jesus' return are felt by those still living. Rather than being neglected, forgotten, abandoned or overlooked, it looks like special treatment!

So if that is what will happen to those believers who have already died, what about those who are still alive at Jesus' return? This is spelt out at 4:17. Those of us in such a situation who are still left will then be caught up with those already raised so that together all God's people will meet the Lord Jesus Himself in order to be with Him forever. The focus is on our relationship with Jesus. His return guarantees that we will meet Him and be with Him. The fulfilment of the glorious gospel message will be seen in believers being physically with Christ forever. Perhaps if Paul had gone further, he might have spoken about the new heavens and the new earth, and the new glorified physical body that believers will enjoy, but for now he closes his account by depicting the whole people of God with the risen Christ in their midst.

There are a few words and phrases which may require some clarification. The people who have been 'left behind' in 4:17 are, of course, not unbelievers but believers still alive at the return of Christ. The reference to all these believers being caught up in the clouds to meet the Lord has also often been misunderstood. From the Latin term for 'caught up', we derive the term 'rapture'. In some pre-millennial views, 'the rapture' has taken on huge significance. Believers are raptured, leaving human society bereft of Christian influence for a period before the eventual return of Christ. However in Paul's theology all these events are virtually instantaneous. Rather than focusing on what happens on the earth, his focus is on the Lord Jesus.

The reference to the clouds is also slightly ambiguous. Often in the Old Testament, the cloud would be a symbol of the presence of God. There are other times when a cloud seems almost to be a symbolic picture of the vehicle used to travel (see Mark 13:26; 14:62). Perhaps these two views are not so far apart. Jesus returns in the clouds, revealing His divine presence and His intention to gather all His people. It would be a great shame, however, to get bogged down by the details of 4:17 when Paul's main thrust is so clear. When Christ has returned, every believer, including those dear brothers and sisters who had recently died in Thessalonica, will spend eternity in the presence of Christ. Not one believer will be forgotten.

4. *The response – the restoration of hope (4:18)*

Given all that Paul has said, it is no wonder that he now concludes this passage with a call for the believers at Thessalonica to encourage each other with this teaching. Paul has not set out what will happen at the return of the Lord Jesus merely for academic interest. It has had an intensely pastoral dimension, having arisen out of the grief which he had heard about within the Christian community. Therefore, the response to what he has written which he is looking for is that his teaching would be lovingly and carefully applied to grieving Christians in order that they would not remain in despair. Amidst the natural sadness of bereavement, he wants believers to draw alongside others and apply this message so that they can take comfort from the fact that their deceased loved ones who had followed Christ (perhaps only for a few days, weeks or months) will

Part Two: Teaching I Thessalonians 4:13-18   177

certainly be fully included in God's eternal purposes. In other words, they are to use this teaching about the personal return of the Lord Jesus to restore hope.

In summary, Paul's aim is to restore hope and confidence to those who had lost it through their ignorance of what would happen when Jesus returns. Somehow they had thought that people would have to be alive when Jesus returns in order to benefit from His coming. Such is not the case. On the basis of both the resurrection of Christ and His personal return, all believers can look forward to a resurrection life with Jesus in eternity.

From text to message

Getting the message clear: the theme

- Our hope and confidence in the future is based on the resurrection and return of our Lord Jesus Christ.

Getting the message clear: the aim

- The aim of the passage is to help believers to have confidence in Christ in the face of death. Preaching or teaching on this passage should help in answering the following questions:
  - On what basis should response to a believer's death be different from how the world would react?
  - How does the resurrection of Christ provide believers with hope for the future?
  - What is the main point to draw out from the teaching about the personal return of our Lord Jesus Christ?

A way in

There are many situations in life where everything seems to be running smoothly and the future appears to be clearly mapped out. It might be purchasing a house, getting a university place or proceeding on a well-marked career path. Everything seems secure and we can envisage how things might develop in a month, a year or perhaps even a decade. Our confidence rests on these plans working out. Then something happens. Tragedy strikes, hope evaporates and we are suddenly plunged into despair. In such situations it is not easy to rebuild and restore hope. Sometimes we need a bigger framework in which to understand things so that we can see how things might yet turn out for the best in the end. This is the situation at Thessalonica. With the death of a few believers, hope has come crashing down. In order to rebuild it, Paul has to construct a bigger, more secure picture of what is actually going to happen in the future so that the believers can see how things will work out for the best for those who have recently died after trusting Christ.

One of the key things Paul wants to highlight is that those who have finished their earthly course will not be disadvantaged in any way when the Lord Jesus returns (see 4:15). Imagine a relay race at the Olympics. The first runner takes up the baton and runs a lap as fast as they can before handing over to someone else. Their race has now finished and there is little to do other than stand at the side of the track encouraging the others still left in the race. They cheer as eventually the last runner breaks the tape to come in first. However when the medals are awarded, it is not just the final athlete who mounts the podium. Each of the

Part Two: Teaching 1 Thessalonians 4:13-18

four members of the team will climb the steps and each will receive gold. None will be forgotten, even though some of them had long finished their role when the race was finally won. In a similar manner, Paul wants to provide assurance that those believers who had already finished their earthly course would certainly not be forgotten at the end when Jesus returns.

Pointers to application

- We are to be distinctive as believers in many ways. One of the most important differences will be highlighted at the funeral service of a believer. Though, of course, there may be enormous pain and sadness because death is an enemy and sometimes visits in particularly tragic ways, nevertheless a Christian's funeral should be different. It should be marked by hope and confidence in his or her future resurrection and a belief that ultimately nothing will ever separate them or us from the Lord Jesus Christ. For us to grieve exactly like non-Christians – who have perhaps only a vague, inarticulate sense concerning the future, built only on wishful thinking – is, ultimately, a denial of the gospel. However distressing and (at least from our perspective), untimely the death of a believer may be, we can have confidence and hope based on the gospel which tells us of the return of Christ.

- In order for believers to gain confidence for the future, we need to be taken back to the cross and resurrection of our Lord Jesus Christ. This is the solid historical reality which is the platform for our future outlook.

Christian hope is never based on wishful thinking but is tied to the historical events relating to the first Easter weekend. Any hope we have concerning the future must flow from Jesus' resurrection and the implications this has in our relationship to death. In Jesus' resurrection, a doorway has been forcibly opened through the wall of death. This enables those of us who follow Him to pass through death.

- Paul bases his teaching in chapter 4 on what God, through Jesus, has already revealed to them (see 4:2, 9, 15). Ultimately any confidence that believers might have concerning the future rests on the faithfulness of Christ in keeping His word. The pattern of events which Paul lists in these verses is rooted in 'the Lord's own word'. Strengthening our confidence in the future is completely linked to trusting God's faithfulness to His Word.

- When we think as Christians about the future, it is possible to focus on ourselves rather than Christ. We might wonder what it will look like to have a new resurrected body and to live in the new heavens and the new earth. Other passages in Scripture may help a bit in satisfying our curiosity. However, the focus in this passage is all on Jesus and what He will do. The future reaches its climax when we meet the Lord Jesus and are with Him forever. Paul wants these believers to be entirely focused on Jesus, both now and then. Therefore, our devotion to Christ should be something that draws us forwards as we consider the amazing prospect of meeting Him face to face.

Part Two: Teaching 1 Thessalonians 4:13-18

- For the Christian, death itself, though often painful and ugly, is redefined as 'falling asleep'. The point about sleep is that, though we are inert to those around us, there will come a point when we wake up to a new day. This is the picture that Paul uses, following Jesus' lead when He 'woke up' the twelve-year-old girl in Mark 5:41. Again this should bring great comfort to us as we face death, knowing that one day we will hear words from Jesus waking us up. It should also provide comfort to us when our loved ones face death as we remind ourselves that death is no longer the end.

- At different times in church history there have been varying interpretations relating to the 'end times'. In recent years much has been made of the rapture and those who are 'left behind', resulting in a complicated series of events. As we have seen, however, there is a simplicity within the text as we keep our focus on Jesus. It highlights the danger of Christians getting themselves entangled with the minutiae of varying interpretations, when keeping a focus on Christ would give them much more confidence about the future.

- This passage has its own built-in application that the Thessalonians should encourage each other through this teaching. It is once again a reminder that this teaching has been given not to fuel speculation but to encourage ordinary believers facing the nitty-gritty of serious illness, death and bereavement. The natural result of teaching on this passage should not be academic arguments about the millennium but greater pastoral concern amongst the church family and renewed devotion to our Lord Jesus Christ whom we will each one day meet.

Suggestions for preaching

Sermon 1: Rekindling hope (1 Thess. 4:13-18)

- The absence of hope – the problem identified (v. 13)
- The basis of our hope – the resurrection of the Lord Jesus (v. 14)
- The focus of our hope – the return of the Lord Jesus (vv. 15-17)
- The restoration of hope – the response (v. 18)

Other preaching possibilities

There is more than sufficient material in this passage for a sermon, but if the preacher needs to move more quickly through the material, then it would be possible to combine this passage with the following one and cover 4:13–5:11. Both passages end with the call for believers to encourage each other (4:18; 5:11) which provides a common application to the sermon. Perhaps the following major headings could be used.

- The reality of the return of Christ 4:13-18
- Living in the light of that reality 5:1-11

Suggestions for teaching

Introducing the passage

- Even as Christians, why do we find it so hard to cope with the prospect of our own death or the death

Part Two: Teaching 1 Thessalonians 4:13-18

of those we love? To what extent do you feel that Christians do face death differently from others?

Understanding the passage
- What do you think has caused Paul to address the issue in these verses? (see v. 13)
- In what way should the death and resurrection of Jesus strengthen our confidence in what God will do for us in the future?
- What is the basis of all the teaching in verses 15-17?
- How does Paul describe what will happen to the two groups in verses 15-17?
- What is the end result for God's people to which we should look forward? (see v. 17)
- What response is Paul looking for amongst the Thessalonians as a result of this teaching? (see v. 18)

Applying the passage
- What hope do most people have with regard to the future and in what ways is 'Christian hope' different?
- In what ways can a good grasp of doctrine be a means of pastoral encouragement?
- How should the reinterpretation of death as 'falling asleep' help us pastorally?
- How is it best to minimise controversy about all the issues that surround the return of the Lord Jesus Christ?
- How can the teaching in this passage be used to encourage people in your church family?
- How should the prospect of meeting Jesus at His return affect the way that I live today?

10.

LIVING IN THE LIGHT OF THE RETURN OF CHRIST (5:1-11)

Introduction

Many of us keep a diary which we find helpful in enabling us to plan for things coming up. It means, at least in theory, that we won't be caught by surprise with an unexpected commitment since hopefully it has been written clearly in the diary to remind us. As a result it is much easier to plan and to make preparations for a future event. Perhaps it's a holiday and the looming date in the diary motivates you to do a whole range of things beforehand, ranging from purchasing the currency to ordering a new passport. Keeping an up-to-date diary, electronic or paper, enables us to live in the light of the future. We make decisions about what to buy at the shops today because we know we have a friend visiting tomorrow.

All of this makes perfect sense to us but the difficulty we find with the coming return of the Lord Jesus Christ is that, though we may be completely persuaded that it will happen, it isn't straightforward to know how to enter it into our diary. And if it doesn't get entered then it doesn't shape the decisions which we make today. In fact, that is often the reality of the situation – the doctrine of the return of Christ doesn't make much difference to the way that we live. So how does Paul address this sort of issue at Thessalonica?

Listening to the text

Context and structure

Paul is still developing the third of the three main issues which he has highlighted both in his opening thanksgiving (1:2, 3) and in his prayer (3:10- 13). It relates to the issue of hope and the return of the Lord Jesus Christ. He has already picked up one aspect of hope at 4:13-18 by showing how their knowledge of the return of Christ should transform their attitude to death. Now at 5:1-11 he wants to show how Jesus' return should transform their attitude to their life. In other words, the return of Christ should shape our future (4:13-18) and our present (5:1-11).

As so often in this letter, new sections are punctuated by the word 'brothers' which appears in this passage at 5:1 and 5:4. However, this does not mean that the subject matter is completely different since both relate in some way or other to the idea of Jesus returning 'like a thief' (see 5:2, 4). Another pointer to the structure of the passage is the use of 'so then' at 5:6, which applies the teaching of 5:4, 5. We then notice 'but since' at 5:8, which amplifies how Christians are to live. The final instruction in 5:11 is that this teaching should be used to encourage other believers within the church. If we put this together this is how the passage appears then:

Part Two: Teaching 1 Thessalonians 5:1-11

- When and how will Jesus return? (1-3)
- How do we get ready? (4-11)
  - We live in the day (4, 5)
  - ...so don't live in the night (6, 7)
  - ...but get up and get dressed (8-10)
  - ...and encourage each other to do this (11)

Again Paul relies on Jesus' own teaching in the gospels. In the previous passage Paul had referred to 'the Lord's own word' (4:15 – probably a reference to Matthew 24:31). Now he twice refers to the Lord's return as being like a thief in the night, which comes from Jesus' teaching in Luke 12:39 and Matthew 24:43. The apostolic teaching is firmly rooted in the teaching of Jesus.

Another key point to observe is the great significance of the faith/love/hope triad once again. It featured at the beginning of the letter (1:2, 3) in the middle (3:10-13) and now appears at the end of the main teaching part of the epistle (see 5:8). This shows how these three aspects of the Christian life have clearly shaped Paul's teaching to the Thessalonians. This framework also shows how Paul is both bringing his teaching to a close and bringing it to a climax with this call for believers to put on the spiritual armour of faith, love and hope amidst all the struggles that they are facing.

Again we notice the encouragement theme (see 2:12; 3:2; 4:1, 10, 18) being repeated at 5:11. This newly planted church needs encouragement to keep on growing towards maturity.

Working through the text

In working through the text, attention will be paid to the structure already identified.

1. When and how will Jesus return (1-3)

Paul has already established that Jesus will return (see 4:13-18) but when is it going to be? It's an understandable question, though, as in a number of other cases Paul feels that he barely needs to write to them (e.g. 4:9), presumably because he had dealt thoroughly with this issue on his original visit. However, he does give an answer, presumably to reinforce the teaching which some may have forgotten or had misconstrued. It may well be that Paul also has a further aim here which is to provide assurance to believers facing persecution that those opposing them will face God's judgment. So, having almost dismissed the issue of the timing of Jesus' return, he nevertheless provides a number of insights into what will happen.

It will be a momentous public event (2)

Paul describes the return of Jesus as the Day of the Lord. In the Old Testament, the Day of the Lord was an awesome day when God decisively stepped in to deal with His people. It would be a time when all those opposed to Him would be destroyed, which is why there was no room for complacency amongst God's people, as Amos declared at Amos 5:18. It would also be a day when God would finally rescue His people. Judgment for some and salvation for others would flow out of God's powerful intervention. One thing is clear from such Old Testament texts, which is that it would not be a private experience. It would be a public event which all would know about, both those opposing believers as well as followers of Christ.

It will be an unexpected event (2)
A plumber may arrive at the door and there is no surprise because you made the appointment for him to come. However, burglars do not make appointments! If a burglar has broken into our property, it is almost certainly an unexpected event – otherwise we would have taken better precautions. Though it is a surprising analogy, it is one used of Himself by Jesus to show the unexpected nature of His return (see Luke 12:39). It won't be something that we can predict through poring over the intricate details of Daniel and Revelation.

It will be a sudden and inescapable event (3)
Paul uses the image of labour pains which again links in to the teaching of Jesus in the gospels (e.g. Matt. 24:8). The picture is graphic. Such pains come suddenly and are inescapable. In the same way, the Lord Jesus Christ will return. There are many things which we can avoid if necessary. For example, you may be in a position to postpone a visit to the dentist because you want to avoid the pain, but you can't do that with childbirth and nor can we do it with the return of Christ. It may well be that at this point in particular Paul is wanting to give assurance to the Thessalonian Christians as they cope with opposition. Apparently the people of Thessalonica had enjoyed many years of 'peace and safety' under Roman rule in the first-century. Perhaps that had been the response by many of them to hearing the Christians speak about a Jesus who would rescue them from the coming wrath (see 1:10). 'We'll

be okay', they would say. Yet Paul knows that they will not be okay when Jesus returns – they will not be able to escape God's wrath (see 2:16).

In gently dismissing the idea that anyone can set a time and date for the return of Jesus, Paul fleshes out the awesome nature of that day. His teaching is designed to do two things. Its aim is to encourage these new believers through rooting his teaching in both the Old Testament and the very words of Jesus that the Lord Jesus Christ really will return. It also aims to give assurance to believers facing persecution that a day of rescue will arrive, a day when all their persecutors will be judged.

2. How do we get ready? (4-11)

If Jesus' return could happen at any point, then how does that affect the way that I am to live? In this next part of his argument Paul gradually builds his case by helping believers to see how they should live in the light of Jesus' return. To do this, he plays on one central contrast between day and night, though it is developed as Paul speaks of different activities associated with one or the other.

Christians live in the daytime not in the night (4, 5)

Developing the 'thief in the night' image, Paul reminds the Thessalonians that, as believers, they are no longer living in the darkness of the night. This means that though the return of Jesus will still be unexpected, it won't be an unwelcome surprise (since believers are those who long to meet the Lord and be with Him forever – 4:17). Believers have been transferred out of darkness into the light (see also Col. 1:12, 13). They, therefore, belong in the light. These

Part Two: Teaching 1 Thessalonians 5:1-11

verses remind us of what the gospel has achieved. Jesus, the light of the world, has brought us into the light.

..so don't live in the darkness (6, 7)
Paul now builds on 5:4, 5 by making his first application. He draws a contrast between behaviour that is typical of the night and that found in the day. At night people sleep, whilst in the day they are awake and alert. At night people get drunk and lose control of their speech and actions, whereas in the day people are sober and self-controlled. Obviously these are generalisations but they make the point that there is a difference between night-time and daytime behaviour. Paul's point is that with the day of the Lord approaching, believers are in the daylight and their behaviour should match their location. Rather than return to the immoral darkness of their old lives, believers are to recognise that for them at least the day has dawned. It is as if Paul is saying to them, 'It's nine in the morning! This is no time to go back to bed or go for a drink. It's time to get up!' Again Paul sets out wanting there to be a clear distinction between the lives of the believers and the heathen world around (and see 4:5; 4:13). The effect of the gospel (5:4, 5) should be evident in holy living (5:6, 7). It should be noted that Paul uses 'sleep' in two distinct ways in this letter. It has a positive connotation at 4:15 and 5:10, when it refers to those believers who have died trusting in Christ and who await the resurrection of their body. However, here at 5:6 it has a negative connotation as it refers to those who fail to understand that through the gospel a new day has dawned in which to serve Christ faithfully.

...instead get up and get dressed (8-10)
Daytime is not only a time to be awake but also a time to get dressed appropriately. If we gather together one of the dominant themes of the whole epistle, the items that the Christians are to wear relate to the familiar trio of faith, love and hope (see 1:2, 3 and 3:10-13). Though Paul is thankful that the Thessalonians possess these qualities to a certain extent, some things are lacking and these spiritual attributes need to be put on day by day. Given the spiritual battle that the Thessalonians face from the devil (see 2:18 and 3:5), it is no surprise that the clothing is specifically linked to the armour required to protect someone facing an assault. So faith and love are linked to a breastplate and the future hope of full salvation is linked to a helmet. This list would be developed subsequently by the apostle at Ephesians 6:13-17 but the basic elements are all here. The armour worn by the Lord (Isa. 59:17) is available for the Thessalonian believers in order to resist the powers of darkness and live as the Lord's people in the light. As those wearing this armour, they are soldiers – hence the need for sobriety and self-control as they serve in a war zone. Protected through their faith in Christ and their loving, supportive Christian fellowship, they can look with confidence to the future. Once again salvation is something to be received and experienced in the future (see 1:10; 2:12; 3:13: 4:17). Believers are therefore to clothe themselves in preparation for their journey towards their final destination. Just as a thick coat and warm hat might be required to enable someone to survive the cold so that they arrive at their intended destination, so the qualities of faith, love and

Part Two: Teaching 1 Thessalonians 5:1-11

hope are the essential clothing designed to see believers to their final venue.

However, though Paul writes to reinforce the point that believers need to have their behaviour shaped by their future destination, nevertheless he concludes his point by underlining the security of every Christian. Our hope of salvation is not empty since it is backed up by the truths of verses 9 and 10. Hope of salvation is based on the fact that God has appointed believers to receive such salvation through the Lord Jesus Christ. God's appointment relates to His decision to get believers to their goal. Although in God's overall plan, some will receive His wrath (e.g. including those who persecute believers – see 2:16), others will obtain the gift of salvation. He has provided this gift through Christ and He will ensure that believers will receive and experience it at the end of their journey. In other words, as believers put on the hope of salvation as a helmet, they can be assured that this hope will come to fruition because of God's overall plan and purposes.

The security of the destination of every believer is further reinforced by the reminder that our salvation is based on the substitutionary death of the Lord Jesus Christ, who died for us, in our place. The result of His death for us is that whatever the situation, whether they have died (fallen asleep) or whether they are still alive, believers can be assured that they will be with Christ forever. This is virtually an identical conclusion to the argument of 4:13-18 at 4:17. There the primary focus was that those who had died in Christ will be with Him forever. Here the primary focus is that those who are awake will be with Him forever. The goal of our hope is not so much a place as a person –

the Lord Jesus Christ. Ultimately the believer is to dress in such a way (5:8) as to be able to travel in order to meet Him, and the security of arriving at such a destination is based on God's purposes (5:9) and Christ's death for us (5:10).

...and encourage each other every step of the journey (11)
Paul has not spelt all these things out from academic interest. His aim is pastoral encouragement. He is aware of the difficulty of living amidst the darkness of a hostile culture and of the spiritual battles that many of the Thessalonian believers are facing. He has sought to give assurance in 5:9, 10 that they will arrive at their final destination to be with Christ and on that basis he has called them to clothe themselves with faith, love and hope (5:8). His final word in this section is therefore that the Thessalonians should recognise that they are travelling to this glorious destination together and that they should assist each other in this journey. This would involve reminding each other of the goal of their journey, meeting the Lord Jesus Christ. It would mean encouraging each other to put on the appropriate clothing needed for their journey. In these ways they would strengthen each other's hope and confidence and so enable each other to arrive at the goal of their journey. Ultimately, therefore, getting ready for the return of Jesus is about helping each other to live for Christ each day through putting on faith, love and hope. In that way we will be ready, whatever the date.

In rounding off this section, Paul has brought his second main part of his epistle to a conclusion. Faith, love and hope form an inclusion (1:2, 3....5:8) which enables us to see the central purpose of the letter. Christians under pressure need to have assurance that their faith, love and hope

Part Two: Teaching 1 Thessalonians 5:1-11

are all genuine, but because they are also new Christians they need to be encouraged to strengthen those qualities. Though all three are vital and inseparable, nevertheless the letter particularly focuses on the importance of hope, which forms the climax not just of each section in the first part of the letter (1:10; 2:12; 2:16 and 3:13) but also forms the climax of the second part of the letter (4:13–5:11 and especially 5:8). The Thessalonian believers know what the future involves. One day they will be with the Lord Jesus Christ forever. Paul's aim is to encourage them to keep this hope clear in their thinking, such that it informs the way that they live in the present and gives them confidence even in the midst of the persecution and opposition that they are enduring.

From text to message

Getting the message clear: the theme

- Christians live in the light of the return of Jesus through clothing themselves with faith, love and hope.

Getting the message clear: the aim

- The aim of this passage is to encourage believers to be active in serving Christ so that we are ready for His return. Preaching or teaching on this passage should help in answering the following questions:
  - In what way will the Lord Jesus Christ return?
  - How should Christians get ready for His return?
  - How can Christians be sure that they will ultimately receive salvation?

A way in

Many of us live in situations where we rely on our watch because we need to be clear about the time. If we have an early meeting at work, we might set the alarm clock a bit earlier. Then when it goes off, though we may be tempted to press the 'snooze' button, we remember what time it is and what we need to do. Certainly it will involve getting up and getting dressed in an appropriate manner before jumping in the car or on the train to attend the meeting. It will be the same with many other appointments in our diary. At any given point, we need to know the time in order to get ready. So in this passage Paul wants us to know what the time is because that knowledge should affect our behaviour and lifestyle.

The sustained image which Paul uses concerns the contrast between night and day and the behaviour that is associated with one or the other. If we drive through a city centre late at night, there might be people spilling out of pubs and nightclubs, perhaps having consumed far too much alcohol. Rarely would those same people behave like that in broad daylight in the middle of a working week. Instead, during the day they might be dressed for work and be involved in a range of extremely responsible activities. The key issue is what time it is and whether it is daytime or night. Or perhaps contrast what you would wear depending upon whether it is day or night. As you prepare for bed, you may put on pyjamas or other appropriate nightwear. However such clothing would not be appropriate for a meeting at the office with your boss at 10 a.m. the next day! Paul's aim is to underline that it is now daytime for believers, whatever the time it says on your watch, and that this should shape our behaviour.

Pointers to application

- The return of our Lord Jesus Christ is not just a matter of private interest which is of relevance to a few people who might believe in that sort of thing. With the rise of postmodernism it is easy for people to think about Christianity in terms of a set of private beliefs which has no bearing on wider society. Yet this passage is a powerful reminder that the return of Christ will be a public phenomenon that will have an impact on absolutely everyone, whatever their beliefs or ideas about the Christian faith. It needs to be recaptured by Christians as a public truth applicable to everyone. Quite clearly from what Paul says at 1:10, it formed part of his gospel presentation and in general his teaching within 1 Thessalonians shows how it formed an essential means of providing both assurance and encouragement to hard-pressed believers. Though this doctrine has personal ramifications it is not a private truth.

- Although all sorts of crises come and go, in general people in the West tend to live longer and have a better quality of life compared to their forbears. As a result, it has been noticeable that spiritually our generation is probably as complacent as it is possible to be. 'Peace and safety' could be the watchwords of our politicians and forms the aspiration of many within our society. Yet one day all such complacency will be disturbed (see 5:3). The gospel is designed to shake people out of such complacency with its announcement that everyone will stand accountable before the living God.

- The light/dark and day/night imagery comes regularly within the New Testament. The Lord Jesus revealed Himself as the light of the world (John 8:12) and the gospel enables us to be transferred from the kingdom of darkness into the kingdom of light (Col. 1:12, 13). We need to remind ourselves quite literally of the black-and-white nature of the gospel of Christ. Though we live in a world where so many moral issues come to us coloured in various shades of grey, as Christians we need to hold on to the decisive effect of the gospel which divides the whole world into two groups (see 5:4, 5).

- As Christians we are not to return to the behaviour associated with the moral darkness of night. Imagine a situation where during the daytime you are driving a car but then feel tired. As a result you fall asleep at the wheel and cause an accident involving collateral damage. Paul is warning us about the equivalent danger of morally falling asleep and losing control as we pursue our journey in the Christian life (see 5:6, 7). Paul's word of application in the middle of these verses is 'let us not be like others'. We should be different in our lifestyle and behaviour.

- Often our clothing is deliberately and carefully chosen. Perhaps it is clothing designed to be appropriate for a particular appointment or meeting, such as a suit.

Perhaps it is clothing which is selected in order to enable you to take part safely in a particular activity, such as the protection worn by cricketers as they walk in to bat. In each case it is the activity envisaged which determines the appropriateness or otherwise of the clothing. So it is each day in the Christian life. Each day we face a spiritual assault and we need to be clothed with the breastplate of faith and love. Each day we are to lift up our heads and look forward to our meeting with the Lord Jesus Christ and, therefore, putting on the helmet of the hope of salvation is a reminder of the destination of our life. Thinking about the activity we are to be involved in each day as a Christian should shape what we put on (see 5:8).

- The goal of our faith is to be with Jesus forever. Though some parts of the Scripture may stress the new creation and what it will mean to have a new resurrection body (e.g. 1 Cor. 15 or 2 Peter 3), our ultimate goal is to be with Christ. Having been united with Him in the gospel such that we are in Him (see 1:1; 2:14; 4:1; 4:16), the goal of our union is nothing less than communion with Him. In both sections 4:13-18 and 5:1-11, Paul stresses above all this personal encounter with the Lord Jesus Christ. No wonder he could encapsulate one of the main aspects of the gospel as 'waiting for his Son' (see 1:10). The salvation which Paul describes is intensely personal. It is not so much about receiving gifts, though of course the gospel includes the gifts of forgiveness and eternal life. It is about receiving the Giver who has died for us. We may have wanted Paul to spell things out in 5:10 a bit more about what the cross achieved for us. Instead, Paul barely develops this theme here, other than underlining its substitutionary element, and focuses on the believer's encounter with the Lord Jesus Christ at the end. Paul's way of describing salvation should fuel our devotion to Christ such that we constantly remind ourselves that one day we will meet the One who died for us.

Suggestions for preaching

Sermon 1: Living in the light of the return of Christ (1 Thess. 5:1-11)

- When and how will Jesus return? (1-3)
- How do we get ready? (4-11)
  - Christians live in the day... (4, 5)
  - ...so they don't go back to the darkness... (6, 7)
  - ...but they get up and get dressed to meet Christ.... (8-10)
  - ...and encourage each other to get ready (11)

Other preaching possibilities

One obvious point, as discussed in the previous chapter, would be to merge this passage with 4:13-18. As we have seen, the climax of both passages is the meeting of the believer with the Lord Jesus (4:17; 5:10) and the call to encourage each other (4:18; 5:11). An advantage of this approach is that it gathers together much of the material about Christian hope in one sermon, which could be very beneficial since it is comparatively neglected.

Part Two: Teaching 1 Thessalonians 5:1-11   201

The alternative is to break this passage into two parts. The first sermon would focus on 5:1-3 and develop the teaching about the return of Christ, perhaps by linking it with Jesus' own teaching about His return in the gospels. The second sermon would then consider more directly how believers are to live in the light of this return. One minor point which would support such a division is the use by Paul of 'brothers' at 5:4 which often signals a new section. Developing this thought one stage further, some preachers might want to run a mini-series on 4:13–5:11, perhaps linking it into the season of advent when the church has traditionally focused on the return of Christ. For example:

+ Why is the return of Jesus pastorally important? 4:13-18

+ How will the return of Jesus take place? 5:1-3

+ How do we live in the light of the return of Jesus? 5:4-11

Suggestions for teaching

Introducing the passage

+ In what sort of situations do we find it easy to think of our actions and behaviour being shaped by a future event? Why do we find it hard to do this with regard to the return of our Lord Jesus Christ?

Understanding the passage

+ What images does Paul use to describe the return of Jesus and what effect should they have on us? (vv. 1-3)

- What does Paul mean when he says that Christians are no longer in darkness? (vv. 4, 5)
- What are the implications for the believer in no longer belonging to the darkness? (vv. 6, 7)
- What clothing is appropriate for the day according to Paul and what might putting on these articles of clothing involve in practical terms? (v. 8)
- On what basis does Paul give believers assurance that the hope of salvation will be fulfilled? (see vv. 9, 10)
- What is the climax of our hope according to 5:10?

Applying the passage
- Why do we find it hard to believe in the doctrine of the return of Christ?
- Why do we find it hard sometimes to be distinctive as Christians within the world?
- To what extent do we think of salvation as a future event rather than as a past experience?
- How do you think future communion with Christ should shape my current experience of Him?
- How should the prospect of meeting Jesus at His return shape my behaviour and the way that I live today?
- How can the teaching in this passage be used to encourage people in your church family?

11.

PAUL'S VISION FOR THE CHURCH (5:12-28)

Introduction
In bringing this letter to a conclusion it would be very easy to imagine Paul moving straight from 5:11 directly to his prayer at 5:23. After all, the main themes of faith, love and hope which introduced the whole letter (1:2,3) have featured at the hinge of the epistle (3:10-13) and at the climax of the section on hope (5:8). There is, therefore, a sense of completeness about finishing at 5:11 with a final prayer of blessing, perhaps followed by one or two personal notes. It is important, therefore, to ask what 5:12-22 is doing within the letter. What is it saying and what purpose does it serve? Again it is important to remember the overall context of the letter that it is written to a newly planted church which is under heavy pressure due to opposition and persecution. When an immature church is under intense pressure, it is easy to imagine things falling apart. Specifically, it is easy to see how relationships could fall apart.

Under intense pressure, people in the church may disagree with their leaders, who are also still young in the faith. Under intense pressure, relationships within the church family may suffer as people express disappointment and frustration with each other. Under intense pressure, many might find their relationship with the Lord suffering as they cannot understand how such persecution could possibly tie in with God's will for them. Seen in this light, the concluding exhortations of 5:12-22 make perfect sense. Paul is aware that some of the relationships in the church are in danger of fracturing due to the pressures that they are facing. As a result, writing into a situation where, due to the pressures all sorts of relationships are in danger of fracturing, Paul wants to provide final encouragements designed to correct and strengthen these relationships. His aim is that together the church and its leaders may be able to walk closely with the Lord and weather the storm in order to produce a mature, healthy, growing church. This appears to be Paul's aim and vision as he proceeds towards the end of his letter.

Listening to the text

Context and structure

In terms of the immediate context, 5:12 indicates that Paul is introducing a new section. Not only does he use the word 'brothers' – which usually marks the beginning of a separate passage – but also, as we look at 5:8-11, there are a number of indications that Paul has finished his previous section. That section had started at the hinge of the letter at 3:10-13 with the references to faith, love and hope, and had then proceeded with Paul urging or encouraging them forward

Part Two: Teaching I Thessalonians 5:12-28 205

in certain areas (4:1). It has now finished with a concluding reference to faith, love and hope (5:8) and a repeated plea to encourage each other with this teaching (4:18; 5:11). Given that the theme of encouragement starts and ends the section 4:1–5:11, it can be seen that 5:12 must be introducing a new concluding section.

There are a few markers within the passage which enable it to be divided up into its various parts. 'Brothers' introduces 5:12, 13 as well as 5:14, 15, before finally starting the farewell remarks at the very end at 5:25-28. In addition, there is the prayer at 5:23, 24 which stands on its own. Putting all these pieces of the jigsaw together helps us to discern a clear structure with a common theme holding it all, together based upon various relationships.

- Relationships with their leaders 5:12, 13
- Relationships with each other 5:14, 15
- Relationships with the Lord 5:16-24
- Relationships with Paul 5:25-28

In the opening exposition, some reference was made to Paul's prayer and word of assurance at 5:23, 24 through linking it to his opening words at 1:1-3. The preacher may feel that it is important to go over this ground again at the end of the series in order to reinforce the overall message of the book.

Working through the text

As we work through the text, attention will be given to the structure of the passage already identified.

1. Relationship with their leaders (5:12, 13)

We have recognised that the Thessalonian church is newly planted. That means that most if not all of the church members were relatively new Christians. We know from what Paul has written that although they had made a good start, nevertheless there were certain issues that needed to be sorted out. For example, sexual self-control must have been an issue (see 4:4, 5). It would therefore have fallen to the church leaders to deal with such moral issues within the church family. Yet the leaders were themselves new and inexperienced. They had not been leading churches for years. Nor had they been believers for decades. They had been thrust into a situation where as new Christians they had to lead and care for other new Christians. In such a situation we can easily imagine relationships being put under enormous strain. Perhaps a leader has tried to correct someone about issues relating to their lifestyle and has met with a strong reaction. 'What right has so-and-so to tell me how I should live my life? After all, aren't we saved by grace? He hasn't been a Christian any longer than the rest of us, so what right has he got to be leading the church anyway?' In response, Paul recognises that there clearly should be leaders within this new church. He doesn't designate them with any formal title such as elder or bishop, though such terms and others would be utilised later within the New Testament. Instead, he refers to their position and function as those 'who are over you in the Lord'. The same word is used to describe the function of leaders, whether bishops, deacons or others, at 1 Timothy 3:4f, 12 and 5:17. It denotes a degree of authority to care and provide for those entrusted to them, which includes the responsibility of correcting or admonishing ungodly behaviour. The main point Paul brings out about them is to recognise their hard work (see both 5:12 and 5:13). In this respect the leaders of the church had modelled themselves on Paul's own ministry amongst the Thessalonians described at 2:9, where he speaks of his toil, hardship and working day and night. So the leaders had been set apart in order to work hard amongst the church membership, presumably so that like Paul they would not be a burden to others but, positively, would be able to encourage and urge the believers on to live lives worthy of God (see 2:9-12).

If that describes the church leadership, how should the church members respond? Again Paul reinforces his advice through repetition in 5:12 and 5:13. Though some of the believers may have resented being admonished, nevertheless they were to respect and highly esteem their leaders. Indeed they were to hold them in the highest regard 'in love' because of their work. Though this new church had the potential to fracture as leaders sought to correct the behaviour of certain members of the church family, the glue that would hold it together would be respect and love for those who had been appointed as leaders. Through such respect, esteem and love would come peace (5:13) as opposed to friction and tension. Leaders would in part need to earn respect, like Paul, through their diligence and hard work in caring for the flock but, in return, the church family would need to give respect and be willing to be corrected in order for this young church to be strengthened.

2. *Relationships with each other (5:14, 15)*
Again we recognise the context of a newly planted church, where a group of believers who may hardly have known each

other before are thrown together through the preaching of the gospel. All sorts of people with all sorts of needs had come together and it could well have been a frustrating experience. Some certainly needed to change. The idle who were mentioned indirectly back at 4:11 were to be warned about being passengers within the church family and acting selfishly. The timid or faint-hearted, who perhaps found opposition and persecution particularly unnerving, were to be encouraged and gently urged onwards to live a life worthy of God in the same way that Paul demonstrated fatherly care for the believers (see 2:10-12). Or perhaps the timid included those struggling to cope with bereavement (see 4:13-18) and had lost much of their confidence in the gospel. The weak were to be helped and supported. Perhaps some were weak physically and needed the care of a loving church family for practical support (e.g. 4:9, 10). Perhaps some were morally or spiritually weak and struggled to hold on to their faith amidst the surrounding opposition (e.g. 4:3-8). Of course we don't know all the details but amidst all these problems it would be easy for other Christians to react badly. Out of frustration with these various groups, we can imagine some being impatient and responding in kind – 'if they won't help, then we won't help them! If they won't stand with us, then we won't stand with them!'

In that context, with the church once again being in danger of fracturing, Paul's remedy is to apply glue which will hold them together even amidst the difficulties. Love for one another, which already existed in part (see 1:3), is to grow and increase (see 3:12 and 4:9, 10) and this would happen to a certain extent through church members demonstrating patience (5:14) and kindness with everyone

(5:15), perhaps including their persecutors. Such qualities would enable this new fellowship to cope with the many frustrations and be bound together in such a way that would facilitate growth and enable the church to withstand persecution. Paul had exhibited gentleness amongst them 'like a mother caring for her children' (see 2:7) and perhaps that had been an enormously frustrating experience for him. Yet that would be a model to help the believers to show gentleness to each other through developing patience and kindness. Oil in an engine enables all the moving parts to function together without too much friction and overheating, and in a similar way these qualities would assist the church in working and growing together.

So 'living in peace with each other' (v. 13) comprises far more than benevolent feelings towards others within the church family. It will involve strong words of admonition to the idle, thoughtful words of encouragement to the weak, practical action to provide assistance to those in need, as well as careful patience and restraint to prevent retaliatory action where someone has been wronged (see v. 15). The fruit of the Spirit should be demonstrated in the nitty-gritty of these relationships as evidence of the reality of their faith in Christ.

3. Relationships with the Lord (5:16-24)

The Thessalonians had joyfully accepted the gospel message (see 1:6) and clearly there had been much initial enthusiasm which had led to the gospel ringing out from them throughout the surrounding area (see 1:8). But had such gospel zeal cooled down? Had the reality of continued opposition from their fellow countrymen (see 2:14) caused them to pause and take stock of what was happening? What might be in store for them (see 3:3, 4)? 'Surely continued suffering cannot be God's will for us,' may have been the thought expressed by some. The initial honeymoon period had come to an end and the reality of living as a Christian in a hostile setting had dawned. Perhaps joy and thanksgiving were giving way to despondency and prayerlessness.

In that sort of context, Paul gives a number of encouragements in order to rekindle their enthusiasm for following Christ.

God's will (16-18)

God's will in Christ Jesus is that the Christian life should be marked by various activities. In every circumstance there should be joy. Joy was the hallmark of their conversion (1:6) and it was also a feature of Paul's relationship with God – whether he was praying in God's presence (3:9) or looking forward to standing in the presence of Christ at His return along with the Thessalonian believers (2:19, 20). This was a joy fixed to the eternal realities of the gospel and the presence and blessing of God. The encouragement to be joyful always was therefore a command to focus on the glory of the gospel and the return of Christ.

Paul had not only demonstrated joy but had been unceasing in prayer, as was evident especially at 3:10 with his description of praying night and day in order to see them again. Further, he had also demonstrated great thankfulness to God for the Thessalonians (1:2, 3). Though there were things that concerned him about their faith (see 3:10), his first instinct was to express thanks to God for every sign of genuine spiritual life and particularly for the way they had responded to his preaching (see 2:13). Though he was enduring distress and persecution in his own experience

Part Two: Teaching 1 Thessalonians 5:12-28

(see 3:7), even in such circumstances he quickly turns to thanksgiving. Again, therefore, we see the apostle modelling the Christian life to the Thessalonians as he shares these terse encouragements. God's will could include going through testing times (see 3:3) but it should always include the basic responses of joy in the gospel, prayer for assistance and thanksgiving to God for every sign of genuine spiritual life. For those who are in Christ Jesus it is to be their basic response in all situations as well.

God's Word (19-22)
But what would sustain such joy and thanksgiving in the gospel? The Thessalonians had come to a living faith in Christ through the word of the gospel being applied by the Spirit. The Spirit had burned with deep conviction in the preacher (see 1:5) and had also lit up the hearers of that gospel word with great joy (see 1:6). The Spirit had brought life and light to preacher and hearer as God's Word went out. The way to quench this work of the Spirit which brings joy and thanksgiving was therefore to neglect the Word of God preached. So Paul issues a warning not to let the fire of the Spirit be put out by rejecting God's Word (see v. 19). This would include the danger of not listening to the apostle himself – hence the need to pay careful attention to this letter (see 5:27). It would also mean recognising the danger of dismissing any prophetic words which were delivered to the church. Within Acts there are a number of references to those who brought God's Word to the people as prophets (e.g. Acts 11:27; 15:32; 21:10).

Those people designated as prophets in the early church were not by and large apostles holding apostolic authority. However, they did bring a message from the Lord to God's people which needed to be received with appropriate respect (see v. 20). Given that they did not have apostolic authority, such teaching would need to be tested (see v. 21a) to see if it was in line with apostolic teaching. Such testing or sifting might highlight some aspects which were in line with God's will that had already been revealed and therefore those parts needed to be welcomed and acted upon (see v. 21b). Other aspects of the prophecy might fail the test and could even cause the church to go astray by embracing evil (see v. 22), and so there needed to be considerable discernment, whilst other parts seemed to come genuinely from the Lord.

There is a lively debate as to whether God still sends prophets to His church today. Some would argue that the gift of prophecy is still available and that to dismiss this possibility is to do exactly what Paul warns against here by 'quenching the Spirit' and 'treating prophecies with contempt'. Others would argue that the apostles and prophets have laid the foundation (see Ephesians 2:20) and that we should not expect these roles to continue on the completion of the New Testament. Whatever conclusion we may come to on that debate, we can see that in the Thessalonian context, the role of the believers, and particularly those involved in leadership, would be to ensure that any genuine word from the Lord was accepted as this would be the fuel that the Spirit would use to rekindle their faith and joy in Christ. Such is how Paul encourages the believers at 5:19-22. His aim is that they should be on fire for God's will in Christ Jesus through the work of the Spirit fanning the flame of God's Word in their hearts and lives.

God's Work (23, 24)

As the apostle steers his letter home, he comes to a final prayer of blessing. The Thessalonians have turned to Christ, which has filled him with joy and thanksgiving. Yet he is also aware that as a newly planted church there is still a long way to go. He has revealed that there are aspects of their faith that are lacking (3:10). He longs for their love to overflow (3:12) and he wants to strengthen their hope and confidence in the return of Christ (3:13). He is aware therefore that God's work in them is not complete at this stage. As a result, he prays for the completion of God's work in their lives. Completion, which will come at the return of the Lord Jesus Christ, will involve completeness. He therefore makes reference to them being sanctified 'through and through'. He prays also for their whole being by referring to their spirit, soul and body in a way which is designed to point to the completeness and thoroughness of God's work in them, enabling them to be ready for the return of Christ. This final prayer naturally links to his earlier prayer at 3:11-13 and to his prayer of thanksgiving that opened the letter at 1:2, 3. Everything within the letter comes within the embrace of Paul praying fervently for the work of God to be done in them. They are new Christians and there is much to be done in their lives before Jesus returns to see them grow to maturity and so Paul prays that the God of peace, the God who brings wholeness, would be at work within and amongst the Thessalonian church family.

Yet even as the Thessalonians were listening to Paul's prayer being read, perhaps they had their doubts. How could they keep going under the intense opposition they faced on a daily basis? How could Paul be sure that they would be welcomed into God's kingdom and glory (2:12) at the return of Jesus Christ? So Paul, aware of all their doubts and concerns as young Christians under pressure, gives them the final word of assurance that they need (5:24). Ultimately, the work of God is dependent on His faithfulness alone. He is the One who has called believers to new life through the gospel and He is the One who will ensure that every believer comes through the storms of opposition or difficulty to be presented before the Lord Jesus Christ. This final prayer picks up the twin themes of so much of this letter. There is the urging and encouragement to new Christians to keep growing and there is the assurance to Christians under pressure that God's work will be done.

So God's will is that, sustained by God's Word, they should rejoice and give thanks for the gospel, even as they pray fervently for God's work to be done amongst them, trusting that God will ensure that His work will be brought to completion.

4. Relationships with Paul (5:25-28)

Once again we return to the context of the letter. Paul had been with them for only three Sabbaths and had then been forced to flee Thessalonica due to the severity of the opposition towards him (see Acts 17:1-10). As he has made apparent at 2:1ff, there were clearly some who felt that Paul was no longer interested in them, and so Paul had been forced to reveal the depth of his love for them both whilst present with them (2:1-12) and whilst absent (2:17-3:10). As if to underline this ongoing affection and love, he now signs off in a way that reveals his partnership with them. He has shown himself to be dependent upon them before (see 3:7) and he now asks them to pray for him (5:25). In return he

Part Two: Teaching 1 Thessalonians 5:12-28

asks that his love for them should be acknowledged (5:26). He then encourages them to listen to his letter being read so that everyone in the fellowship can hear that he has not abandoned them at all (5:27). Finally, he prays as he began by commending all of them to God's grace (5:28). Though persecution and misunderstandings had threatened to split the Thessalonian church from the apostle, his final remarks are designed to seal the relationship and provide assurance of his ongoing love and concern for them and his desire that this partnership in the gospel be continued for the future.

So, in all sorts of ways, Paul concludes by cementing and strengthening a whole range of relationships that were in danger of being fractured. Due to their immaturity as believers or through the pressures caused by opposition, Paul is aware that there was tension in each of these vital relationships and so his conclusion seeks to build them up. His longing is for a church which respects its leaders who are working hard. It is for a church where its members encourage each other and show patience and kindness even in trying circumstances. It is for a church committed to hearing God's Word and doing God's will trusting that God's work will be done. It is for a church that will continue to walk with its apostle, fully assured of his depth of love and concern. In all these ways Paul seeks to strengthen the church as he concludes his letter.

From text to message

Getting the message clear: the theme

- Strong relations with church leaders, one another and the Lord are required for a church to thrive.

Getting the message clear: the aim

- The aim of this passage is to strengthen the relationships in the church so that it would be prepared for the return of Christ. Preaching or teaching on this passage should help in answering the following questions:
  - How should church leaders relate to their members?
  - What are the signs of a healthy relationship between a believer and the Lord?
  - On what basis can Christians be sure that they will be ready for the return of Christ?

A way in

In 2012, London hosted the Olympic and Paralympic Games. Though the Games were relatively short events (the Olympics lasted about as long as Paul's original visit to Thessalonica recorded in Acts 17!), nevertheless those who organised them were keen to ensure that there was a lasting legacy which would endure long after 2012. So it is with Paul's visit to Thessalonica. Though brief, his intention was to leave a legacy which would completely changed the area for the better. In order to secure the legacy, one of his main concerns is to ensure good relationships between the believers and their leadership, amongst one another and chiefly with the Lord. Without these relationships being secured nothing of any lasting value would be left.

Paul's prayer at 5:23 is interesting because of its sense of thoroughness. Imagine cooking a beef burger on a barbecue. You want the meat to be cooked thoroughly. It's no good for it to look all right on the outside. It needs to be cooked all the way through. So it is with our holiness. As those already set apart for the Lord, we are to grow in holiness in every aspect of our lives. So Paul prays that believers will be sanctified through and through. He wants their whole spirit and soul and body to be ready for the return of the Lord Jesus. Rather than being half baked and unpalatable, Paul longs for us all to be thoroughly devoted to the Lord, evidenced in a life that is worthy of Him.

Pointers to application

- Leaders within the church family are marked out particularly by their work (what they do) and also by the way that they fulfil their ministry in working hard (how they do it). Being given the opportunity to serve as a leader over others should entail a sense of responsibility which leads to a desire to work hard on behalf of the church family, emulating the apostle in his own ministry (1 Thess. 2:8, 9). These verses may be a rebuke to some of us who are coasting along in Christian leadership. Notice also that working hard is linked with the hard work of being called, from time to time, to admonish members of the church. Again it is easy for pastors to duck away from such responsibilities for the sake of avoiding confrontation and preserving reputation but, as always, faithfulness is the key (see 1 Thess. 2:4), even if it means applying God's Word in ways which some may find uncomfortable.

- Verses 12 and 13 also feature a call for the membership of the church to respect their leaders and hold them in the highest esteem because of the nature of their work. Giving respect may be easy when everything is running smoothly but perhaps it is especially when words of admonishment are required that the leaders should be supported and respected because of the difficulty of this sort of ministry. How should such respect and love be conveyed? It may show itself in many different ways but it will first be an underlying commitment to those in leadership, followed by personal support and encouragement, as well as a willingness to listen to and engage with their preaching of the Word of God (see 1 Thess. 2:13). Those who bring the very Word of God should be highly esteemed in love.

- In verses 14 and 15 there is the recognition that church life involves all sorts of tensions where friction can easily develop, leading to a culture of grumbling and arguments. Into that mix Paul seeks to pour in oil, in order to lessen the friction and overheating that may result. In part it takes the form of avoiding recriminations and seeking to show kindness. All this needs to be applied within our fellowships to enable us to be a support and encouragement to our brothers and sisters in Christ. Certain issues need to be resolved occasionally by the leadership (see 5:12) but mostly difficulties that arise between believers need to be resolved through forgiveness and kindness.

- Especially when believers are going through testing times, it is easy to default to a situation of grumbling against God. Yet Paul wants to encourage the Thessalonians and us to view everything through the gospel. As we view life through the lens of the gospel there will always be cause for thanksgiving and joy. Further, it will colour our response in prayer as we seek to pray for the progress of the gospel in our own lives and in the lives of others, recognising that God is well able to use such testing times to further His sovereign purposes of grace.

- Paul highlights the danger of quenching the Spirit through holding God's Word in contempt (5:19, 20). We have a proverbial saying that 'familiarity breeds contempt' and it may well be the case that this can occur within the church. Over the course of time church members can hear God's Word being preached on numerous occasions over many years, and the danger is that they can become so familiar with it that they become hardened to what is actually being said and immune to its promptings. We need to remind ourselves on the basis of 1 Thess. 2:13 that the preaching of the Word of God is the Word of God. Therefore with appropriate testing, in recognition that all preachers are human, sinful and certainly not infallible, there should be a sense of awe as God's Word is communicated and as God's Spirit warms our hearts and ignites our devotion to the Lord Jesus Christ.

- Paul's final prayer at 1 Thessalonians 5:23 should be an encouragement for each of us to wholehearted commitment to the Lord. The way that he lays a stress on their whole spirit, soul and body being sanctified through and through suggests that he is concerned about seeing more progress made in their Christian lives. So it will also be with each of us. Though we may have made great progress through God's grace over

- the years, there will still be further work that the Lord needs to do. Our danger is often complacency, resting either on our past experiences or our Bible knowledge. Our need is, in humility, to recognise that God has further work to do in and amongst us.

- Paul's final word of assurance at 5:24 should also be a word of encouragement for us. Ultimately, our progress in the Christian life and our welcome into glory is all through God's faithfulness and not due to our own achievements. Especially when we face testing times and the church and individual believers are under enormous significant pressure, it is a huge relief to be reminded that God's sovereign purposes of grace will all be achieved. In the midst of anxiety and doubts we are to lay our heads down on the pillow of God's faithfulness.

Suggestions for preaching

Sermon 1: Key relationships for the church (1 Thess. 5:12-28)

- Relationships with their leaders (12, 13)
- Relationships with each other (14, 15)
- Relationships with the Lord (16-24)
  - God's will (16-18)
  - God's Word (19-22)
  - God's work (23, 24)
- Relationships with Paul (25-28)

Part Two: Teaching 1 Thessalonians 5:12-28

Other preaching possibilities
Given that the triad of faith, love and hope occur both at 1:3 and 5:8, it seems clear that 5:12 introduces the final section of the epistle and therefore it appears natural to handle the material in 5:12-28 in one block. However, as we have seen there is plenty of material in these verses and it would be relatively straightforward to break the passage into two sermons. The first would deal with relationships within the church family – both with leaders and one another (5:12-15). The second would deal with relationships with the Lord, using the suggested framework above (5:16-24 or 16-28).

Suggestions for teaching

Introducing the passage

- How important are relationships in any organisation? In what ways can a breakdown in relationships affect the whole organisation? What are the main things which preserve good relationships?

Understanding the passage
- Why might Paul have needed to give these encouragements to respect leaders and what might this have involved in practice? (vv. 12, 13)
- In verses 14, 15 what are the key words which enable a fellowship to function well and what does Paul encourage them to avoid?
- Within the Thessalonian context, why do you think Paul issues the instructions in verses 16-18? How is it possible to exhibit joy always, pray continually and give thanks in all circumstances?

- How had the Thessalonians been quenching the Spirit and what is Paul's remedy? (vv. 19-22)
- In what ways would verses 23 and 24 have provided both encouragement and assurance to the church?
- What do the final verses reveal about Paul's relationship to the Thessalonian church? (vv. 25-28)

Applying the passage

- In what ways could your church be a better support and encouragement to your leaders? (vv. 12, 13)
- What are the practical ways in which patience and kindness could be exhibited more within your fellowship? (vv. 14, 15)
- How is 'putting out the Spirit's fire' linked to our attitude to God's Word? (vv. 19-22)
- How should knowledge of God's faithfulness provide assurance to God's people especially when they are under pressure or if they are new Christians? (v. 24)
- What changes could you make to enhance your relationships within your church family?
- How do you think God might answer if you used the prayer in 1 Thess. 5:23 concerning yourself?

3.

Introducing 2 Thessalonians

I.

GETTING OUR BEARINGS IN 2 THESSALONIANS

Introduction

Having written 1 Thessalonians, the obvious question to ask is why Paul would need to write another letter to the same church. Of course, some commentators argue that Paul did not write this second letter, but on the whole such views are largely subjective. The current state of play is handled admirably by Gordon Fee in his NICNT Eerdmans commentary where he shows how authentically Pauline this letter is, whilst casting serious doubt on the 'forgery' view which holds to the position that someone was copying Paul. As preachers our chief task is to handle the text which we have received and work with the natural assumption, which is plain from the letter, that it has been authored by the apostle (see 1:1; 3:17). This fits with Paul's frequent references to what he had taught them on his original visit (e.g. 2:5; 2:15; 3:7-10). Further, the many links between

1 and 2 Thessalonians in content and structure make it clear that they have the same author.

Fee dates the letter as having been written only a few months after 1 Thessalonians in A.D 50. If this is the case, then we need to recognise that the presenting issues highlighted in 1 Thessalonians are almost certainly still present. The Thessalonian church is still a relatively newly planted church which is under pressure due to opposition to the Christian faith. A few months later, there is still likely to be immaturity, perhaps both in belief and behaviour, as well as continued pressure. In fact this is what we find.

What are the issues Paul is writing to address?

Within the letter there appears to be three distinctive concerns picked up by Paul.

1. Persecution has continued and may be growing

The context of hostility to the Christian faith has been evident since Paul's initial visit (see Acts 17:1-10) and was referred to at 1 Thessalonians 1:6; 2:14-16 and 3:3-5. This theme now resurfaces at 1:4-6. The Thessalonian church is still facing persecutions and trials (NIV) or afflictions (ESV) in 1:4.

It is experiencing suffering in 1:5 and has been troubled (NIV) or afflicted (ESV) in 1:6. The fact that Paul opens with this issue suggests that the church was under increasing pressure. Given the way Paul develops his teaching about the return of the Lord Jesus Christ in this section, he may be responding to a real sense of injustice that was being felt amongst the Thessalonian believers. They were being persecuted by people who were apparently getting away with it. Christians were being treated unjustly with impunity. How long would they be able to cope as day by day their persecutors carried on with no apparent intervention from God to protect His people or stop the persecution?

2. *Deception has entered and must be countered*
Paul's answer to the issue of current injustice was to unpack what would happen when the Lord Jesus returned – see 1:6-10. However, this was precisely the problem as far as some at Thessalonica were concerned. They had received a report which, as far as they were concerned, had originated from Paul, which said that the Day of the Lord had already happened – see 2:2. This had thrown them into confusion because if the return of Christ was the solution to persecution and injustice, how is it possible for Jesus to have already returned and for the persecution to continue? This is therefore a serious issue which Paul must sort out. The fact that the Thessalonian church had been deceived in this way actually falls into line with the broad sweep of events which will precede the return of Christ. Paul's solution is to encourage them to hold firmly to the teaching which he had previously passed on to them. Having been deceived into letting go of certain teachings, they are now to hold on more firmly.

3. *Disobedience has continued and must be stopped*
The issue of deception is new but the matter of disobedience by a particular grouping within the church is not. Paul has raised concerns about some of the believers at 1 Thessalonians 4:11, 12 and 5:14. Though it is not completely clear why these believers were behaving as they did, the

fact is that some were idle and disrupting others. In due course the causes will be explored but for the present it can simply be noted that Paul sees this group as a running sore within the Thessalonian church. Despite repeated appeals, they were refusing to listen to the apostle and therefore he uses extremely strong language to try to restore harmony within the church through the obedience of this group both to Paul's teaching and previous example.

On the surface of the letter, these are the three presenting problems which require attention. Two are not new but may have developed over the intervening months, whilst one – the issue of deception – has emerged since the writing of 1 Thessalonians. Though it may be the most obscure of the three issues, the fact that it has suddenly emerged may have been the crucial factor which caused Paul to write once again.

One other consideration may also point to the significance of the material in chapter 2. Within the three chapters, two of them concern issues relating to the proper understanding of the teaching about the return of the Lord Jesus Christ (see 2 Thess. 1, 2). A true view of Christian hope will enable the Thessalonians not to be unsettled but to be encouraged, even amidst the difficulties which they faced. However, we can also see that within the three chapters two of them concern matters relating to a proper response to the teachings of Paul (which are the Word of God – see 1 Thess. 2:13). In chapter 2 the Thessalonians have been deceived into letting go of these teachings which is why they are told to hold on to them (2:15). In chapter 3 some of the Thessalonian believers have been ignoring Paul's teaching (3:6) which is why they need to be vigorously rebuked. Seen in this light, 2 Thessalonians 2 touches on both issues – an accurate understanding of the return of Christ and the need for correct handling of the Word of God. For this reason again it may be that 2 Thessalonians 2 contains the key issues which actually precipitated the decision of Paul to write.

- 2 Thessalonians 1 – Persecution – Living for Christ's glory
- 2 Thessalonians 2 – Deception – The return of Christ
- 2 Thessalonians 3 – Disobedience – Holding on to Christ's message

What is the structure of 2 Thessalonians?

In one sense the structure of 2 Thessalonians is relatively easy to discern because in each of the three chapters Paul is dealing with one of the presenting issues referred to earlier. However it may be helpful to refer back to the structure of 1 Thessalonians for assistance in this area. In Paul's earlier letter, we noted the significance of 1 Thessalonians 3:11-13. These verses include a prayer which acts as a hinge – summing up the key issues in chapters 1 to 3 but also setting the agenda for chapters 4 and 5. On careful examination we can see that the prayer at 2 Thessalonians 2:16, 17 may have a similar function. In its reference at 2:16 to the good hope which they have received from God, Paul is summing up the message of 2 Thessalonians 1 and 2. The answer to the injustice of persecution lies in the fact that Christ will return to be revealed as judge. The resolution to the issue of deception lies also in the fact that Christ will return. So though there are many details to be worked out, the first half of 2 Thessalonians reaches its climax in the opening words of the prayer at 2:16 with a focus on the future.

The prayer continues into 2:17. Paul longs for them to be strengthened in every good work and word. This sets the agenda for 2 Thessalonians 3. First, we have a positive example where strengthening in the Lord's work is required (3:1-5) and then Paul tackles one of the presenting problems at Thessalonica through encouraging the group that are idle to get working (3:6-15).

On either side of this pivotal prayer at 2:16, 17, there is reference to the need to hold on to Paul's teachings which he has handed down to the Thessalonians (see 2:15 and 3:6). It is as if Paul is wanting to say that his prayer at 2:16, 17 will be fulfilled as the Thessalonian believers hold on to his word, which is God's Word.

There may even be a deeper parallel between 1 Thessalonians and 2 Thessalonians in terms of their overall shape. In the first part of 1 Thessalonians, Paul handles two issues facing the believers. They are facing direct persecution from their enemies but they are also struggling to cope with indirect persecution as doubt is cast on whether Paul's ministry is genuine or not. Similarly, in 2 Thessalonians Paul responds to the issue of direct persecution in chapter 1 but then in chapter 2 has to deal with an issue that casts doubt about whether his teaching is genuine or not. In addition to this, we noted that back in 1 Thessalonians Paul used the second half to provide encouragement and correction to this young church (1 Thess. 4, 5), and in 2 Thessalonians 3 we find him doing the same sort of thing, even to the extent of returning to an identical issue which still needed to be resolved. Identifying this parallel structure to the two letters should help us in terms of understanding their flow.

An outline of 2 Thessalonians

Introduction (1:1, 2)
Part One   A. Persecution   Thanksgiving prayer (1:3, 4)
Confidence in return of Christ to bring justice (1:5-10)
Prayer for Christ to be glorified (1:11, 12)
                B. Deception   Understanding the future (2:1-12)
Having confidence in the gospel (2:13-15)

Central Prayer (2:16-17)
Part Two   A. Work of the gospel. Encouraging gospel work within the world (3:1-5)
                B. Failing to work. Challenging disobedience within the church (3:6-15)

Conclusion (3:16-18)

Questions for studying 2 Thessalonians

Each preaching unit includes a set of Bible Study questions which may be of some assistance. In addition, the following questions may also be useful for a group which has read through 2 Thessalonians together in its entirety, as a prelude to the study of individual passages.

- What are the key issues that the church in Thessalonica was facing?
- In what ways might the teaching about the return of the Lord Jesus Christ have been an encouragement to the Thessalonian believers during times of persecution? (ch. 1)
- What was the problem that faced the church at 2:2 and why was it likely to unsettle or alarm the believers?
- What were the key truths which the Thessalonians were encouraged to hold on to at 2:13-15?
- What was Paul's main prayer request for himself at 3:1-5?
- How does Paul challenge the disobedient group in Thessalonica at 3:6-15?
- In what ways can you see any relevance of the teaching in 2 Thessalonians to your own church?

2.

WHY WE SHOULD PREACH AND TEACH 2 THESSALONIANS

Sometimes it is blindingly obvious why a New Testament letter should be preached. However, there are a number of reasons why 2 Thessalonians may seem particularly remote. Though some parts of the worldwide church are facing severe persecution and great injustices, other parts of the church are under far less external pressure from society. Further, the idea that the return of the Lord Jesus Christ may already have happened is not the sort of view that one is often likely to meet. Finally though there may be some Christians who refuse to work, the prevailing high unemployment figures around the world make it much more likely for people to be desperately seeking work than avoiding it. So at first glance this is not a promising picture. If ever a New Testament document seemed irrelevant to modern Christians, then it is probably 2 Thessalonians! After I had been in a vicarage in Carlisle for a year, I discovered an old scythe hidden in the garage. I took it out and looked at it. Though it was impressive in its own way I had no further use for it since the church already possessed a lawnmower and strimmer. It was an interesting artefact but had little relevance to my life and so I put it back where I found it! Should this be the case with 2 Thessalonians?

I think the situation with 2 Thessalonians is quite different. First, though some of us may not be experiencing significant persecution, nevertheless it is growing in intensity around the world. Wherever Christians face injustice and hostility we need to be reminded of the certainty of the return of our Lord Jesus Christ. He is the One who will establish justice. Our hope and confidence ultimately rest on His return. This is a Book, therefore, which can provide comfort and assurance to suffering believers. Further, the message of 2 Thessalonians 1 culminates in a vision of Christ being glorified both in the future at His return (1:10) and also now through believers (1:12). Such a focus on pursuing the glory of Christ should be intensely relevant to every believer in every situation.

Second, concerning the danger of being deceived into letting go of God's Word, we may feel that we are unlikely to make the same mistake as the Thessalonians (see 2:2). However, the history of the church is littered with examples of situations where believers have let go of God's Word. The call to stand firm and hold on to the teachings (see 2:15) is one that we constantly need to be reminded about. Satan continues to seek to deceive the saints by encouraging or enticing us to let go of God's Word. Therefore teaching that exposes his methods and encourages us to hold on to God's Word should always be relevant.

Third, though the specific reason for the idleness of the group of believers in 2 Thessalonians 3 remains unclear, it is vitally important that every believer recognises the value of working to the glory of God. As we shall see, Paul is praying for them to glorify Christ through their work (see 1:11, 12) and to be strengthened 'in every good work and word' (see 2:17 ESV). God works, the apostle works and so we must work. In 2 Thessalonians we see the significance and value of work in a way which connects creation and redemption. This letter is intensely practical in wanting to apply the faith to everyday life, which again reveals its ongoing relevance.

Finally, within this letter is one of the great prayers for mission. At 2 Thessalonians 3:1, Paul asks that the Thessalonians would pray that the Word of the Lord would speed ahead (ESV)/spread rapidly (NIV) and be honoured. As believers we should always have a passionate concern for the spread of the gospel around the world. The gospel spreads and the church grows as God's Word runs. It is always relevant to be praying this prayer, in whatever situation we find ourselves.

So, far from being remote and irrelevant, there are many great reasons to study 2 Thessalonians if we want to see a church holding on to God's Word, seeking to bring glory to Christ and looking forward to seeing the glory of Christ at the end. If that is our vision, or if we want it to be our vision, then 2 Thessalonians may be exactly the Book to study and teach.

3.

IDEAS FOR PREACHING AND TEACHING A SERIES ON THIS BOOK

One of the practical issues facing the preacher committed to the expository method concerns division of a book of the Bible into appropriate sections for preaching. A number of factors must be considered:

- Would the congregation benefit more from an overview of the letter taking only a few sermons or by allowing plenty of time to explore all the details of the letter?

- How long would a congregation be able to cope with a particular series?

- Are there any particular constraints which need to be borne in mind e.g. a time frame such as an academic term, church diary constraints due to special events, holidays, preaching allocations (if there is more than one preacher available)?

Series 1: 3 Sermons
1. Sermon 1   1:1-12
2. Sermon 2   2:1-17
3. Sermon 3   3:1-18

This is perhaps the simplest and most straightforward way of approaching 2 Thessalonians. The series is able to link with each of the three presenting issues outlined above. The drawback is that there is a considerable amount of material in each chapter which may mean that the preacher is often skating over significant sections. However there are times and seasons when it is good not to get too bogged down in the minutiae in order to focus on Paul's main response to each problem. This series does not have an overview as a separate sermon but that is by no means essential as long as the big picture of the book is kept in mind throughout each exposition.

Series 2: 5 Sermons
1. Sermon 1   Overview [1:1,2;2:16,17;3:16-18]
2. Sermon 2   1:3-12
3. Sermon 3   2:1-15
4. Sermon 4   3:1-5
5. Sermon 5   3:6-15

This slightly longer series starts with an overview by allowing the first sermon to focus on the 'hinge' of the letter at 2:16, 17. This may be a helpful way of introducing the letter in such a way that the congregation can see the flow of the whole letter before plunging into one of its sections. Personally, I feel it is often a good idea to introduce a series in this sort of way but it requires having a good knowledge of how the book fits together in the first place though, as already noted, it is perfectly possible to preach a series without it.. This series also enables the preacher to look at 3:1-5 separately as it is a particularly rich portion. In this series I have kept the connection between 2:1-12 and 2:13-15 because the latter, especially noting 2:15, is the answer to the problem highlighted at 2:2. The division of material could be used, for example, at a weekend houseparty where there is a short introductory meeting on the Friday night followed by two talks each on Saturday and Sunday.

Series 3: 7 Sermons

1. Sermon 1   Overview [1:1,2;2:16,17;3:16-18]
2. Sermon 2   1:3-10
3. Sermon 3   1:11,12
4. Sermon 4   2:1-12
5. Sermon 5   2:13-15
6. Sermon 6   3:1-5
7. Sermon 7   3:6-15

This is still not a particularly long series but here there is the opportunity to spend much more time on sections such as 1:11, 12 and 2:13-15 which may have been left slightly in the shade when connected with longer passages.

4.

TEACHING 2 THESSALONIANS

1.

BRINGING HOPE AND PURPOSE TO GOD'S PEOPLE – AN OVERVIEW OF 2 THESSALONIANS (1:1, 2; 2:16, 17 AND 3:16-18)

Introduction

As so often in Paul's letters, the introductory words and the final exhortations often provide significant clues to the message he is seeking to bring. If the central prayer at 2:16, 17, which provides the hinge of the letter, is also considered, we will find that we are given a very helpful way of getting an overview of what is happening. As has already been observed in our study of 1 Thessalonians, this is a newly planted church which was facing severe pressure. As we survey the details at the beginning, middle and end of 2 Thessalonians, we will notice that great grace is required because the pressures of opposition and persecution are continuing. In addition, being a newly planted church, it is particularly susceptible to other dangers which might stunt its growth. Two such dangers are revealed as they face hostility through deception (ch. 2) and disobedience (ch. 3). Indeed, this highlights that the traditional assault of the world (ch. 1) the devil (ch. 2) and the flesh (ch. 3) are all at work, and Paul needs to supply the resources through his teaching to counter all these assaults and enable this young church to stand and grow.

Listening to the text

Context and structure

For the background to this letter we turn first to Paul's visit recorded at Acts 17:1-10 and then 1 Thessalonians. Perhaps it is helpful to note similar themes emerging in both letters. For example, part of the solution to persecution in 1 Thessalonians is the strong and repeated references to hope and confidence in the future. Similarly in 2 Thessalonians, hope will be an essential ingredient to strengthen Christians under pressure. Likewise, 1 Thessalonians identified problems of laziness within some members of the church family which are here directly addressed.

The opening introductory words (1:1, 2) closely parallel those used in 1 Thessalonians. However, there are differences at the end of the letter where Paul wraps up some of the main themes. In fact on closer inspection the conclusion divides into three brief items. The first, at 3:16, links to the unity and harmony of the fellowship as it faces disruption from some church members (3:1-15). The second, at 3:17, links to the need to avoid being deceived about what authentically comes from the apostle (2:1-15). The third, at 3:18, links to the grace of our Lord Jesus Christ which is supplied to provide 'good hope' (see 2:16) amidst adversity (1:3-12). In this way we can see that 3:16-18 provides a fitting conclusion for the letter.

In addition the important prayer at the heart of 2 Thessalonians divides naturally into two parts. Verse 16 points to the future hope which God in His love and grace has provided. Verse 17 points to the present and the encouragement for the Thessalonians to be active in serving Christ at every opportunity. Clearly these two verses are not free-floating verses that can be ripped out of context but a careful study of the letter reveals that they occupy a central and pivotal position, which is why it may be helpful to use them in an overview sermon. So as we shall see, 2:16 gathers together the material of chapter 1 and 2 whilst 2:17 prepares the reader for the message of chapter 3. Only once the verses have been carefully considered within their context is it wise to see how their message contributes to the whole of the letter.

Both grace and peace are mentioned at the beginning and the end and also feature in the central prayer (2:16). In addition, as has been noted concerning the significant role of Paul's prayer at 1 Thessalonians 3:11-13 in providing a hinge for the whole letter, so 2:16-17 has a similar function within 2 Thessalonians. It is worth paying particular attention to these key verses to get an understanding of the main direction and thrust of Paul's teaching.

Working through the text

As we work through the text, attention will be paid to the structure of both the conclusion of the letter and the central prayer as a means to gain an overview.

1. Three presenting problems and their solutions (1:1-2; 3:16-18)

Fierce opposition...and God's grace which brings security and hope (1:1, 2; 2:16; 3:18)

We already know from 1 Thessalonians 1:6; 2:14 and 3:3 that the church is facing considerable opposition and this has intensified, as can be seen at 2 Thessalonians 1:4-6. The solution, according to Paul, rests in the grace of the Lord Jesus Christ. By God's grace they have eternal security. As in 1 Thessalonians, though Paul could have identified them as 'the Church of God in Thessalonica', in fact they are addressed as 'the Church of the Thessalonians in God the Father and the Lord Jesus Christ' (1:1). Through God's grace they have been put into a place of complete safety, located within God the Father and the Lord Jesus Christ.. Here they can know the security of being wrapped up in God's eternal purposes. Just as the letter is encircled by God's grace (1:1; 3:18), so their lives are also upheld and embraced by God's loving arms in which there is complete security no, matter how great the opposition is. Such grace which has already provided security in the present also provides the promise of security at the end. It is through God's grace that these believers have received eternal encouragement and good hope (2:16). This will enable them to know that their future is also secure.

Unsettling deception….. and God's Word which brings clarity and confidence (3:17)

The next presenting problem concerns the fact that the church had been deceived. They had a high view of the significance of the return of Christ, as is evident from 1 Thessalonians. They also had a high view of the teaching of Paul, regarding it quite properly as the Word of God (1 Thess. 2:13). Yet what had happened is that somehow they had been deceived into accepting a message that the Day of the Lord had already arrived as an authentic word of Paul (see 2 Thess. 2:2). Clearly such teaching was likely to cause considerable damage, as it would undermine confidence that Christ would bring salvation and justice at His return, since if the Lord had already returned why were they still suffering? So Paul needs to counter this false message, which he does in chapter 2, but this raises the question as to how the Thessalonians would know with any degree of confidence that 2 Thessalonians was a genuinely Pauline letter. So to respond to that issue Paul finishes by underlining the fact that 2 Thessalonians has really come from him (see 3:17). Through handwriting part or all of the letter Paul, wants the Thessalonians to know which word is authentically from him and has apostolic authority so that they will know to which word they need to hold on (see 2:15 and compare with 2:2).

Deliberate disobedience…and God's peace which sustains unity (3:16)

The final presenting problem concerns the deliberate disobedience of a group within the Thessalonian church. They have already been identified earlier at 1 Thessalonians 4:11, 12 and 5:14. The fact that this was still a problem highlights that there was continuing, deliberate disobedience. Paul needs to deal with this group and uses strong language both to them (3:12) and to the others within the church family (3:6, 14). However, even within these warnings, Paul is careful to remind the majority that, though disobedient, the others are still brothers (3:6, 15). Therefore it is natural for him to be concerned for the peace, harmony and unity of the fellowship. Though it would be understandable if there were to be strong words between the two groupings, Paul's prayer is that the peace and unity of the Lord will be experienced by all of them on all occasions (3:16). Having given a strong exhortation, Paul's desire is that this will have done the trick. Yet even as the internal squabbles are being sorted out, he is praying for peace for all of them.

So at the beginning and end of the letter we are introduced to the three presenting problems in a manner which also indicates the solution – which focuses on the provision of God's grace, God's Word and God's peace.

2. Paul's prayer and the glory of Christ (2:16, 17)

This prayer straddles the whole letter, enabling us both to look back at what precedes it and also to look forwards to what follows.

The confident hope of seeing the glory of Christ (2:16 and see 1:10; 2:14)

Through God's love and grace believers have 'eternal encouragement and good hope'. The solution to the continuing persecution has been for Paul to emphasise the fact that the Lord Jesus Christ will return, bringing justice (see ch. 1). Though they were temporarily sidetracked through being deceived by a message purporting to come from the apostle, Paul has reminded them once again that the return of Christ will resolve all the issues which they currently face (see ch. 2). Yet Paul is concerned more than about persecutors being judged. The good hope of every believer is that when the Lord Jesus returns they will see and experience His glory (see 1:10 and 2:14). Our hope is nothing less than being with

Christ and seeing His glory. Ultimately, amidst all the issues that they are facing, Paul wants them to have a clear idea of their destination which will sustain them and direct them.

The clear purpose of working for Christ to be glorified (2:17 and 1:11, 12; 3:1)

Though Paul is concerned that they should know what the future may hold in order to sustain them in the present, nevertheless he has a concern for the Thessalonians to get on with living for Christ now. So he prays that they would be strengthened in every good work and word (2:17). He has already used very similar vocabulary at 1:11 where he prayed for God to fulfil every good purpose and every good work prompted by their faith. Why has he prayed like this? It is so that the name of our Lord Jesus Christ may be glorified in them through God's grace (see 1:12). In other words, Paul's prayers at 1:11 and 2:17 are united in seeking to see a people who have a great passion for glorifying Christ through the way they live out their lives. Positively, Paul wants them to be praying even as he is working so that Christ's Word is honoured (3:1). Negatively, he wants them to avoid any activity which brings the name of Christ into disrepute (see 3:6ff). His passion is that they will be strengthened so that they will work to bring glory to the name of Christ.

Within the wider context of the whole letter, Paul's 'hinge' prayer focuses on the glory of Christ. He gives assurance that believers will see the glory of Christ – this is their good hope which should bring them eternal encouragement. Also he prays that believers will work for the honour and glory of Christ in their everyday lives – this is their role which should give purpose and direction to their lives.

From text to message

Getting the message clear: the theme

- Christians should have assurance of seeing the glory of Christ and should aim now to glorify Him in how they live.

Getting the message clear: the aim

- The aim of these passages is to get Christians to focus on the glory of Christ both now and in the future. Preaching or teaching on these passages should help in answering the following questions:
  - What were the problems that the Thessalonian church was facing?
  - How does Paul resolve these problems?
  - What were Paul's aims for these Christians as revealed in his prayer at 2:16, 17?

A way in

Due to the rapid technological advances of our society there are many items which now appear to be completely redundant. Why would you want to use a hand-pushed lawnmower when, for a relatively low cost, you could purchase an electric version which would involve far less energy and effort? Many old things can seem completely irrelevant to modern life. So it may be with the Bible but particularly with a book such as 2 Thessalonians. It seems to come from another age with its references to a message about the return of Christ having already come and with people giving up work rather than being keen to find it. It all seems as remote and as useless as a decrepit old lawnmower.

Yet though it may seem that there is no point of contact at all, as we look more carefully we find that any book which focuses on the glory of Christ must have a message that is relevant for today. So perhaps rather than an old-fashioned lawnmower, we should picture an old ornament which is about to be thrown out until it is discovered that it is full of high-quality, precious jewels. So it is with 2 Thessalonians – it may not appear valuable at first sight but there are great treasures to be found.

In 1488, Bartolomeu Dias rounded southern Africa and came across what he described as the Cape of Storms. However, Portugal's King John II renamed the piece of land as he could see that, despite its reputation for bad weather, it was the gateway to India and to great riches. It therefore became the Cape of Good Hope. So it is that though the Thessalonian believers were experiencing great storms from outside (ch. 1) and from inside (ch. 2), nonetheless they were to understand that they had a good hope (2:16) as they put their confidence in the fact that the Lord Jesus Christ would indeed return, both to judge their persecutors and to bring full salvation to those waiting for Him.

Pointers to application

- As believers we constantly need reminding of our location. Though we may face many difficult days and enormous pressures in our current situation, we are to remember that God's church is kept secure in God our Father and the Lord Jesus Christ. Through God's grace we are eternally secure. It is similar to the situation of Elisha and his servant at Dothan in 2 Kings 6:15-17. Though we may be completely surrounded we are

- One of the great dangers is being deceived into letting go of God's Words. In this instance it came through what purported to be a message from the apostle himself. We need to be alert to the dangers that Satan brings across our paths and especially in this area. Right from the beginning in Genesis 3, Satan has aimed to separate God's people from God's Word. It is vitally important, therefore, that even if the messenger has a tremendous spiritual pedigree we should carefully test what we hear. Indeed this is what Paul himself had encouraged in 1 Thessalonians 5:21. 'Test everything (including messages which are supposed to have originated from him!). Hold on to the good.' We need to be aware that Satan may often masquerade as an angel of light (see 2 Cor. 11:14).

- It is interesting to note that Paul prays that the Lord would 'be with all of you' (2 Thess. 3:16). He is clearly concerned with the deliberate disobedience of an element within the church, and we could imagine that after such a fierce passage (3:6-15) he would be particularly concerned to pray only for those seeking to please God through their behaviour. Yet Paul longs for unity and for all of them to know the Lord's presence and blessings. He is concerned for all the church family – even for those brothers and sisters who needed a word of exhortation. How important it is that we show a similar breadth of concern and a love for all of God's family.

- We need to remind ourselves that we do indeed have a good hope and that whatever we are facing we can look with confidence into the future with Christ. So often our heads are down and our eyes are focused only on our immediate circumstances. As a result our perspective can become dominated by the enormity of the difficulties we are up against and the storms of life. Within both 1 and 2 Thessalonians, Paul constantly directs the believers' attention forwards, to the sure expectation of being with the Lord Jesus Christ and beholding His glory. It is vitally important therefore that we teach regularly about our hope as believers as an integral part of the glorious gospel of Christ.

- Paul doesn't want the Thessalonians to be coasting or drifting in their Christian experience, perhaps working hard for the Lord within the setting of the gathered church but failing to serve Christ within the workplace. Paul's vision is the holistic, all-encompassing vision of praying that the believers would be strengthened in every good work and word. His longing is for there to be a fully fledged devotion to the Lord Jesus Christ (see a similar thought in his prayer in 1 Thessalonians 5:23) which seeks to please Him in all aspects of life. Our consumer culture with its penchant for laid-back 'coolness' stands a long way from Paul's vision of Christians passionately seeking to invest their lives in service to Christ.

Suggestions for preaching

Sermon 1: Bringing hope and purpose to God's people: an overview of 2 Thessalonians (1:1, 2; 2:16, 17 and 3:16-18)

- Three presenting problems and their solutions (1:1, 2 and 3:16-18)

- Fierce opposition....and God's grace which brings security and hope (1:1, 2; 2:16; 3:18).

- Unsettling deception...and God's Word which bring clarity and confidence (3:17).

- Deliberate disobedience...and God's peace which sustains unity (3:16)

- Paul's prayer and the glory of Christ (2:16, 17)

- The confident hope of seeing the glory of Christ (2:16).

- The clear purpose of working for Christ to be glorified (2:17).

Other preaching possibilities:
Naturally it would be possible to dispense with an overview altogether and to deal with these three short passages within the expository series as they occur within the text. Another possibility would be simply to use the overview to focus on one or other of the two parts of this suggested sermon. So one could deal either with 1:1, 2 and 3:16-18 or, alternatively 2:16, 17 by itself. Pursuing either passage would be a helpful way to provide a good introduction to the book.

Part Four: Teaching 2 Thessalonians 1:1,2; 2:16,17 & 3:16-18   255

Suggestions for teaching

Introducing the passage

- In what sort of situations would you need to repeat what you had said earlier, or explain in greater depth what you had already spoken about before? In what ways does this help us to understand why Paul penned this letter of 2 Thessalonians?

Understanding the passage

- What is the distinctive point about the location of the Thessalonian church in 1:1?
- Why do you think it may be important for Paul to include 3:17 within the letter?
- Given the divisions within the church (e.g. 3:6), what is surprising about 3:16?
- In 2:16 what are we told believers have received from the Lord and what do these things mean?
- What does Paul pray for at 2:17 and what might an answer to such a prayer look like in the life of a Christian?

Applying the passage

- Why does Paul speak about the church being 'in God' rather than 'in Thessalonica'? (1:1)
- Could there ever be a danger that our fellowship might drift away from God's Word and how might we prevent this? (2:2; 3:17)
- Why do we lay such little stress on Christian hope in our presentation of the gospel and in our teaching in church? (2:16)

- What are the signs that we are coasting or drifting within the Christian life and what should we do? (see 2:17)
- How could we regain clearer convictions about our hope as believers?
- In what ways could we use 2 Thessalonians 2:16, 17 as a focus for our own prayers?

2.

THE GLORY OF CHRIST
(1:3-12)

Introduction

How do you cope when persecution rages and there seems to be no end in sight? How can you keep going as a believer when those who persecute are perpetrating grave injustices which are not dealt with by the state or which may even be sanctioned by the authorities? How do you pray when the Lord does not seem to answer and no relief appears to be forthcoming? It may well be that all these sorts of questions were in the minds and perhaps on the lips of the Thessalonian Christians. The church had been birthed amidst suffering (see Acts 17:1-10) and had continued to experience opposition (see 1 Thess. 2:14; 3:3). Such persecution had not abated in the intervening period between the writing of 1 Thessalonians and this subsequent letter. Indeed things may have been getting even worse. If that was the case, we can well understand why there were concerns about injustice and God's lack of intervention. Similarly we can also understand why Paul tackles this issue first within 2 Thessalonians. Though there is a particularly perplexing difficulty which needs to be resolved concerning a false message that purported to come from the apostle (see 2:2), Paul's first thought in this epistle is pastoral. Some were perplexed and struggling amidst the troubles they faced and so, right at the start, Paul addresses these concerns.

Listening to the text

Context and structure

This is the first of the three presenting issues which have been identified within 2 Thessalonians. It comes first because it may well be the most pressing and urgent concern for the church. It focuses particularly on the hope that is linked with the return of the Lord Jesus Christ and therefore has strong links with the way this theme is developed within 1 Thessalonians. Apart from the substantial section which specifically referred to hope and the return of Christ (see 1 Thess. 4:13–5:11), each section in the first half of 1 Thessalonians ended with some sort of reference to what would happen when Christ returned (see 1 Thess. 1:10; 2:12; 2:16; 3:13). For Paul the theme of Christian hope and the return of Christ was absolutely central and this sets the scene for the focus here in 2 Thessalonians 1.

After the brief introduction (1:1, 2), Paul starts as usual with thanksgiving (1:3, 4) before moving to prayer for the Thessalonians (1:11, 12). In the middle there is a section which explains that God is just and highlights what will happen when the Lord Jesus Christ appears in order to provide them with assurance and encouragement (1:5-10). The structure is therefore relatively straightforward:

1. The past – giving thanks for signs of spiritual vitality (vv. 3-4).

2. The future – looking forwards to the sight of Christ's glory (vv. 5-10).

3. The present – working today for Christ to be glorified (vv. 11, 12).

Working through the text

There are important connections with 1 Thessalonians which should be recognised. The 'more and more' aspect of spiritual growth at 1:3 has already been touched on at 1 Thessalonians 3:12; 4:1 and 4:10. As has been mentioned above, the theme of Christian hope linked to the return of Christ is also particularly strong in 1 Thessalonians. Similarly, there are important links within 2 Thessalonians. The theme of sharing in Christ's glory is at 1:10 and 2:14. Also the focus on 'work' which pleases God occurs at 1:11 and 2:17. In addition the theme of work occurs at 3:6-15, where the same word is used on numerous occasions.

Another link to consider is the Old Testament background, especially in relation to the return of the Lord Jesus Christ and the judgment that results on those who do not obey the gospel (1:7-9). Isaiah 2:10 speaks of the splendour of the majesty of the LORD and Isaiah 66:15 refers to the LORD coming with fire as He exercises judgment. Both cross-references shed light on Paul's teaching and also helpfully reveal the Lord Jesus Christ as a fully divine figure.

1. The past – giving thanks for signs of spiritual vitality (vv. 3-4)

Such are the signs of life in this relatively newly planted church that Paul feels under obligation ('ought') to start with thanksgiving. He could have started by sorting things out with regard to the false prophecy mentioned at 2:2 which would have had the effect of restoring his reputation ('you see – I didn't say all that stuff about the return of Christ having happened already. It wasn't me who got it wrong!'). Equally he could have begun by rebuking the recalcitrant minority, which he will eventually do at the end at 3:6ff. Instead, Paul focuses on the good things which he can see and rejoices in them, giving thanks to God. So, what is it that excites him about the Thessalonians?

Their faith is growing

Their faith has been evident from the beginning (1 Thess. 1:3) and yet there were things lacking (1 Thess. 3:10) which had caused Paul to write before and pray for them. He rejoices in the fact that these prayers were being answered because he now has evidence that their faith is growing more and more (1:3). Their faith is evident in the way that they were holding on amidst persecution (see 1:4) and Paul is also aware of their faith leading to action in various ways (see 1:11). Despite the persecution there was evidence of spiritual life. Like snowdrops poking through a blanket of snow, so Paul can see that their faith has not disappeared but is growing more and more.

Their love is increasing

Their love for others had also been evident early on (1 Thess. 1:3) though once again Paul was aware of some

Part Four: Teaching 2 Thessalonians 1:3-12

deficiencies which led him to pray for it to increase and overflow (1 Thess. 3:12). Again he is able to rejoice that God has answered prayer as he sees evidence of their love increasing (1:3).

Their hope is enduring
Paul doesn't use the word 'hope' and nor did he at 1 Thessalonians 3:13, though in both cases this is clearly the dominant motif. At the beginning he had noted their endurance was inspired by hope in our Lord Jesus Christ (1 Thess. 1:3). So when he now speaks of their perseverance and their endurance under severe afflictions it is reasonable to conclude that 'hope', though not mentioned, is located somewhere in the forefront of the picture. Having prayed that their hearts would be strengthened in the light of the return of Christ (1 Thess. 3:13), Paul rejoices yet again in the evidence of answered prayer. They have been enabled to keep on going amidst their afflictions, such that Paul is able to boast to the other churches about their resilience. Earlier their faith in Jesus had rung out across the region (see 1 Thess. 1:7, 8,) and now news of their faithfulness under pressure is similarly spreading – which must have been a great encouragement to other believers. The fact that the apostle boasts about this enduring faith that he had seen in the Thessalonians must also have been an encouragement to the Thessalonians themselves.

2. The future – looking forwards to the sight of Christ's glory (vv. 5-10)
Yet, though they were persevering under pressure, this didn't mean that it was necessarily easy. Paul heaps up the references to the opposition that they were facing –

persecutions (v. 4), trials or afflictions (v. 4), suffering (v. 5) and trouble [or afflictions ESV] (v. 6). In such circumstances we can easily imagine some of the implications. Perhaps some of the believers were losing their jobs and livelihoods or were being 'shut out' from particular organisations or opportunities due to their faith in Christ. Ostracised and excluded, they must have found it a difficult experience with the inevitable yearning for justice and perhaps the nagging voice within seeking to persuade them that God won't do anything about it. If that is a likely reconstruction, then we can see why Paul seeks to remind them that God is just and that one day His justice will be vindicated and that those who are currently shutting out Christians will find themselves shut out from the presence of Christ. He sets things out in four steps:

God's judgment is just (vv. 5-7a)
Paul wants to lay down a marker at the start of this section by repeating twice, in slightly different ways, that God is just and that His judgment is righteous. Currently He is exercising His wise judgment so that one day when Christ returns it will be obvious to all that God has been absolutely just.

- Judgment in the present (v. 5). Paul wants to persuade the suffering Thessalonians that the very fact that they are persevering when they are under so much pressure is evidence that God is judging or assessing them in order to ensure that they are counted worthy of the Kingdom of God. It is similar to passages such as 1 Peter 1:6, 7 which also speak of a context of suffering and trials where their purpose is to strengthen faith and prepare the believer for future glory. We can picture a workman working with a precious material. It is heated and brought to the right temperature as part of the necessary process required in enabling the metal to be refined and fit for future use. Throughout the process he is assessing the appropriate temperature to enable the refining work to be thorough. His judgment, involving heat, needs to be correct. So it is, maintains Paul, with regard to God. His judgment is right. The process to enable these believers to be prepared for His kingdom, therefore, will involve a degree of suffering. The trials do not mean that the process is out of control. Instead they provide evidence that God is at work doing all that is necessary to bring all His people into glory.

- Judgment in the future (vv. 6, 7a). However God's judgment will only be completed in the future when everyone will be able to see His justice worked out. According to Paul this will be payback time. Those who have been doing the afflicting or troubling will themselves be afflicted or troubled (v. 6). Those who have been crying out for relief will experience relief (v. 7a). When those things happen, then everyone will be able to see that without any shadow of doubt God has been and is just, and no one will be able to speak to the contrary. Just as we long for justice when someone has perpetrated a crime, so we rejoice when they are eventually apprehended and receive an appropriate sentence. At that point justice will be seen to have been done. So it will be with God as everyone recognises that He has always acted justly.

This is the platform for Paul's exposition of what will happen in the future in order to give the believers confidence and assurance, even when they are under pressure – God will be seen to be just. But when will such justice arrive?

The Lord Jesus will return (v. 7b)
Justice will be exercised through the revealing of the Lord Jesus. When His presence is unveiled then we can look forward to everything being resolved. His appearing is described in three ways. It will be from heaven, which could simply be a reference to the location where He comes from but could also be a reference to the authority which He wields. In the same way as someone coming out of No. 10 Downing Street to meet the press speaks with authority in a British context, so someone coming out of heaven has God's full authority. Second, He will be revealed in blazing fire (see Isa. 66:15) signifying, that He has come to purge sin and destroy everything that has opposed God's rule. Finally, He will come with His powerful angels alongside, which links to the vision of 1 Thessalonians 3:13. Again it is a sign of strength to accomplish the overthrow of a power that has sought to usurp God's rightful position as the Lord over all. Imagine a situation where a bank has been robbed by a criminal gang. As soon as they are alerted to what has happened, the police respond with sirens sounding and lights flashing. Their aim is to restore order and bring about justice through the use of greater force to overpower the criminals. In 1982, Argentinian forces invaded and captured the Falkland Islands. A few weeks later, once preparations had been made, the British Prime Minister organised a task force – a huge convoy of ships and soldiers – to recapture the islands. This show of strength indicated the resolve to

restore British rule. Of course, often we see the forces of good impotent in the face of evil but we can have complete assurance that justice will come when the Lord Jesus is revealed in all His full power and authority.

The door will be shut (vv. 8, 9)
But what exactly will happen on the day when the Lord Jesus is revealed? Twice Paul says that He will 'punish' (vv. 8, 9 NIV). It could be translated 'they will pay the penalty' which indicates once again the justice of the punishment and also God's activity in doing it. In verse 8 he explains who will be punished and in verse 9 how they will be punished. The people referred to in 1:8 are those who do not know God and do not obey the gospel of our Lord Jesus. This could refer to two different groups, perhaps Gentiles and Jews, but it seems more likely that this is one group referred to in two different ways. So those who will face final judgment are those who don't know God because they have not obeyed the gospel. Interestingly, Paul refers to 'not obeying the gospel' rather than not believing it. Trusting the gospel message will be revealed in obedience to the gospel and submission to the Lord Jesus Christ. It is also noteworthy that in Isaiah 66, the One who comes in glory and who is looking for obedience is the LORD God. In 2 Thessalonians it is the Lord Jesus, demonstrating Paul's high view of Jesus within the Godhead.

Having identified who is to receive punishment, Paul turns to explain what it involves (v. 9). Again Paul mentions two things which may or may not be identical. First, they are to be punished with everlasting destruction and second, they will be shut out from the presence of the Lord. Though it is possible that these two descriptions refer to different things, it is more likely that one helps to explain the other. Eternal judgment is all about being shut out from the glorious presence of the Lord. The essence of the doctrine of judgment and hell is that it is exclusion from the presence of God and His goodness forever. In 1 Thessalonians 4:17, we noticed that the Christian hope of heaven is focused on communion with the Lord Jesus Christ forever rather than a particular place. Here we see the reverse, that the focus of the doctrine of hell is the absence of being with Christ. To be shut out and excluded is once again a just penalty for those who had shut out and excluded believers. Yet it is an act of the Lord Jesus with such awesome eternal consequences that, in teaching on this subject, we should be fully aware of the terrible nature of what it means, so that we avoid speaking with any glibness or superficiality. The finality of the door being shut links to some of Jesus' parables (e.g. Luke 13:22-30; Matt. 25:1-13).

We will see Christ (v. 10)
The climax of the return of the Lord Jesus Christ, however, is not in His work as Judge, important though it is. For those who have been welcomed into His kingdom (partly through their perseverance as believers amidst suffering – see 1:5), the focus will be on beholding His glory. Yet again Paul gives two descriptions of the same experience in order to explain one by the other and in this way intensify the message. Though others will be shut out from the Lord's presence and the majesty of His power, believers will be 'shut in' so that they can experience the full glory of the Lord Jesus Christ on display. The experience of Christ being glorified amongst or in His holy people is from our standpoint that of marvelling at the person of Christ. Those who are present

are described both as His holy people and those who have believed, again describing the same people from different angles – from God's angle, we are those who have been set apart to belong to Him, whilst from our perspective we are those who have put our trust in Christ. So the great climax of this section is to point to the Christian's future hope, which is focused on seeing the Lord Jesus Christ in all His power and glory. The Christian's hope is not on a place but on a Person and being in His presence forever.

And the amazing thing, says Paul as he rounds off this paragraph, is that this vision of people marvelling at the glory of the Lord Jesus includes the Thessalonians. Though they were afflicted, persecuted and suffering great injustices, because they had believed Paul's testimony they were therefore included. This pastoral application would surely have been an enormous encouragement and word of assurance to them to help them to continue to persevere with even greater confidence, knowing that their future would ultimately be determined by Christ, not their persecutors.

3. *The present – working today for Christ to be glorified (vv. 11, 12)*

Having turned to an explanation of what would happen in the future, Paul returns to prayer. It is all very well to know that the future will work out but Paul is also concerned that the Thessalonian believers are active in serving Christ in the present. So having provided assurance to encourage them in 1:5-10, he now wants this to be a launch pad to help them live for Christ now in Thessalonica. So 'with this in mind', referring back to 1:5-10, he now prays for them. In what way does he pray? We can divide the material into what?, how? and why? We will see that the answer to each question connects with his previous teaching.

What does Paul pray for? (v. 11a)
The apostle prays that God may count them worthy of His calling. His calling relates to His personal call and invitation to be with Him in glory (see 1 Thess. 2:12). He has already explained that God is using their experiences of suffering to prepare them for entrance into His kingdom (1:5). Now he prays more generally that God would be so at work within them that even now they may be living lives which are fitting and appropriate for those who claim to follow Christ, bearing in mind their glorious destination.

How does Paul pray for them? (v. 11b)
What does a life worthy of God's calling look like? It will be a life filled with good purposes as believers, knowing God's purposes, seek to implement them in their lives. It will be a life filled with work prompted by faith in Christ. At 1 Thessalonians 1:3, Paul had given thanks for their work prompted by faith and now he prays that such faith – which has been growing more and more (see 1:3) – would bear fruit in even more work which is pleasing to the Lord. Once again it may well be that the two phrases in the verse should be used to explain each other or intensify the meaning of what Paul longs for. Running them together, we see that Paul is praying for an active faith which leads to clear thinking, purposeful resolutions and good works. As is clear from Ephesians 2:8-10, the believer can never be saved by good works, but we are certainly saved for good works. Of course, as believers we are desperately weak and our good resolutions often falter, and so Paul prays that

Part Four: Teaching 2 Thessalonians 1:3-12

through the power of God (the same power which will one day be displayed for all to see and experience – see 1:9), Christians may be enabled to see their faith in Christ lead to good works pleasing to Him.

Why does Paul pray like this? (v. 12)
Though his prayer could have ended at verse 11, Paul continues. He longs that they would live in the way described in 1:11 so that a particular result can be achieved. He prays like this so that the name of our Lord Jesus may be glorified in them. Earlier Paul had explained that the great climax of history would be to see the glory of Christ unveiled (1:10). Yet even now the great purpose of the Christian life is to bring glory to Christ through good works prompted by faith in Him. Again this cannot be accomplished through our own doing but only through the grace of God and the Lord Jesus Christ, but this is the goal for each day of our Christian lives – to bring glory to Christ. This is no small ambition or one that can be hindered by adversity or opposition. This is the true purpose which is to give shape and meaning to our lives as believers and should cause us to lift up our eyes and hearts each day. Though others may have important jobs and roles to perform, none can compare to the great purpose of the believer to bring glory to the Lord Jesus Christ. Yet Paul is not quite finished. He longs not just that Christ would be glorified in us but also that we would be glorified in Him. The thought is similar to 2 Corinthians 3:18. As believers reflect the Lord's glory, so they are also transformed into His likeness. This theme of glory both present and future connects the whole chapter together and lifts our view from current persecution and suffering to the great purposes of God to glorify His Son.

So, having given thanks for the Thessalonians (vv. 3, 4), Paul's teaching has ended up focusing on the glory of our Lord Jesus Christ. Our future life is to be focused on seeing His glory (vv. 5, 10) and our present life is to be focused on bringing glory to His name (vv. 11, 12). Such teaching should inspire and encourage every believer even if, like the Thessalonians, we might be facing suffering and trouble.

From text to message

Getting the message clear: the theme

- Even when believers face persecution and suffering they can have assurance that Christ will be glorified both now and in the future.

Getting the message clear: the aim

- The aim of this passage is to assure suffering believers that God will bring about justice and He will also usher every Christian into the glorious presence of the Lord Jesus Christ. Preaching or teaching on this passage should help in answering the following questions:
    - What are the main signs of spiritual vitality?
    - In what way will evil be overcome and what role will Jesus Christ play in this process?
    - What factors should govern how Christians are to live each day?

A way in

The weather in the U.K. is always a fascinating topic of conversation because it is so uncertain. We may be able to put some confidence in the forecast for the following day but we are far less certain about relying on long-range forecasts

Part Four: Teaching 2 Thessalonians 1:3-12

as they often bear little relation to reality as time unfolds. In this passage, the Thessalonians are enduring a heavy storm and they would love to know the long-range forecast, which is exactly what Paul provides. He wants to assure them that one day the weather will be significantly better. The storms will be dispersed and give way to the unbroken sunlight of the radiance of the glory of Christ. Just as a really accurate weather forecast can provide hope for the future, so Paul provides a reliable guide to what will happen in order to give confidence to suffering believers.

One of the most powerful images within this passage concerns the idea of being 'shut out' (see 1:9). All of us have probably experienced situations where we have been locked out or where we have not been permitted to enter a building or a particular part of it. Especially if we are really longing for admission, the experience of being excluded can be painful and isolating. We long to be included and welcomed, rather than being left outside. Some of the Thessalonian believers were currently enduring suffering and persecution which may well have involved them being 'shut out' from certain jobs, opportunities or public buildings. Nevertheless, Paul looks forward to a day when all of that will be reversed and when it will be those persecuting who will be shut out from the glory of Christ. This is an image that is also used by the Lord Jesus (see Luke 13:22-30). It provides a helpful means of painting a picture of the reality and consequences of hell. Using this picture helps us to see that hell is not about 'enjoying a good time with my mates'. Instead it is about being excluded from a place where you realise you should be, as a result of decisions you have taken during your lifetime.

Pointers to application

- Paul's first instinct in any situation would appear to be to express thanksgiving to God for the good things that he has observed within that particular church. Though he could very easily have started by expressing frustration that they had not followed his previous instructions (see 3:6ff) or by defending his own reputation (see 2:2), he starts with thanksgiving. It is perhaps a lesson to us, especially if we are fairly critical by nature. It is also of importance to remember this when a degree of correction is required. Though it may be easy to fasten on to the problems, Paul's example helps us to see the need to take a broader look at God's work in our lives and begin with thanksgiving.

- Paul is delighted to pick up on answers to prayer. In his previous letter he had pointed out deficiencies (see especially 1 Thessalonians 3:10-13). Now that he is writing again, he is able to see how some of his earlier prayer requests had now been answered as he looks at their faith, love and perseverance amidst trials. Specifically recalling answers to prayer is a powerful reminder of the reality of God and of His good purposes towards us.

- As believers we always need to take the long view and see everything in the light of eternity and the return of the Lord Jesus Christ. Focusing merely on our current and recent experiences may lead us to despair, whereas lifting our eyes to the horizon enables us to get an entirely different perspective on what is happening to us. If we focus on the present we will often see injustice, unfairness and pain. However, if we take into account what will happen at the end, we will be able to see God's justice as well as His goodness to all His children.

+ God's judgment is a good thing! So often judgment is portrayed negatively. However, every time we see a miscarriage of justice we instinctively grumble and complain. In contrast, we breathe a sigh of relief when a vicious criminal is eventually caught, convicted, sentenced appropriately and put behind bars. We yearn for justice, especially if we have been on the receiving end of an abuse of power. Similarly, we will be able to breathe a sigh of relief when we see God's justice being finally worked out.

+ Our confidence concerning the future rests upon the personal return of the Lord Jesus Christ as described in these verses. If we only have the 'gentle Jesus meek and mild' view, we will have little confidence that great injustices will be righted. However the way that Paul links Jesus to Old Testament texts about the LORD helps us to gain a far bigger view of His majesty, splendour and power. Our confidence in the future will be proportionate to our understanding of the true majesty of Christ. A full-orbed biblical view of Christ is the only thing that will ultimately provide us with hope during dark days.

+ Hell is described as the experience of being punished with everlasting destruction which involves being shut out from the presence of the Lord. It is not easy to teach carefully and lovingly about the reality of hell. We will want to avoid caricatures, and we will certainly only be faithful to biblical teaching if we can teach about it with tears in our own eyes as we recognise the enormous consequences of what it means for people we know to be actually shut out from God's presence. Nevertheless, this image of being 'shut out' is enormously helpful in painting a clear picture of what hell will involve for those who do not obey the gospel of our Lord Jesus. Though our culture dismisses hell with contemptuous derision, we need to be faithful in warning people and eager to invite them now to obey the gospel so that they might experience the presence of Christ both now and in eternity.

- Heaven is all about Christ. Again, our culture has various caricatures concerning heaven which emphasise how boring it will be. Yet in the gospels there was never the slightest chance of boredom when Jesus was around! Similarly we need to be reminded that the heart of the Christian faith is the person of the Lord Jesus Christ and our relationship with Him. Our destination is to be with Christ and to see Christ, and our view of heaven needs to be defined by that rather than anything else.

- Paul longs for believers to be active in serving Christ in the present. There is no hint of it being acceptable to drift along towards heaven on the basis of Christ's finished work. Instead the prospect of meeting Christ in the future should give us extra impetus to please

Him now through actively working out our faith in every situation. So for Paul there is no sacred/secular divide. Our faith in Christ is to prompt good purposes and deeds which are in line with our calling in every part of our lives. Paul wants the whole of our lives to be shaped and affected by our calling as believers.

- Knowing that Christ will be glorified in the future, Paul's aim is that Christ should be glorified also in the present. Our aims can often be very small and self-centred but Paul wants us to have a much bigger vision. He wants to see Christians devoted to seeing the name of Christ glorified now through their lives. How might our lives as Christians and the reputation of the church be transformed if individually and collectively our great aim was in every aspect of life to see Christ's name glorified?

Suggestions for preaching

Sermon 1: The glory of Christ (1:3-12)

- The past – giving thanks for signs of spiritual vitality (1:3, 4).

- The future – looking forwards to the sight of Christ's glory (1:5-10).

- The present – working today for Christ to be glorified (1:11, 12).

Other preaching possibilities

The main challenge with looking at the chapter as a whole is that there is so much material in it that some preachers will want to divide the three paragraphs into three separate sermons. In going down this route, it would be important to remember that at the start of both verse 5 and verse 11 Paul carefully connects the paragraph to the preceding one. In this way the flow of the whole chapter can be maintained whilst enabling the preacher to spend more time on unpacking the riches contained in these verses.

Suggestions for teaching

Introducing the passage

- Can you think of any situations where what will happen in the future shapes your ability to keep going in the present? In what ways is this a helpful insight into the way Paul encourages the Thessalonian Christians who were facing persecution?

Understanding the passage

- In what ways can you see links between Paul's prayer at 1 Thessalonians 3:10-13 and his thanksgiving at 2 Thessalonians 1:3, 4?
- How is God's justice revealed in this passage? (see 1:5-7)
- In what way is hell described? (see 1:8, 9)
- What do we learn about Jesus in these verses? (see 1:7-10)
- How is heaven described? (see 1:9, 10)
- According to Paul what is the purpose of living a Christian life? (see 1:11, 12)

Part Four: Teaching 2 Thessalonians 1:3-12

Applying the passage
- Why does Paul start with thanksgiving (1:3, 4), rather than the other topics he wishes to raise?
- Why is God's judgment a good thing?
- What are the main features of heaven and hell according to this passage?
- How do verses 11 and 12 counteract any tendency to have a sacred/secular divide?
- In what ways could you pray for the suffering church as a result of studying this passage?
- How could you refocus your life on the Lord Jesus Christ?

3.

Hold on to the truth!
(2:1-15)

Introduction

Recent years have seen a rise in cases of 'phishing'. It is defined as the attempt to get information (passwords, usernames, credit card details, etc.) by masquerading as a trustworthy entity in an electronic communication. Many of us will have come across it. By and large we will be able to spot such attempts but occasionally we can be deceived. Afterwards we feel so stupid but sometimes it all seems so plausible that we fall for it. Of course, it can be a deeply unsettling experience because, having been deceived once, we are less sure of ourselves concerning what is genuine. In such situations, it can be helpful to gain a bit of understanding about how such deceitful schemes work, so that we can be forewarned for the next time.

All this might seem very remote from first-century Thessalonica but there are clear parallels. The church has been 'fed' what appeared to be a genuine word from the Apostle Paul which they had swallowed (2:2). Unfortunately, the message had not come from Paul and as a result they were unsettled, perhaps wondering how they could avoid further deception in the future. This chapter is designed to put them straight and forewarn them about possible future deception in order that they could be helped to stand in their faith (2:15) and remain clear about their future hope in Christ.

Listening to the text

Context and structure

This is another presenting issue which has caused Paul to write to them again. It may well be the most urgent as in this chapter he needs to mend some reputational damage and help them not to be deceived again. However, it is subordinated to the teaching in chapter 1 with which it is clearly linked. The most important issue in Paul's thinking is that the Thessalonian believers be encouraged to cope with their suffering and persecution. This can only be done by reminding them of the return of the Lord Jesus Christ which will bring justice and a glorious future. So that is how Paul opens his letter. However, there is a problem which is that a report supposedly from Paul had indicated that the Day of the Lord had already come (see 2:2). If such was the case, and if they were still suffering persecution (which they were), then that would mean that the Lord Jesus on returning had failed to bring about justice, which would presumably cast doubt on their faith in Him. So in order to affirm the teaching about the return of Christ in 2 Thessalonians 1, Paul needs to explain that they have been

Part Four: Teaching 2 Thessalonians 2:1-15

deceived and help them to see what would happen before the return of Christ in order not to be deceived again.

This chapter may appear to be very complicated but in fact, as we shall see, it is relatively straightforward. The issue of being unsettled by the false teaching – which may have come by prophecy, report or letter (2:2) – is definitively answered by the call at the end of the chapter to stand firm and hold on to the teachings that have been handed down by Paul through word, mouth or letter (2:15). There is also a contrast between those who refuse to love the truth and do not believe the truth (2:10-12) and the Thessalonians who have believed the truth (2:13). We can also observe that Paul is keen to explain the sequence of history which involves the 'man of lawlessness' being 'held back' (twice in verses 6, 7) before finally being 'revealed' (twice in verses 3, 8). So the following structure seems to make sense of these features:

- The problem: unsettled believers who have been deceived (1-3a)

- The overview of history: though currently held back, the man of lawlessness will be revealed and will then be defeated by Christ (3b-8)

- Some will perish through being deceived (9-12)

- ...but you will be saved through holding firmly to God's Word (13-15)

Working through the text

We have already noted the connection between the coming of Christ at 1:7 and 2:1 which links the chapters together. We have also noted that the deception that came through some report or word supposedly from Paul (2:2) is definitively answered by the genuine word which comes from Paul (2:15 and see 3:17, to underline the point in Paul's farewell). Within the passage we can also see the significance of attitudes to 'the truth' (see 2:10-12; 2:13) which will, from a human angle, determine salvation.

As will be made clear in the following exposition, a key issue in handling this passage is recognising that it is shaped by the teaching of the Lord Jesus in Matthew 24 and Mark 13. For us it seems strange to think that Paul had already taught the Thessalonians all about the man of lawlessness in his first visit (see 2:5) because we would find it difficult to conceive expounding such teaching to new believers. However, the key is that if Paul was simply passing on the 'traditions' (see 2:15), which means the teaching that had been handed down to him in the gospels, then it would have been natural for him to have spent time unpacking material such as Matthew 24, and therefore it would indeed have been part of his initial teaching on their conversion.

1. *The issue: don't be deceived (2:1-3a)*

In Paul's teaching in 2 Thessalonians 1, the coming of the Lord Jesus was absolutely pivotal. His return and intervention would be the means of establishing justice and ending the suffering and persecution currently experienced by the Thessalonian believers. Clearly if it was discovered that Jesus had already returned and the persecution was still continuing, that would have an enormous impact on their faith. It would mean that their faith in Jesus was an irrelevance since Christ was unable to overcome the evil they were experiencing. So we can easily imagine that when

Part Four: Teaching 2 Thessalonians 2:1-15

a report came – apparently from the Apostle Paul himself – to the effect that the Day of the Lord had already come, it threw the persecuted church into confusion. No wonder they were alarmed and unsettled because, if the message was true, it had major consequences for their faith. Ultimately it might mean that their faith in Christ was of no value and their hope was meaningless.

Paul's response is to call for them not to be deceived (see 2:3a). As he will later point out, Satan's strategy is to deceive (2:10) so that people reject the truth. It is vital therefore that Paul highlights that a deception has taken place in order to warn the believers and help them hold firmly to the truth (2:15). Paul is always well aware of the activity of Satan in seeking to disrupt the work of the gospel (see 1 Thess. 2:18 and 3:5) and here he must counter another initiative designed to thwart God's purposes.

2. *The explanation: evil will come, but the Lord is in control* (2:3b-8)

Having informed the Thessalonians that this particular word about the return of Christ had not come from him, what does Paul need to do? Of course, having given a quick denial, Paul could simply have jumped to a call to hold on to the teachings that he had passed on to them, which is where he concludes at 2:15. However, before getting to that point, Paul uses what has happened in order to provide a framework to enable them to understand the overall shape of history leading to the return of Christ, in order that they might be better placed to stand firm against the assaults of the evil one. First, he needs to give some sort of explanation of why such deception might have occurred, which is why he makes reference to the man of lawlessness.

Second, he needs to provide a framework which helps the Thessalonians to see how the coming of the Lord Jesus Christ relates to the rise of evil. Third, he needs to provide some sort of assurance that the Lord is in sovereign control over all history and all evil. All these tasks are accomplished within these verses.

It is helpful to consider the structure of these verses:

- Man of lawlessness revealed…..to oppose God (3, 4)
- Man of lawlessness currently held back (x2) (5-7)
- Man of lawlessness revealed…to be defeated by Christ (8)

It is also helpful to notice the very important parallels with Matthew 24 and Mark 13 which probably lie behind the reference in 2:5 to Paul's previous teaching:

Matthew 24	2 Thessalonians 2
24:9-14 – Time of Persecution, deception and false prophecies… and the call to stand firm.	1:4 – Time of Persecution ….deception and false prophecy (2:1-2)…..and the call to stand firm.
24:15-22 – Time of Rebellion – the abomination in the temple.	2:3-4 – Time of Rebellion by man of lawlessness in the temple
24:23-26 – Time of satanic deception – don't believe it.	2:9-14 – Time of satanic deception – don't believe it
24:27-31 – Time of judgment at the return of the Lord Jesus Christ	2:8 – Time of judgment at the return of the Lord Jesus Christ

Part Four: Teaching 2 Thessalonians 2:1-15

When we put these passages side by side, it highlights the fact that the same events are being described. This in turn throws light on the identity of the 'man of lawlessness' in the sense that the apostle is not talking about an entity who is not referred to anywhere else within the New Testament. Instead, the close parallel with the character behind the 'abomination that causes desolation' of Matthew 24:15 shows that they are one and the same. At this point Matthew is quoting from Daniel 9:27, and Daniel's prophecy may have been partially fulfilled in the events linked with may have been referring to Antiochus Epiphanes in 167 B.C. and in the gospels there may be a pointer to another partial fulfilment with the arrival of the Roman general Titus at the Temple in A.D. 70. Either way, Paul is well aware that there are aspects of lawlessness and rebellion already at work (see 2:7). One day this will culminate in an ultimate rebellion against God.

We could also glance at Revelation 13 for another parallel, although again different language is used. It depicts the work of the unholy trinity of the dragon, the beast from the sea and the beast from the earth. Together they oppose God and His people (Rev. 13:6) and deceive the inhabitants of the earth (Rev. 13:14). Ultimately all these forces of evil are to be defeated at the return of Christ (see Rev. 19:11– 20:10). Although the preacher of 2 Thessalonians will not want to be diverted from the passage in front of him, nevertheless the fact that the pattern of history described both in Matthew 24 and Revelation 13–20 is in principle the same as 2 Thessalonians 2 should provide assistance. It will reassure both him and the congregation that even though the terminology of 'the man of lawlessness' may be obscure, nevertheless the teaching at this point in the New Testament fits in with the general pattern revealed elsewhere in the Scriptures.

So, what is the point behind Paul's teaching with its parallels in the gospels and Revelation?

Fierce opposition to God will come (vv. 3b, 4)
Don't be deceived by thinking that somehow you might have missed the return of Christ. It will be a momentous event, as has already been described (see 1 Thess. 5:1-3 and 2 Thess. 1:7-10, and see also 2 Thess. 2:8), but it will also be preceded by a period of heightened rebellion against the Lord. The marks of this rebellion include all the details set out in 2:4 – opposition to God in every way. Paul is doing something similar to what Jesus was doing at Matthew 24. The disciples were seeking information about the end of the age and when Jesus would return. An identical pattern is given to them here. So as Paul deals pastorally with the Thessalonian believers whose confidence has been knocked by accepting this false prophecy, he is wanting to provide reassurance that they have not missed out.

As we look in more detail at these verses, the focus is on rebellion against God – but even here Paul signals a note of assurance in highlighting that this figure is 'doomed to destruction'. He is described as opposed to God and as someone who wants to set himself up as a god. In opposing God it is not surprising, therefore, that his habitual method is to rebel against God's Word or law. His title of 'man of lawlessness' reveals his complete opposition to God's will through a strategy of undermining, twisting and rejecting God's Word. Though at verse 7 we are told of 'a secret power of lawlessness', the picture that we are given in verse 4 reveals

Part Four: Teaching 2 Thessalonians 2:1-15   287

a person whose chief purpose is to overthrow God. In other words, this is a portrait of Satan. Near the beginning, in Genesis 3, his aim was to resist God through causing God's Word or law to be disobeyed. This identical strategy will be pursued right to the end before his final defeat (see Isaiah 14:12-14 for further material on Satan's desire to be like God). The Thessalonians are warned that such fierce and bitter opposition to God will come before the day when the Lord Jesus is revealed.

The Lord is in complete sovereign control (v. 5-7)
Paul wants to provide further reassurance and in doing so remind the Thessalonians of teaching that he had already passed on to them at his original visit (see v. 5). The idea of this man of lawlessness staging an enormous rebellion against God and His people sounds extremely frightening. However, though elements of such rebellion were already present (as evidenced by the deception involved in the false teaching of 2:2), Paul wants to show that everything is under God's control. Twice in verses 6 and 7 he teaches them that this rebellion against God is being 'held back'. It is designed to help the Thessalonians see that when the main rebellion against God does occur, it will not have taken Him by surprise and therefore ultimately it should not be a matter of undue anxiety to them. The difficult issue within verse 7 is to determine how God holds things back and whether He does this through some agent or angel who is then removed. Whatever one's conclusions, it is important not to get distracted from the central point that God is in charge – restraining evil, permitting rebellion and then finally overcoming everything that has set itself up against Him. Amidst difficult verses where commentators offer lots

of different interpretations, it is wisest to be reminded of the flow of the letter. Facing persecution and Satan's deception, Paul wants to make sure that the Thessalonians have a 'good hope' focused on the return of the Lord Jesus Christ.

These verses will have shown the Thessalonians that although Satan will arise at the end in one final rebellion, his strategy of opposing God through seeking to undermine and reject God's Word is going to be pursued constantly in various ways. Though the tide of evil is held back so that it doesn't completely overwhelm believers, hostility to God's Word or law will be a regular occurrence throughout history as the evil one seeks to deceive and draw people away from God. By reminding the Thessalonians of his previous teaching, Paul wants to help them understand the reality of the activity of Satan but in a context which reveals God's overall control of history as He 'holds back' the man of lawlessness.

The Lord Jesus Christ will overthrow all evil (v. 8)
Paul brings his timeline to an end by reminding the Thessalonians that though the man of lawlessness will be revealed to rebel against God (see v. 4), he is 'doomed to destruction' (see v. 3) and this is made very clear at verse 8. Whoever the person is who is leading this rebellion and however powerful he seems, he will very quickly be both overthrown and destroyed. This will occur through the coming of the Lord Jesus. The decisive overthrow will occur through the breath of His mouth as the Word of God is announced. In the same way that the Word of Christ calmed the sea in an instant (see Mark 4:39), so all the satanic forces will be calmed with a Word – depicted as a 'loud shout' (see 1 Thess. 4:16). Jesus will arrive in all the

splendour of a King vanquishing his enemies. Ultimately our hope as Christians is based on the return of Christ in all His power and authority. This is what provides us with 'good hope' and 'eternal encouragement' (see v. 16) amidst all our present struggles. It is worth noting that the section from 2 Thessalonians 2:1-8 begins and ends with a reference to the coming of Christ. The return will bring about not only the defeat of evil (v. 8) but will also be the moment when believers are gathered to Him (see v. 1 and also 1:10). Again we notice the parallels with Jesus' own teaching in Matthew 24:30, 31. When Jesus appears in splendour with power and great glory, two things will occur. First, the nations of the earth will mourn (24:30) as they contemplate their inevitable defeat. Second the elect will be gathered up to be with Christ (24:31). Both these aspects are highlighted at 2 Thessalonians 2:1, 8. The day of judgment will also be the day of salvation.

So these verses provide an overview of history from the perspective of God's dealings with Satan. Satan will mount a terrifying campaign against God and His people at the end (vv. 3b, 4) and even now is working against God's purposes through resisting His Word (v. 7). But God is in charge of all things. Currently He is restraining evil (vv. 6, 7) and at the end the coming of the Lord Jesus will bring immediate and total victory (v. 8). This is the context in which the Thessalonians are living, which helps to make sense of the assault that they have experienced through being deceived concerning God's Word (vv. 1, 2). The call is to understand where they fit into this timeline so that they will not be deceived (v. 3a).

3. The danger of deception (2:9-12)

Having provided an overview of how events will unfold in the future, Paul now returns to the issue of how they were deceived in the first place and how this can be avoided in the future. Who had deceived them (see v. 3)? It must be the same person who deceives all through history and who will eventually bring deception to a climax at the coming of the lawless one (see v. 9). It is a reference to Satan, who uses all sorts of means, including counterfeit miracles, signs and wonders, to achieve his purposes. Again we should notice the clear parallels with Matthew 24. All the way through the chapter there are references to deception – (see Matt. 24:5, 11, 24). These culminate in the references to false Christs (including the man of lawlessness?) and false prophets using signs and miracles in an attempt to deceive the elect. A false Christ pretending to be God's anointed King looks very much like the man of lawlessness as he is described at 2:4 as he takes the place of God in the temple. This teaching within the gospels clearly informs the apostle in 2 Thessalonians (and see also Rev. 13:13, 14). If the Thessalonians have been deceived, they need to know that it is part of the spiritual struggle that has been going on since Genesis 3. They also need to recognise that Satan has many other strategies which he might use to seek to deceive, and so Paul's additional teaching at this point is designed to forewarn them of these sorts of dangers.

However this raises the question of whether it would be possible for the Christians in Thessalonica to fall, through being deceived by Satan. Such a thought might provoke considerable anxiety. So Paul handles this issue by making two complementary points.

Part Four: Teaching 2 Thessalonians 2:1-15

First, the reason why people in general are deceived and perish is because they refuse to love the truth (see v. 10). And if they refuse to love the truth about Jesus then they cannot be saved. A further point is that it is not just that they failed to love the truth of God's Word but at the same time they had delighted in wickedness (see v. 12). The responsibility lies firmly with them because it is due to their own actions that they will end up perishing. As we will soon see in verse 13, the main way of protecting yourself against Satan's attacks is to believe and love the truth.

At the same time however, Paul also adds a complementary truth. So, second, the reason that some people perish is that God has sent them a powerful delusion so that they believe the lie rather than the truth (see vv. 11, 12). Paul wants to show that even though some will perish through Satan's work of deception, it does not mean that God is a powerless, passive observer. Instead, these verses highlight that ultimately God is directing all things and even Satan is merely one of His messengers used by Him to achieve His own eternal purposes. No one will be able to blame God that they perished because they must take responsibility themselves for not believing the truth and delighting in wickedness (see v. 12). Equally, no one will be able to credit Satan with success since it is God who is ultimately in control of all things, even Satan and his lies. All these things are woven into His purposes.

So it is helpful to notice the way that Paul carefully interweaves these two themes. Together they provide a warning to the Thessalonians not to stray from the truth but to trust God's sovereign purposes. And it is these two purposes which are followed up in a more positive way in the final main section of the chapter (see verses 13-15).

4. *The assurance of salvation (2:13-15)*

So how does Paul wind up this issue in this chapter? Perhaps by now the Thessalonians were feeling pretty stupid for having been deceived. Perhaps they were feeling slightly vulnerable. After all, if those who fail to love the truth perish, what will happen to them having been deceived into rejecting the truth? To provide assurance in order to address some of these concerns, Paul starts with thanksgiving, once again echoing the thanksgiving at 1:3, 4, and then goes on to stress God's sovereignty in salvation and the significance of believing and holding on to the truth. Understanding these truths in verses 13-15 is designed to help them to withstand Satan's schemes and enable their hope and confidence concerning the future to be renewed (see v. 16). Paul reminds them of God's sovereignty in salvation by taking them through every decisive event from beginning to end.

They are loved by the Lord (13)

Though they may have got things wrong with the false prophecy (see 2:2), the Thessalonians have been eternally loved by the Lord Jesus Christ. Whilst human love may be fickle and unreliable, God's love is completely certain and dependable. There is a further reference to the love of Christ at verse 16 which amplifies this point.

They have been chosen by God (13)

This love of Christ for them was worked out first through God choosing them to be saved. In passing, it is worth pointing out once again that back at Matthew 24:22, 24, 31,

Part Four: Teaching 2 Thessalonians 2:1-15

the Lord Jesus specifically refers to those who will be saved at the end as 'the elect', His chosen ones (and see Rev. 17:14). Similarly here, Paul focuses on the fact that they have been chosen by God. At this point we can note that there are two possible readings. NIV refers to the fact that God chose them 'from the beginning' which links to Ephesians 1:4 and God's election before the creation of the world. This would certainly provide the Thessalonians with great assurance by reminding them that their eternal safety is bound up with a decision God made at the beginning. This might also link in to the theme of 'eternal encouragement' which comes at verse 16. However, the ESV and the NIV margin also refer to another possibility that 'God chose you as his firstfruits'. If so, the meaning is that they are particularly loved as the first of the crop. It also implies that there are many others whom God will 'gather' (see 2:1) which provides further assurance of the progress and success of the gospel in Thessalonica and elsewhere despite Satan's schemes. Either reading is possible but both provide further encouragement to the believers in helping them to know what it means to be loved by the Lord.

They have been set apart by the Spirit (13-14)
Salvation comes not just through being chosen in eternity but how that is worked out in history. The sanctifying work of the Spirit refers to His work of setting people apart to belong to God. Though the idea of sanctification is often linked in our minds to the life of a believer as he or she grows in holiness, in the New Testament it is more commonly a word that is linked to conversion (see for example 1 Corinthians 6:11 where 'sanctified' comes

between 'washed' and 'justified' and must be a conversion word). This seems to be the case here since the phrase is linked with belief in the truth and through God's calling in the gospel (see v. 14). So as the gospel is preached, the call to turn to God and trust in Christ (see 1 Thess. 1:9, 10) goes out. People respond to this call through the Spirit setting them apart to belong to God which is experienced as they believe the message. The work of the Spirit and our response to the truth go hand in hand as the Spirit enables us to put our faith in Christ. It should be noticed that verse 13 is fully Trinitarian. Believers are loved by the Lord (Jesus Christ), chosen by God (the Father) and set apart by the Spirit. Again it provides great assurance amidst assaults by Satan that the triune God is fully involved in their salvation and His purposes cannot therefore be thwarted.

They are destined to share in the glory of our Lord Jesus Christ (v. 14)
God's decision to choose and the work of the Spirit at conversion lie in the past. What assurance would this have given the Thessalonians if nothing else was said concerning the future? So Paul adds that the whole purpose of the Trinitarian work is that believers might share in the glory of our Lord Jesus Christ (see v. 14). This is where everything for the believer is heading. In line with one of the dominant themes of the letter, Paul wants the Thessalonians to be fully persuaded that they have a good hope (see 2:16). So this is the destination to which the Thessalonian believers will be taken. It links back to 1:10 and the picture of believers marvelling at the glory of Christ on His return and also to 2:8 and the reference

Part Four: Teaching 2 Thessalonians 2:1-15

to the splendour of His coming. God (Father, Son and Spirit) is planning through the gospel to bring every believer into the very presence of the glory of Christ and none of Satan's schemes will derail this eternal purpose of grace.

So stand firm and hold on to God's Word (v. 15)
So Paul's main theme in these verses relates to God's sovereignty in salvation but the other key point relates to our response to God's Word. The problem at Thessalonica was that, through letting go of God's Word due to deception, some were failing to believe and love the truth. Paul now gives his response to wrap up the issue and hold the whole chapter together. In contrast to those who have not believed the truth, he reminds the Thessalonians that they have believed the truth (see 2:13). Whereas Satan had led some to turn away from the truth, the Spirit of God had enabled them to believe it. Therefore as they have started out on the Christian journey through believing the truth, Paul's commission to them is to continue the Christian life by standing firm and holding on to it (see 2:15), in contrast to being deceived and unsettled (see 2:2). Verse 15 is therefore the logical conclusion of this whole section with its call to hold on to traditions, whether passed on by word of mouth or by letter. The word 'tradition' is often translated 'teaching' and this is fair since what Paul hands down to them comes with the force of teaching. However, 'tradition' may be a better translation as it reminds us not so much of the message taught by the apostle but of the source and authority of the message. The 'tradition' is something that is not new, such as the false prophecy or false teaching relating to the Day of the Lord in 2:2. Rather, it relates to something

older that has been passed down. Within the context of 2 Thessalonians 2, we have had cause to note time and time again that the teaching of the Lord Jesus in Matthew 24 stands behind the whole chapter. Therefore the appeal at 2:15 is in reality not so much a personal appeal from Paul to hold on to his teachings but a call to the Thessalonians for them to hold on to the words of Jesus. The breath of His mouth will overthrow and destroy all evil (2:8) and in the meantime believers must hold on to His words (2:15) as a means to stand firm amidst the assaults on the church.

The concluding prayer (2:16, 17) has already been dealt with in a previous exposition but in particular it is easy to see how 2:16 forms a natural conclusion to the rest of the chapter and especially 2:13-15. To a church whose hope had been shaken and who were facing discouragement through continuing persecution and satanic deception, Paul gives assurance of God's sovereign love and grace. On the basis of the inevitable defeat of all the forces of evil by the coming of the Lord Jesus Christ, he prays that they would be encouraged to stand firm and have full confidence in the good hope of sharing in the glory of our Lord Jesus Christ.

From text to message

Getting the message clear: the theme

- God is sovereign over all the forces of evil and will save His people, who need to stand firm, holding on to the words of Jesus.

Part Four: Teaching 2 Thessalonians 2:1-15

Getting the message clear: the aim

- The aim of this passage is to give confidence to believers that God is in sovereign charge over all things. Preaching or teaching on this passage should help in answering the following questions:
  - Why is it possible for Christians to have confidence and hope whilst Satan is still active?
  - How is God's sovereignty demonstrated?
  - What is the key thing Christians need to do when confronted with satanic deception?

A way in

We need to understand the devastating effect that this false teaching would have had on the Thessalonian church. Imagine a few survivors from a shipwreck huddled together in a life raft. Desperate to be rescued and coping with a violent storm, they look forward to a search-and-rescue plane coming over the ocean to rescue them. Then they hear it approaching but soon realise it has gone straight past, leaving them abandoned in the middle of the ocean. At that point surely all hope would have evaporated. It must have been a similar sort of situation for the Thessalonians believers. In the middle of the storm of persecution, they had received a message which in effect told them that the rescue plane had flown over without picking them up. It must have led to major disappointment and disillusionment. Yet it needn't have happened because it was all a result of being deceived and letting go of the truth. Only the truth of God's Word can protect us against such disillusionment.

If the problem relates to being deceived into letting go of the truth, then the solution at 2:15 is all about standing firm and holding on to the Word of God. There are many situations in life where you need to hold on and not let go. For example, a child on a climbing frame or a rock climber on a sheer face must ensure that they hold on at all times. Or perhaps we can picture a small child with his or her parents in a town with busy roads. They need to hold on in order to avoid danger, even if it is also the case that the parent is holding on with an even stronger grip. Or perhaps think of a harbour with a strong tidal flow. Any boats must be moored carefully so that they do not drift away with the tide. In order to remain where they need to be, they have to be safely and securely tied on to the mooring. So it is with God's people being tied securely to God's Word to prevent them drifting away or being carried away by error and false teaching.

Pointers to application

- It is vital that as Christians we are aware that we are in a spiritual battle. Satan does prowl around like a roaring lion (1 Pet. 5:8) and in all sorts of ways he aims to thwart God's purposes (see 1 Thess. 2:18). Sometimes this may be done through temptation (1 Thess. 3:5) and at other times through deception (see 2 Thess. 2:1-3a, 9, 10) but it is all equally insidious and dangerous. We need to be aware that Satan can even use miracles, signs and wonders (see 2 Thess. 2:9) to achieve his purposes and so it is vital that as believers we are not gullible but always on our guard. Paul had previously encouraged the Thessalonians to test every prophecy (see 1 Thess. 5:20, 21) but it may well be

Part Four: Teaching 2 Thessalonians 2:1-15

that they had failed to do this consistently, which had led to their current problems.

+ It is extremely helpful to see the importance of comparing Scripture with Scripture in order to enable the more difficult parts to be interpreted by those parts which are clearer. This is particularly true of this chapter where the close parallels between Matthew 24 and 2 Thessalonians 2 help us to interpret parts that would appear to be very obscure. Especially in areas such as the doctrine of the return of Christ, it is much safer to use the combined wisdom of several passages than to build an enormous structure on the basis of a contested understanding of a very difficult passage.

+ Though terrible things happen and the church is constantly threatened and occasionally overwhelmed, nevertheless verses 3-8 remind us that God is in sovereign charge of all things. Even now He is restraining the full force of evil and when He deems it the right time to permit Satan to be unleashed, He will ensure that Christ will be instantly victorious. We are like sports fans watching a recording of a game where our team is struggling badly and yet we already know that it will result in victory for us. How the result will be achieved we do not know and at times we can hardly think it possible that it will work out like that in the end. Nevertheless, despite all our anxiety, as we watch the game we can have complete confidence in the end result and so can every believer as we look forward to the day when our Lord Jesus Christ returns.

- Though this passage clearly speaks of the sovereignty of God in history and in salvation, nevertheless it is vital that this does not lead to passivity and laziness. Our responsibility within this chapter is very clear and it concerns how we stand in relation to the truth. On the one hand, it is possible not to believe the truth and not to love the truth (2:10, 12). On the other hand, we see people believing the truth and holding on to it (2:13, 15). This means that it is vital for preachers themselves to love the truth and hold on to it because if they let their grip slacken it will have disastrous effects on their churches. It applies, however, to every believer. Each one of us is called to believe, hold on to and love the truth of the Word of God, and we need encouragement each day and each week to treasure it accordingly.

- We need to be reminded of the importance of applying doctrine to our lives in order to encourage us to keep going through difficult days. Paul teaches about the doctrine of election not for its academic interest but as a means of providing reassurance to Christians under pressure. It is certainly possible to teach doctrine in such a way that it is indigestible, but rightly handled it should provide nourishment to strengthen us in our Christian journey. Doctrine needs to be applied and in so doing should make a difference to the way we live.

- When we speak of sanctification, we generally refer to the process of growing in holiness. However, though

Part Four: Teaching 2 Thessalonians 2:1-15 301

we certainly do not want to downplay progress in our obedience to the Lord Jesus Christ, we also need to recognise the value of understanding 'sanctification' as a term associated with conversion. To be sanctified means to be set apart in order to belong to Christ. Indeed it is only through being sanctified and set apart for Christ that we are able to progress in holiness. It is important, therefore, to understand sanctification as being linked to conversion in order to prevent us going down a legalistic or moralistic route in our pursuit of holiness.

- Our destination is glory. Paul constantly reminds the Thessalonians of this in both his letters. We also need to be reminded that this is where we are headed. It is easy to get so embroiled in what is happening to us and around us in the world, the church and in our own lives that we sometimes forget to look up and recognise that there is a destination to which we are travelling. Reminding ourselves of this truth will often be the means of encouraging us when tempted to become despondent. It will also help to clarify and perhaps simplify our understanding of our priorities and aims. If this is our destination, it may cause us to consider some things as being of far less significance then the world around might think and, conversely, it might lead to other decisions which the world may not understand. Being clear about where we are heading should affect the direction in which we travel in our daily Christian life.

Suggestions for preaching
Sermon 1: Hold on to the truth! (2:1-15)

- The issue: don't be deceived! (2:1-3a).

- The explanation: evil will come, but the Lord is in control (2:3b-8).

- The danger of deception (2:9-12).

- The assurance of salvation (2:13-15).

Other preaching possibilities
One of the challenges in preaching through this chapter is how to divide up the material. There is material specifically relating to the deception and how it fits with God's overall plan in verses 1-12. However, Paul's message only makes sense when coupled with verses 12-15. The presenting issue of 2:2 is ultimately answered at 2:15. So though the preacher may want to spend a bit more time in preaching through the material in 2:1-12 in one or two sermons (e.g. 2:1-8 and 2:9-12), he will want to make sure that he connects the whole chapter together each time and preserves the flow of Paul's argument.

Suggestions for teaching
Introducing the passage

- Can you think of situations in life where it is vitally important to hold on? What would be the consequence of letting go? How does this help you to understand the climax of this chapter at 2:15 with its call to hold on?

Part Four: Teaching 2 Thessalonians 2:1-15

Understanding the passage

- What has been happening at Thessalonica according to Paul's report in 2:1, 2 and why did it matter?
- Read Matthew 24:1-31. What are the parallels with 2 Thessalonians 2?
- What can we learn about the timeline of the events described in verses 3-8?
- What are the reasons that people might perish according to verses 9-12?
- What are the things that God has already done for every believer in verses 13-14?
- What did Paul want the Thessalonians to do in verse 15 and what might this have involved?

Applying the passage

- In what ways do we think Satan is still active in our day?
- What difference should knowing the future (e.g. 2:8 and 2:14) make to the way we think about the difficulties and struggles that the church faces?
- In what ways have we found that certain doctrines have strengthened and nourished us in the Christian life (see 2:13, 14)?
- What do you think is entailed in practice by 'holding on to the teachings' (2:15)?
- How should we pray for the church to be protected from satanic deception?
- How could you strengthen your hold on God's Word in order to avoid being deceived?

4.

THE PROGRESS OF THE WORD OF THE LORD
(3:1-5)

Introduction

In all sorts of areas of life we want to see progress. It might be in a business, a sports team or a child learning the piano. Year on year, we long for development, growth and advances. It should also be like this in the Christian life. Failure to make progress generally means stagnation and drift. As Paul viewed the Thessalonian church, this was a key consideration. Having spent two chapters fighting fires, he now wants to see them going forwards. However important it was to encourage them not to give up amidst persecution and prevent them being downhearted through the false teaching they had received, he recognised that one of the most important issues was to encourage them in their Christian life. In this paragraph, therefore, Paul is longing for progress. He asks them to pray for the progress of the Word of the Lord (3:1) and he in turn prays for them to progress in obedience to the Word of the Lord (3:4).

It is good that they know where they are heading (2:16) but now they must get going in that direction (2:17) and this paragraph (3:1-5) spells out how Paul envisages that should happen.

Listening to the text

Context and structure

This passage immediately follows the 'hinge' of the letter at 2:16, 17. As in the parallel section in 1 Thessalonians where 4:1, 2 follows 3:11-13, this is of particular significance, in that it will set the course for the rest of the letter. Up to 2:16, the focus has been the 'good hope' of Christians sharing in the glory of Christ (see 1:10, 2:14, 16), and this is the antidote to both persecution (to show that persecutors will be judged by Christ at the end) and false teaching about the return of Christ (to show that believers will be protected by Christ up to the end).

At 2:17 Paul turns to his vision about how believers should live out their lives before Christ's return. In doing so he picks up the strand of teaching from 1:11, 12 which reveals how Christians should work now to bring glory to Christ. They will do this through their words and works prompted by their faith. It is this theme that is now developed in the final chapter.

Ultimately, the reason behind developing his argument in this way is that some of the Thessalonians had made no progress at all in some areas of their Christian life and Paul will come round to dealing with this issue at 3:6-15. However, to start with, Paul wants to encourage them all and so he prepares for the coming rebuke and correction

Part Four: Teaching 2 Thessalonians 3:1-5

by offering words to guide them in the right direction. Encouragement needs to come before reproof.

So these verses (3:1-5) are here to develop the theme of 2:17 and to encourage and strengthen them so that they continue to make progress until the Lord Jesus Christ returns.

At the beginning of this passage Paul wants them to pray for him (and Silas and Timothy). However by the end Paul is praying for them. The transition occurs between verse 2 and verse 3, where the theme of praying for protection and deliverance is to be a common theme in their prayers for Paul and Paul's prayers for them. Either side, however, are prayers for progress – for the preaching of the Word of the Lord to make progress and for their obedience to the Word of the Lord to make progress. This appears to assist in identifying a structure to the passage.

- The Thessalonians pray for Paul (vv. 1-2)
- for the Word of the Lord to progress (v. 1)
- for the Lord of the Word to protect (v. 2)
- Paul prays for the Thessalonians (vv. 3-5)
- for protection by the Lord (v. 3)
- for them to be kept (God's love v. 5)
- for obedience to the Lord (v. 4)
- for them to keep going (Christ's perseverance v. 5)

In both sections Paul is aware of the opposition but is praying for the Word of the Lord to make progress.

There are a number of important links with other parts of 2 Thessalonians. We have already noticed the context of the hostility of Satan (2:9) and this is now described as the evil one (3:3) who is no doubt standing behind the evil men described at 3:2, who are persecuting and opposing Paul and the gospel. As at 1 Thessalonians 2:18; 3:3-5, Paul is very aware of the influence of Satan in seeking to oppose the work of Christ.

In contrast Paul's aim is to strengthen the Thessalonians. This aim was behind his commission in sending Timothy to them (1 Thess. 3:2) and also his earlier praying (1 Thess. 3:13). Now he continues to pray that the Lord would strengthen them (2 Thess. 2:16 and 3:3), in order to be protected against Satan's attacks.

Working through the text

As we work through the text, attention will be paid to the structure of the passage previously identified.

1. *Praying for Paul to make progress (vv. 1, 2)*

As mentioned above, Paul needs to address a particular situation amongst a minority of the church family in Thessalonica which he will do at 3:6-15. Before doing that he wants to encourage them in a very positive way (see vv. 3-5). However, even before that he asks them to pray for him (vv. 1, 2). If he had gone directly to 3:6, the impression would have been of an apostle laying down the law in an aggressive manner. The fact that he first encourages them slightly softens that picture. Further, his request that they pray for him takes much of the sting out of his later rebuke. This is not an apostle laying down the law but a father who is seeking to encourage (see 1 Thess. 2:10-12) and a brother who needs their assistance.

How exactly should they pray for him and his ministry?

Pray for the Word of the Lord to progress (v. 1)

In asking for prayer concerning the Word of the Lord (NIV 'message of the Lord' = ESV 'word of the Lord'), Paul is clearly referring to his own preaching ministry since he is specifically asking for prayer for 'us'. He is longing that the sort of response which the Thessalonians had given to the Word of the Lord, as described at 1 Thessalonians 1:4-10, would be replicated elsewhere. Specifically he asks for prayer for two things to happen.

First, he asks for prayer that the Word of Lord would 'spread rapidly' (NIV) or 'speed ahead' (ESV). Both in different ways are vivid images of progress. Think of a YouTube clip or news story going viral and spreading incredibly rapidly around the world, and this is the sort of advance that Paul is longing for. Or using the slightly different picture of the Word running, we can think of a champion sprinter like Usain Bolt sprinting ahead of his rivals. Either way it is a dynamic portrait of advance and progress that is being painted, which dovetails neatly with Luke's repeated phrases at Acts 6:7 and 12:24 of the Word of God spreading. Paul's vision is that the Word would keep on advancing, and within his own lifetime that was certainly the case.

Second, he asks for prayer that the Word of the Lord would be honoured. Again, returning to Luke's description of events in the early church, we can turn to Acts 13:48. Some at Pisidian Antioch heard Paul preach and as a result they believed and put their trust in Christ. Luke describes such a response as 'honouring the word of the Lord'. So it is not just that Paul wants them to pray for the Word to be preached but also for it to be received appropriately, perhaps reflecting the joy with which the Thessalonians had heard Paul preaching the gospel (1 Thess. 1:6) as they recognised Paul's word as none other than the Word of God (1 Thess. 2:13). So this is the main priority in Paul's ministry, which is why these requests for prayer go right to the top of the list.

Pray for the Lord of the Word to protect (v. 2)
However Paul is realistic and he knows only too well the reality of opposition to the gospel both for himself (see 1 Thess. 2:2) and for them (see 1 Thess. 2:14; 3:3; 2 Thess. 1:4-6). In praying for the gospel to progress he recognises therefore that those who preach that Word need the protection of the Lord. In the context of wicked and evil men seeking to obstruct the path of the gospel through attacking gospel ministers, Paul asks for deliverance. Notice that he does not pray that there would be no suffering at all. He recognises that not all have faith and that therefore there will be a continual spiritual battle. However he does seek prayer for deliverance amidst opposition in order that he can continue preaching the Word of the Lord. Though the truth will always provoke some sort of reaction (see 2:12 for those who, having not believed the truth, delight in wickedness) Paul is seeking strength from the Lord to keep at his work of proclaiming the truth.

2. Praying for the Thessalonians to make progress (vv. 3-5)
At this point there is a transition from Paul requesting their prayers, to him praying for them. However it continues the request made at 3:2, as the basic issue whether for apostle or Thessalonian is basically the same – the need for protection.

... for the Thessalonians to be kept (vv. 3, 5)

Perhaps, having mentioned his own need for deliverance from evil men Paul, was sensitive to the fact that this was clearly an issue also for the Thessalonians. So though he and they might be surrounded by those with 'no faith', they can have full assurance that they will be kept by the Lord. On what basis can they know this? Their assurance is based on the faithfulness of the Lord. He is well able to strengthen and protect from the evil one because, as has already been shown in 2 Thessalonians 2, He is sovereign over all the forces of evil. Even when rebellion against God reaches its climax (see 2 Thess. 2:4), it will be brought down by the first word that comes from the mouth of the Lord Jesus Christ (2 Thess. 2:8). The Lord will watch over His own people who now belong to Him through the work of the Spirit who set them apart (see 2 Thess. 2:13). Constantly Paul has been working and praying that they would be strengthened (see 1 Thess. 3:2, 13; 2 Thess. 2:17) and he is confident that the Lord will faithfully watch over and preserve them.

It may also be appropriate at this point to turn to 3:5. Paul's prayer for the Thessalonians has two angles – for protection (3:3) and for continued obedience to his teaching (3:4). This is then followed by two further prayers (3:5) which seem to run in parallel to the previous requests. If this is correct, then Paul amplifies his prayer for their protection by asking that the Lord would direct their hearts into God's love (3:5a). This request links to Paul's reminder to the Thessalonians that they have been loved by the Lord and chosen by God from the beginning (2:13). He had directed them to consider God's love as an antidote to anxiety about the work of Satan and the prevalence of evil, in order to give assurance to them that they would certainly share Christ's glory at the end. So now he asks that the Thessalonians would constantly be directed to these truths so that, amidst all the assaults on their faith, they could bathe in the knowledge and experience of God's love for them in Christ.

... for the Thessalonians to keep going (vv. 4, 5)
Having developed the theme of praying for protection for both himself and the Thessalonians, Paul now returns to the theme of the progress of the Word of the Lord. He longs that it would make progress evangelistically in the lives of non-Christians (3:1) but also that it would do so in the lives of Christians (3:4). What Paul commands as we shall see is 'the teaching' that he had passed on to them (see 3:6). However these teachings or traditions, as we have already seen (see 2:15 and the clear links to Jesus' teachings in Matthew 24), are none other than the Word of the Lord (see 1 Thessalonians 2:13 for the explicit link between the word of men and the Word of God).

Paul is connecting with his main prayer at 2:17, which is based on his earlier teaching at 1:11, 12. On the basis that believers will be kept so that they will one day share the glory of Christ, they are now to keep going in obedience to the Word of the Lord, as demonstrated in their words and deeds. In the way Paul indicates that he has confidence that they will keep doing the things that he has commanded them, this verse seems to be a prayer that this will indeed be the case. As they do this, so they will bring glory to the Lord Jesus Christ (see 1:11, 12).

Part Four: Teaching 2 Thessalonians 3:1-5

But how can they keep going? Paul's prayer is that the Lord would strengthen them in obedience (2:17) and perseverance so that they may be able to exemplify Christ's own perseverance (3:5). Christ is the one who persevered through suffering and opposition all the way to glory. As the Lord, He is therefore the One who can strengthen believers to keep persevering, but at the same time He also provides the model for how believers are to keep going. He is able to keep us going and also provides the pattern for us to follow. This was something that the Thessalonians were already working out in practice (see their perseverance at 1:4).

So Paul prays for them to be kept by Christ but also to keep going so that the Word of the Lord would make progress in their own lives. Here is the remarkable blend of assurance and encouragement which is designed to bolster their faith and also propel them forward in the service of Christ. It mirrors Paul's prayer for himself. So whoever it is, Paul's desire is that Christians under pressure would be kept and that in every situation the Word of the Lord would make progress in people's lives.

From text to message

Getting the message clear: the theme

- Paul's prayer is that the Word of the Lord would take effect more and more in the lives of both non-Christians as well as believers.

Getting the message clear: the aim

- The aim of this passage is to encourage us to pray for God's Word to spread rapidly. Preaching or teaching on this passage should help in answering the following questions:

- What is Paul's chief desire revealed in this request for prayer?
- What is Paul's chief need as he seeks to preach the Word of the Lord?
- What is Paul's vision for the Thessalonian Christians as they look to the future?

A way in

As we embark on a journey there will be some things that are essential, which should be packed. Other items might be desirable but the essential ones must not be overlooked. As Paul prepares to bring this letter to its conclusion, he is looking to the future both for himself and the Thessalonians. What are the really essential things which are needed for their respective journeys? For Paul, it is prayer for the Word of the Lord to progress whilst he, as a servant of the Lord, is protected. For the Thessalonians, it is prayer for the Word of the Lord to continue to make an impact on their lives whilst they also know God's love and protection. So, for both of them, the first things which must be packed and kept readily available are the Word of God and prayers for progress and protection.

Verse 1 contains the vivid picture of the Word of the Lord speeding ahead or running (ESV) and spreading rapidly (NIV). The images are slightly different but, taken together, convey the sense of rapid progress. For an illustration of the Word of the Lord speeding ahead we need look no further than an Olympic champion overtaking competitors and leaving them trailing in his or her wake. Or we could think of a car accelerating away down the motorway and getting to its destination long before others would have thought possible. In terms of the Word of the Lord spreading rapidly, one could think of an email or YouTube item going viral or of a particular fashion or accessory suddenly hitting the streets. All these pictures help us to see that Paul wants them to pray for the gospel to make real progress around the world.

Pointers to application

- As we have seen at the beginning (1:3, 4), Paul always finds a way to start which seeks to encourage. Though he will have serious things to say to some within the church (see 3:6ff), he does not want to tar the whole church with the same brush and so he prays for them in a positive way. Yet even before this he requests prayers for himself from them. Paul is not aloof or independent. He does not throw his weight around as an apostle. Rather he recognises that he needs them and is dependent upon them praying for him. Perhaps this is a lesson to those in church leadership not to become detached in any way from the rest of the fellowship. Paul's aim is mutual encouragement and it should be the same with us.

- The request for the Word of the Lord to spread rapidly or speed ahead should be a priority in our churches that should shape the agenda of each fellowship. It should remind us that this is the key priority in all our initiatives. Church growth will only come about through the Word of the Lord doing its work in the lives of individuals and groups of people. In other words, as we see in Acts, church growth is dependent upon 'Word growth'. It should also focus our minds on the key needs within any congregation – it is to gather and train those who will be able to preach and apply the Word of the Lord whether as preachers, evangelists, youth ministers, children's workers, etc. Other roles are required for the running of any church and each gift has its place but focusing on developing Word gifts is the key. This verse should also help to focus the church's prayer meeting. Though it is right and proper to pray about many things, nevertheless this should always be the main request – that the Word of the Lord should spread rapidly

- Paul also wants the Word of the Lord to be honoured. His focus is not just on the preaching of the Word but also on the response that it generates. Recognising that the Parable of the Sower (Mark 4:1-20) shows differing responses to the sowing of the seed of the Word of God, he wants prayer specifically for good soil where the seed will be received and grow to bear fruit. Preaching is not an end in itself and so we must pray for a good response. As people recognise the truth of the message and put their trust in Christ, so they honour the Word, and as they honour the Word they honour the Lord.

- Paul is realistic about the challenges believers will face as they seek to preach God's Word and live for Christ and so he prays for protection. We also need to recognise the reality of the spiritual battle that we face. If we are involved in Word ministry we should not be surprised at such assaults from those within our culture. If we are seeking to apply God's Word to every aspect of our lives, we should not be surprised when work colleagues or friends react against the light, preferring the darkness (John 3:19-21). As believers we are not invulnerable and therefore we need this healthy reliance on God's ability to be faithful to His people and protect those that belong to Him.

- Paul prays that the Lord would direct their hearts into God's love. There are times when some of us love to relax and be refreshed through having a bath, immersing our body in the hot, soothing water. Similarly Paul longs that the Thessalonians would be sustained amidst all the opposition by bathing in the wonderfully refreshing waters of the knowledge of God's love for His people. Amidst the stresses and strains of living for Christ in a hostile culture, we need to plunge into these waters regularly in order to be revitalised spiritually.

- Paul prays for the Thessalonians to keep going through persevering. There are always times for every believer when we feel like giving up and that we can't go on. At such times we especially need to pray for Christ to grant us perseverance so that we can keep following Him. It is a prayer for the Word of Christ to continue to make progress in our lives so that we do not stall in our Christian journey. Just as a car needs to have its engine continually running to make progress, so Paul is praying for God's Word to continue to run in their lives so that they don't come to a halt.

Suggestions for teaching
Sermon 1: The progress of the Word of the Lord (3:1-5)

- Praying for the Word of the Lord to make progress in Paul's ministry (vv. 1, 2).
- For the Word of the Lord to progress (v. 1)
- For the Lord of the Word to protect (v. 2)
- Praying for the Word of the Lord to make progress amongst the Thessalonians (vv. 3-5).
- For the Thessalonians to be kept (vv. 3, 5)
- For the Thessalonians to keep going (vv. 4, 5)

Other preaching possibilities
Those wishing to proceed at a quicker pace may wish to consider preaching 2 Thessalonians 3:1-15 (or up to 18) in one go. If so, it is important to recognise the linking word 'command' which comes at 3:4, 6, 12 and also the context of Paul's prayer at 2:17, which sets the agenda for the final chapter. Alternatively, some preachers may feel that 3:1 is such a significant verse that they would wish to devote a whole sermon to unpacking it, though the danger would be to lose sight of the original context within 2 Thessalonians.

Suggestions for teaching
Introducing the passage

- Describe situations where you have seen examples of rapid progress – perhaps in an individual or

Part Four: Teaching 2 Thessalonians 3:1-5

a company or a sports team. How may these situations illustrate what Paul is longing for in 3:1?

Understanding the passage
- What would an answer to the prayer of 3:1 look like in practice?
- Why do you think Paul also thought that the prayer contained in 3:2 was necessary?
- What attributes of the Lord undergird these requests and why are they so helpful? (See 3:3-5)
- How do you think verse 4 would have been received by the Thessalonian church?
- Do you think 'Christ's perseverance' means the perseverance which Christ provides, the example set by Christ's perseverance, or both?
- If Paul's first task in this letter is to address the problems of 3:6, why do you think he started the chapter in the way that he did?

Applying the passage
- How does Acts 13:48, 49 amplify what Paul is longing for at 3:1?
- How should the prayer of 3:1 shape the priorities of the local church?
- In what ways do you think we are in the sort of spiritual battle described in 3:2, 3?
- What do you think 'direct your hearts into God's love' means, bearing in mind what Paul had already said in 2:13, 14, and why might we need to pray for this today?
- Pray for the Word of the Lord to speed rapidly and be honoured in your own situation

- In what areas do you need to keep going and not give up in your own Christian life?

5.

THE APPLICATION OF THE WORD OF THE LORD (3:6-15)

Introduction

The apostle now turns to deal with his final main issue which relates to how their faith in Christ has been applied to their lives. Although Paul has already provided teaching on this subject (e.g. 1 Thess. 4:9-12), somehow there was a group in the Thessalonian church who had remained oblivious to all his encouragements. Rather like a situation where the fan belt comes off a vacuum cleaner, there can be plenty of noise as the motor turns round, yet at the same time there is no discernible difference to the carpet. So it was with a group of members within the church in Thessalonica. They made plenty of noise as they made themselves busy in conversation amongst the church family. Yet despite all this noise the gospel did not appear to have made much of a difference to their lifestyle and conduct. Rather than accept the fact that this group were simply being stubborn, Paul regarded their actions with considerable concern. This was not a matter which could be overlooked and so, with all his apostolic authority, he confronts the situation head-on.

Listening to the text

Context and structure

The central prayer at 2:16,17 forms the 'hinge' of the whole letter. Amidst persecution they are to be reminded of their 'good hope' as they look forward to sharing in the glory of Christ (2:16 and see 1:10; 2:14). However, Paul doesn't simply want them to hold on and wait for the future to arrive. So at 2:17 he prays for encouragement and strength in the present so that their whole life, whether in deed or word, is lived for the glory of Christ (and see 1:11, 12). This verse then sets the agenda as Paul tackles the remaining presenting problem from 3:6 onwards. However, he starts the chapter by encouraging them through asking for prayer himself and through praying for them. Both aspects of these prayers feature Paul's desire to see the Word of the Lord making progress. In the lives of non-Christians, he longs that it would make progress and be honoured through people coming to a living faith in Christ. In the lives of the Thessalonian believers, he longs that his words or commands, which derive from the Lord Himself (see 1 Thess. 2:13) would also continue to make progress in their everyday Christian living (see v. 4). Yet this is the problem! Not everyone in the Thessalonian church is doing what has been taught and it is this issue which is now addressed from 3:6.

There seems to be a structure in the way in which this passage has been constructed which helpfully provides real shape to the teaching of this chapter. There appears to be a chiasm.

Part Four: Teaching 2 Thessalonians 3:6-15

A   Keeping away from certain brothers (v. 6)
B   You know how you ought to live (vv. 7-10)
C   Instructions to the idle (vv. 11, 12)
B   You know how you ought to live (v. 13)
A   Don't associate with certain brothers (vv. 14, 15)

So it would appear that at the beginning and end Paul gives clear, strong instructions about the need for the majority to keep away from those who are described as 'idle'. In the middle, the 'idle' are directly addressed with another strong command to get working. In between, we see Paul encouraging the believers to continue to follow his own example of working hard.

There are a number of important links which tie this passage in with the rest of the letter. Paul uses the word translated 'command' at 3:4 before doing so again at 3:6 and 3:12 (and also at 1 Thessalonians 4:11). This shows that 3:1-5 and 3:6-15 are clearly linked through the refusal of some to follow these commands. When referring to his teaching which had previously been passed on to them, Paul speaks of the 'traditions' at 2:15 (ESV). Again at 3:6 he uses the same word. In chapter 2 the Thessalonians had been deceived into letting go of these teachings which had originally come from Jesus, and now in chapter 3 we see that there are some who had deliberately deviated from his previous teaching. Finally, when we look at Paul's example at 3:7-10 we see a number of links with material in 1 Thessalonians 2:7-12 which also describe his hard work, night and day, so that he would not be a burden to them. In particular we should focus on the word 'work'. It has already occurred earlier in 2 Thessalonians at 1:11 and 2:17 (and also at 1 Thessalonians 4:11). Now it appears in almost every verse in the middle of this section: verses 8, 10, 11, 12. If Paul's vision is that believers should be devoted to working so that the name of the Lord Jesus Christ is glorified (see 1:11, 12), we can see why working or not working is of such significance to him.

Working through the text

As we work through the text, attention will be paid to the structure of the passage previously identified. However, to start with, it may be helpful to spend a brief amount of time seeking to identify the issue which had caused Paul to write.

What was the issue?

Paul had previously identified a problem in the church at 1 Thessalonians 4:11, 12 and 5:14. Some people were not working and were idle, perhaps disrupting others. Having already encouraged them in the right direction, Paul is frustrated that he has to deal with this issue yet again and identifies the same group once more – see 'idle' at 3:6, 11 (and Paul refers to himself as not being 'idle' in 3:7). Given the force with which he speaks to this group once again (3:11, 12) and especially given his powerful instructions to the majority to disassociate themselves from them (3:6, 14, 15), he clearly sees it as an issue of vital importance for the health of the church. Before coming to a consideration of what needed to be done, it may be worth thinking why this group had emerged.

It may be that this group was gripped by Paul's teaching about the return of Christ so that they considered it to be imminent. As a result, perhaps they thought that there was simply no point in carrying on with work. Why bother

Part Four: Teaching 2 Thessalonians 3:6-15 325

working hard, given that the end is to come very soon? Yet if this theological justification were at the root of their behaviour, one would have imagined that Paul would have referred to it and corrected their thinking.

Another possibility is that this group was simply being lazy. Perhaps the very success of the church is developing a culture of deepening love (see 1 Thess. 4:9, 10 and 2 Thess. 1:3) that had contributed to a situation where some were coasting along in their Christian lives and failing to contribute to the church family. They were getting but not giving. This may well be the reason for their behaviour.

Another possibility that may have been a contributing factor is that these Thessalonians were seriously compromised by their surrounding culture. In Acts 17:21 we hear of some of the Athenians who loved to talk about the latest ideas but for whom the idea of manual labour would have been anathema. This 'Greek' culture may well have had a profound influence in places such as Thessalonica as well. For those who adopt this way of thinking, the spiritual becomes more important than the material or practical, and talking more important than action. Even within a Christian context, the thinking may have developed that redemption was good but creation was bad, that being passionately interested in Bible Study was what God wanted and spending time working with your hands was an irrelevance. Certainly we must view these people as 'brothers', as Paul specifically makes clear at the beginning and end of the section (see 3:6, 15), and so we must recognise that what happened to them could happen to us. If such a super-spiritual group had gathered, it would make sense of Paul's down-to- earth example of his own ministry. Specifically, if his ministry among the Thessalonians was a time when the Word of God spread rapidly (see 3:1 'just as it was with you'), then they needed to be reminded that this spiritual progress was achieved through Paul not being idle but through his labour and toil (see 3:7, 8). In other words, within Paul's ministry the spiritual and material, redemption and creation, words and works were all held together. Yet as he looks at this particular group in Thessalonica he can see that a gap has opened up. This may be why he considers that it is such a serious issue which needs to be graciously but firmly dealt with once and for all – hence the need not just to rebuke the minority but also the instructions to the majority about how to handle this difficult situation.

One final point on the background to this issue may shed light on why Paul views it with such seriousness. It concerns a brief consideration of the stress in these verses on his own example which they are to imitate (vv. 7-10). Back at the beginning, Paul was able to commend the Thessalonians through showing them that their faith in Christ was genuine. He did this by describing how they had not only received his message with joy but had also imitated him (see 1 Thess. 1:6). In other words, a genuine response to the gospel had been evidenced not only in receiving Paul's message but also through imitating his behaviour. Since that was the case we can perhaps understand the degree of concern that Paul now feels as he addresses the issue at 2 Thessalonians 3:6-15. They have not abandoned his message. Indeed he takes for granted that they will be willing to pray for its ongoing progress (see 3:1). However, some of them do appear to have abandoned his lifestyle and behaviour.

Though that in itself does not change the fact that they remain 'brothers' (see 3:6, 15), nevertheless it reflects on their real understanding of the impact that the gospel should have on their lives and it also would certainly have an impact on their ability to pass on the gospel to others. Back in 1 Thessalonians 1:7, 8, the gospel spread from Thessalonica through the message and the changed lives of the Thessalonians. If there was now a growing number of people in this church whose behaviour had not been shaped by the gospel, this would strike at the foundations of the purpose of the church to bring God's Word to the world (see 3:1). Such strong calls for the majority to keep away from the minority can be more readily understood once we recognise that ultimately Paul felt that this issue posed serious concerns for the health of the church and for its ability to pass on the gospel effectively through Word and lifestyle.

What was the remedy?

Following identification of the chiastic structure, we can see that Paul deals with the issue in three stages:

Keep away! (vv. 6, 14, 15)

Paul uses extremely strong language at the beginning and end of this section. The majority are commanded to act in a particular way and the effect is heightened by the appeal to the authority of the name of the Lord Jesus Christ (v. 6). Specifically the instruction is to keep away from the minority and not associate with them at all. The reason is because they are idle due to their failure to live according to the teachings which Paul had previously passed on to them.

The reason for not associating with them is that Paul wants the minority to feel ashamed of their conduct as a precursor, no doubt, to genuine repentance and the adoption of Paul's teaching.

The tenor of Paul's words appears to be very strident and confrontational, and yet the tone may well be loving as he longs for restoration. He refers to them as brothers and specifically notes that they should not in any sense be regarded as enemies. However, he clearly sees their behaviour as incredibly serious. To be told to keep away is suggestive of their behaviour being like a strong virus which might infect others and spread – in contrast to the Word of God spreading at 3:1! Persisting in sin and disobedience to God's Word is incredibly serious in God's eyes and the virus of God's Word being ignored has to be countered with strong words and actions.

Their rejection of God's Word which had been handed down through Paul ('the teaching/tradition you received from us') was clearly a rejection of God Himself. Further, it affected the harmony of the fellowship since it laid burdens (see 3:8 for Paul's testimony about his desire not to be a burden) on others who felt obliged out of love to provide for this group, which presumably must have caused some tensions. Finally, it affected the witness of the church, as can be seen by the reference at 1 Thessalonians 4:11, 12 where the strong inference was that the laziness of this group had caused a loss of respect for the church and the gospel amongst the surrounding community. For all these reasons Paul views their conduct as particularly serious. Sin comes in many forms and it doesn't have to be an obvious major breach of God's law for it to have profound consequences. Finally, to link in with what has been said previously, it should also be noted that the separation of creation and redemption is an incredibly serious theological error which does have profound consequences right across the board. As with marriage, what God has joined together must not be separated without very painful consequences. Their behaviour should have been in line with the message that they had received (see 1 Thess. 1:6) and the fact that it was not was a serious concern for the apostle. For all these reasons therefore, we can begin to see why Paul uses such strong language and advocates such decisive action.

Presumably the call to keep away and not associate with this group would have had the effect of withdrawing practical support from them. Through the shock of no longer being able to rely on the generosity of other believers, they would have recognised how dependent they had been and how much they had taken others for granted. Perhaps that would lead some to feel deeply ashamed of their inactivity which had resulted in them being a burden to others (see v. 14), which in turn may have led to their repentance. In any case it is clear from verse 15 that Paul's disciplinary action is with a view to restoration, being motivated out of love for the Lord and for them.

Keep following! (vv. 7-10, 13)

Moving in from the outside of the chiasm we arrive at Paul's positive teaching. It is not just that the majority must keep away (vv. 6, 14, 15) but also that they should continue to act in a way which demonstrates love to others (vv. 7-10, 13), which will also serve as a model to enable the minority to follow the correct path themselves (vv. 11, 12). This model comes from Paul himself. He is not content just to issue commands about how to live the Christian life since he has also modelled it on his own lifestyle. Indeed this short section has many links with 1 Thessalonians 2:7-12 where Paul described his labour, night and day, on behalf of the Thessalonians and his concern not to be a burden to anyone.

So Paul's encouragement is for them to keep following his own 'example' (v. 7) as a 'model' (v. 9) for their own behaviour. Specifically Paul demonstrated a willingness to provide for his own needs in order not to be a burden to others, even though he could have made legitimate demands for such assistance (v. 9). This model of sacrificial service and love is in itself a demonstration of the gospel of our Lord Jesus Christ who also served sacrificially. It therefore reveals the harmony within Paul's ministry. The Word of the Lord which he longed to spread (3:1) brought a message about the sacrificial love of a crucified Messiah who took our burdens. Similarly, the lifestyle of the messenger demonstrated sacrificial love which lifted burdens rather than imposed them. In other words, Paul's teaching and lifestyle were synchronised. His lifestyle supported his message. His works and words were in harmony, which had been the substance of his prayers for them at 2:17 (ESV). The gospel had come to the Thessalonians in work and Word (1 Thess. 1:5) and now they were to continue to follow Paul in every good work and word (2:17) as they held on to God's Word (3:6) and kept on imitating Paul's behaviour (3:7-10).

It is this example which Paul wishes to see developed in the Thessalonian church. Having painted a picture of his own example in 3:7-10, we also see him apply it directly to the church at 3:13 with his call that they should not tire in doing good (ESV 'good' is more accurate than NIV 'right'). Just as he did not tire in his sacrificial love for them, so they are not to tire in doing good. At this point it is worth recognising the significance of 'good works' within 2 Thessalonians. Of course, good works don't save anyone. Nevertheless, believers who have been saved by faith in Jesus Christ should demonstrate good works flowing out of their lives. So at 1:11 Paul speaks of 'every resolve for good and every work of faith'. (ESV) At 2:17, as part of the central motif of the letter, Paul prays that they would be established 'in every good work and word'. Now in a section where Paul constantly uses the word 'work' (see 3:8, 10, 11, 12 ESV), he speaks of not growing weary in doing good (3:13). If good works do not flow out from the life of a believer, it immediately raises concerns about how genuine the person's profession of faith is. Good works, therefore, are a sign of genuine faith in Christ (and see 1 Thess. 1:3).

Get working! (vv. 11, 12)

Having issued his directions (vv. 6, 14, 15) and provided a model of the correct way forward (vv. 7-10, 13) Paul now directly addresses the group who had been at the centre of his concerns. We already know something about them from 1 Thessalonians 4:11, 12 and 5:14. Now he gives us a little bit more information about them. In contrast to his own conduct (see 3:7), they were idle (NIV) or walked in idleness (ESV). Rather than being busy at work, Paul uses a pun to describe them as busybodies (and see also 1 Timothy 5:13, 14 for a similar situation that Paul had to deal with involving 'idleness'). Not only were they failing to work to provide for their own needs but through their disruptive conduct, they were also preventing others working. Rather than Paul's vision of Christians working to the glory of God (see 1:11, 12), they were simply living for themselves and for their own pleasure.

Throughout much of the Thessalonian correspondence Paul has sought to encourage (e.g. 1 Thessalonians 2:12; 3:2; 4:18; 5:11 and especially 2 Thessalonians 2:16,17 (NIV), and here he returns to this familiar theme through coupling it with the word 'command' to underline the gravity of the situation. The instruction is that they should settle down and get back to their work in order to provide for the practical necessities of life. Doing so would strengthen the reputation of the church within the community as well as the church family itself, by bringing unity and removing friction. Such a move may have been resisted by the minority as unspiritual but they needed to be reminded that God is a worker. The creation is full of His good works. As those originally made in His image and as those who are now being recreated in His image through the work of Christ, it is no surprise, therefore, that we should demonstrate this in embracing work as a godly activity. For the Thessalonian believers there is to be no secular/spiritual divide. All of life is to be lived to the glory of God.

Therefore, chapter 3 is a development which comes out of Paul's central prayer at 2:16-17 where he asks that they would all be strengthened and encouraged in every good work and word as they live now in readiness for the glorious hope of being with Christ forever. The presenting problem may seem mundane but beneath the surface Paul is aware of major theological issues which will determine the health

Part Four: Teaching 2 Thessalonians 3:6-15

and vitality of the Thessalonian church as it continues to develop even in the midst of persecution.

From text to message

Getting the message clear: the theme

+ Good works revealed in sacrificial and practical service should flow from our commitment to follow Christ.

Getting the message clear: the aim

+ The aim of this passage is to get Christians working hard to serve Christ and one another. Preaching or teaching on this passage should help in answering the following questions:
  + Why does Paul use such strong language over what appears to be, at first glance, a minor problem?
  + Why was Paul's lifestyle so important within his overall ministry?
  + What significance should good works play within the life of a believer?

A way in

It is very easy for us as believers to accept a secular/sacred divide. We are grateful for all that Christ has given us in the gospel and our focus is on enabling others to receive the good news for themselves. Prayer and the Word of God have become very precious to us and our focus is on getting to heaven. As a result, other things which relate to our physical life in the world can be relegated in our thinking. So work, food, family and the world around us become unimportant. Perhaps all of us struggle in this area. The gospel is absolutely vital and it is a good instinct which puts it at the very centre of our lives. Yet there is a danger that we can become super-spiritual and neglect the fact that God is the Creator who has created work as a good thing, even if it has been disrupted through the effects of the Fall. How we hold together both creation and redemption will be very important in determining our spiritual health.

The strength of Paul's commands is surprising. The times when you have to keep away from someone or must not associate with them are usually associated with the other person having a serious contagious disease or virus. For example, a friend comes back from a holiday abroad not feeling at all well. After some tests they are rushed into hospital and put into quarantine. You are not permitted to be in direct touch with them for fear that the virulent disease might spread and severely damage your own health. Paul viewed the conduct of this group within the Thessalonian church in this sort of light, which reveals how concerned he was about this situation.

Pointers to application

- We usually associate church discipline with serious doctrinal or moral error. Neither seems to be the case in this situation and yet the apostle is extremely exercised by the situation. Clearly therefore we need to learn from this chapter about why Paul is so concerned and this may have repercussions in our church life. Are we too laissez-faire about how we behave as believers? Are there times when we should be far more serious about the need for every member of the church family who professes faith in Christ to be living and working for the glory of God?

- In even thinking about the issue of church discipline from this chapter we need to exercise great sensitivity. Not only do we need, like Paul, to regard others as brothers and sisters rather than enemies but we must also be mindful of our own sinfulness. Paul is concerned about some who had departed from the tradition that he had handed down to them. Yet how easy it is for us to point the finger at some for their departure from obedience to God's Word when we ourselves are doing exactly the same thing in another area of Christian conduct. So whilst departing from God's Word in terms of our handling of money, we point the finger at those who have turned aside from biblical sexual ethics. We may be right to highlight the error of others but we need to be those who are quick to hear God's Word applied to our own hearts and quick to repent, otherwise our own behaviour will become hypocritical and Pharisaic.

- Paul's model of sacrificial service and love for others is very instructive. He does not want to be a burden to others and so he does everything he can to serve them. He is not only a model and example to the Thessalonians but also to us. Granted that there are reasons in life where through age, illness or circumstances, we may need to be dependent upon those around us, the Christian model is that we should give ourselves to others rather than become a burden through our own selfishness and inactivity.

- We constantly need to be clear about the place of good works within the Christian life. We need to stress that they have no value at all in enabling us to get right with God, and this will be especially important in our evangelism and our teaching to those who are not believers. However, we must also be clear that as believers we have been saved for a life of good works (e.g. Eph. 2:10). This is not an optional extra but a vital part of what it means to be a disciple of Christ and evidence of whether we are living under His Lordship.

- We will need to exercise great sensitivity in applying this passage to a situation where so many people are not in employment and would long to work. It would be easy to teach this passage in a way which simply loads up the guilt on those who are desperate to work. Partly this can be handled by referring to underlying attitudes, as many unemployed are eager to find a job. Partly the issue in the passage may be resolved by recognising a distinction between paid employment and work. Many of those who do not receive a salary, including mothers at home with children, are indeed working to the glory of God in a wonderfully sacrificial manner and are great examples of sacrificial service. So the Bible teacher will want to handle this material with care to avoid adding extra burdens on those who are already seeking to follow Christ faithfully.

- We need to explore where we have permitted a secular/ sacred divide to open up. All of life is to be lived for the glory of God. It may be that we need the emphasis which Paul provides in 2 Thessalonians. Our focus in the future should be on having assurance of seeing the glory of Christ. Yet our focus in the present is on living to glorify Christ now, whether in word or work.

Suggestions for preaching

Sermon 1: The application of the Word of the Lord (3:6-15)

- What was the issue?
- What is the remedy?
- Keep away! (vv. 6, 14, 15)
- Keep following! (vv. 7-10, 13)
- Get working! (vv. 11, 12)

Other preaching possibilities

Due to the fact that this section holds together with verse 6 and verses 14-15 bringing the same message at the beginning and end of the passage to reinforce each other, it would probably not be wise to divide up this passage further. However, it would certainly be possible to preach the whole chapter in one go as a way of picking up the key text at 2:17 which provides the agenda for all the following material.

Suggestions for teaching

Introducing the passage

- Can you think of situations where knowledge about something is not translated into action? To what extent does that seem to be the case with the group identified as 'idle' in this passage?

Understanding the passage
- How does Paul reveal the seriousness of the situation within verses 6, 14 and 15?
- What do we know about the group to whom Paul was opposed? (see 1 Thess. 4:11, 12; 5:14 and 2 Thess. 3:6,11)
- What example had Paul set for the believers? (see vv. 7 and 8 and 1 Thess. 2:7-12)
- In what ways were this group being a burden to the others in the church family? (see vv. 7 to 10)
- What is the instruction which Paul gives to these people at verses 11, 12?
- How do you think verse 16 fits in directly with verses 6-15 and especially verse 15?

Applying the passage
- Why do you think that this problem had arisen at Thessalonica?
- Do you think that there was anything within the surrounding culture which may have led them into this sort of behaviour? (e.g. Acts 17:21)
- What place should 'good works' have within the Christian life?
- How can we interpret this passage in situations where paid employment is virtually impossible to find?
- Pray for faithfulness in understanding God's words and applying them to the whole of life.
- In what ways can we close down any secular/sacred divide in our own lives?

Further reading

Introduction

This book is not a commentary in the sense of fully expounding the text of 1 and 2 Thessalonians and giving detailed justification for all the interpretations suggested. Nor is it a series of sermons on 1 and 2 Thessalonians. Rather, it gives guidance and encouragement to those who want to preach the message of these two letters, but are uncertain how to go about it. There are many commentaries on 1 and 2 Thessalonians, and the purpose of this brief chapter is to give guidance on some which I have found useful and stimulating, both in preaching through these books myself as well as in researching this book. It should be remembered that no single commentary will be helpful on every passage. However, commentaries can provide enormous assistance in helping us to understand the text accurately so that we can expound it effectively. Below are some suggestions with brief comments which may help in assessing whether or not a particular resource would be useful to you.

Commentaries on 1 and 2 Thessalonians

It is worth considering having one larger commentary which can assist with the finer details. I have benefited considerably from the New International Commentary on the New Testament (NICNT), *The First and Second Letters to the Thessalonians* by Gordon Fee (Grand Rapids, Eerdmans, 2008). It is very thorough but extremely readable and accessible. He enables the reader to see the flow of the letters so that the big picture is not lost in the detail. His introduction to 2 Thessalonians is particularly helpful in lucidly defending Pauline authorship – indeed he regards any other view of the letter as a 'forgery' and in a footnote says 'NT scholars tend to be offended by this term; but what other term, one wonders, is appropriate for someone's passing off as authentic a letter written in that person's name without his or her approval?' Fee is a very able Bible scholar and in my experience his commentaries are always worth consulting. Readers should note that this 2008 NICNT by Fee replaces an earlier NICNT volume by Leon Morris.

I was also assisted by the New Century Bible Commentary, *1 and 2 Thessalonians* by I. Howard Marshall (Grand Rapids, Eerdmans, 1983). Though smaller than Fee's commentary, there is plenty of helpful detail and analysis combined with judicious interpretations. At a slightly more popular level is the Bible Speaks Today book, *The Message of Thessalonians* by John Stott (Leicester, IVP, 1991). It has all the advantages of an exposition by

John Stott – clear, thoughtful and reliable. It is especially helpful for the preacher.

Clearly, it is not possible to read everything and decisions need to be made concerning how much time you have or can make available. The preacher will want to remember that, though understanding the text is absolutely vital, it is only one stage in the journey to preaching a message to God's people which will encourage, strengthen, teach, train, correct and rebuke. Sometimes one commentary will help to unlock the meaning whilst another will help you to think through issues of application.

If you have decided to embark on an expository series on 1 and 2 Thessalonians, my own suggestion would be to obtain Fee and Stott.

Audio Resources

Nowadays there are many opportunities to hear how others have preached 1 and 2 Thessalonians through CD, MP3 or the worldwide web. The Gospel Coalition website carries a large number of sermons on passages in 1 and 2 Thessalonians. Such sermons can be educative and provide good insights on applying the text. However, there is the danger that preachers will simply repeat what they have heard without wrestling with the biblical texts themselves. Only as the Word of God dwells richly within the preacher will it start to make an impact on the life of the preacher and in turn, on those who hear. As Paul states at 1 Thessalonians 2:13, our aim is that people will receive our preaching not just as the word of men 'but as it actually is, the word of God, which is at work in you who believe.'

PT Resources
Resources for Preachers and Bible Teachers

PT Resources, a ministry of The Proclamation Trust, provides a range of multimedia resources for preachers and Bible teachers.

Teach the Bible Series (Christian Focus & PT Resources)
The Teaching the Bible Series, published jointly with Christian Focus Publications, is written by preachers, for preachers, and is specifically geared to the purpose of God's Word – its proclamation as living truth. Books in the series aim to help the reader move beyond simply understanding a text to communicating and applying it.

Current titles include: *Teaching Numbers, Teaching Isaiah, Teaching Amos, Teaching Matthew, Teaching John, Teaching Acts, Teaching Romans, Teaching Ephesians, Teaching 1 and 2 Thessalonians, Teaching 1 Timothy, Teaching 2 Timothy, Teaching 1 Peter, Bible Delight, Burning Hearts, Hearing the Spirit, Spirit of Truth, Teaching the Christian Hope, The Ministry Medical* and *The Priority of Preaching.*

Practical Preacher series
PT Resources publish a number of books addressing practical issues for preachers. These include *The Priority of Preaching*, *Bible Delight*, *Hearing the Spirit* and *The Ministry Medical*.

Online resources
We publish a large number of audio resources online, all of which are free to download. These are searchable through our website by speaker, date, topic and Bible book. The resources include:

- sermon series; examples of great preaching which not only demonstrate faithful principles but which will refresh and encourage the heart of the preacher

- instructions; audio which helps the teacher or preacher understand, open up and teach individual books of the Bible by getting to grips with their central message and purpose

- conference recordings; audio from all our conferences including the annual Evangelical Ministry Assembly. These talks discuss ministry and preaching issues.

An increasing number of resources are also available in video download form.

Online DVD
PT Resources have recently published online our collection of instructional videos by David Jackman. This material has been taught over the past 20 years on our PT Cornhill training course and around the world. It gives step by step instructions on handling each genre of biblical literature.

There is also an online workbook. The videos are suitable for preachers and those teaching the Bible in a variety of different contexts. Access to all the videos is free of charge.

The Proclaimer

Visit the Proclaimer blog for regular updates on matters to do with preaching. This is a short, punchy blog refreshed daily which is written by preachers and for preachers. It can be accessed via the PT website or through www.theproclaimer.org.uk.

'Teaching' titles from Christian Focus and PT Resources

Teaching Numbers
ISBN 978-1-78191-156-3

Teaching Isaiah
ISBN 978-1-84550-565-3

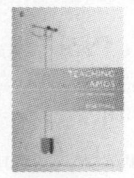

Teaching Amos
ISBN 978-1-84550-142-6

Teaching Matthew
ISBN 978-1-84550-480-9

Teaching John
ISBN 978-1-85792-790-0

Teaching Acts
ISBN 978-1-84550-255-3

Teaching Romans (1)
ISBN 978-1-84550-455-7

Teaching Romans (2)
ISBN 978-1-84550-456-4

Teaching Ephesians
ISBN 978-1-84550-684-1

Teaching 1 & 2 Thessalonians
ISBN 978-1-78191-325-3

Teaching 1 Timothy
ISBN 978-1-84550-808-1

Teaching 2 Timothy
ISBN 978-1-78191-389-5

Teaching 1 Peter
ISBN 978-1-84550-347-5

About the Proclamation Trust

We exist to promote church-based expository Bible ministry and especially to equip and encourage Biblical expository preachers because we recognise the primary role of preaching in God's sovereign purposes in the world through the local church.

Biblical (the message)
We believe the Bible is God's written Word and that, by the work of the Holy Spirit, as it is faithfully preached God's voice is truly heard.

Expository (the method)
Central to the preacher's task is correctly handling the Bible, seeking to discern the mind of the Spirit in the passage being expounded through prayerful study of the text in the light of its context in the biblical book and the Bible as a whole. This divine message must then be preached in dependence on the Holy Spirit to the minds, hearts and wills of the contemporary hearers.

Preachers (the messengers)
The public proclamation of God's Word by suitably gifted leaders is fundamental to a ministry that honours God, builds the church and reaches the world. God uses weak jars of clay in this task who need encouragement to persevere in their biblical convictions, ministry of God's Word and godly walk with Christ.

We achieve this through:

- PT Cornhill: a one year full-time or two-year part-time church based training course
- PT Conferences: offering practical encouragement for Bible preachers, teachers and ministers' wives
- PT Resources: including books, online resources, the PT blog (www.theproclaimer.org.uk) and podcasts

PT RESOURCES

JOSH MOODY &
ROBIN WEEKES

BURNING HEARTS

Preaching to the Affections

Burning Hearts

Preaching to the Affections

Josh Moody and Robin Weekes

Affection is often a neglected theme in our generation of Bible believing Christians. It has not always been so. Previous generations thought a great deal about the centrality of the heart in the Christian life and the need to preach to it. This book will prove a valuable resource as we learn about the place of the affections in our walk with Christ and in preaching Him to ourselves and others.

For some, this little book will be a healthy reminder; for others, it will revolutionise their preaching.

> D. A. Carson, Research Professor of New Testament
> Trinity Evangelical Divinity School, Deerfield, Illinois

It has not only convinced me of the importance of preaching to the affections, but has also inspired me to think that I must and can do this better.

> Vaughan Roberts, Rector of St Ebbe's Oxford
> and Director of Proclamation Trust

Messrs Moody & Weekes, with plenty of good sense, would encourage us preachers to reach the hearts of our listeners... Are they making a timely point? I think they are.

> Dick Lucas
> Formerly Rector of St Helen's Bishopsgate, London

Josh Moody is Senior Pastor of College Church in Wheaton, Illinois and Robin Weekes is Minister at Emmanuel Church, Wimbledon, London.

ISBN 978-1-78191-403-8

PT RESOURCES

JONATHAN GRIFFITHS

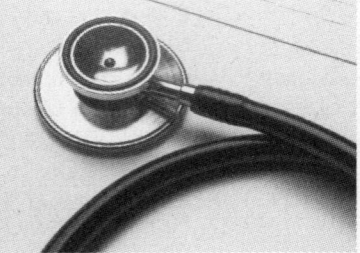

THE
MINISTRY
MEDICAL

A health-check from 2 Timothy

Ministry Medical
A Health check from 2 Timothy
Jonathan Griffiths

It is simple and straightforward: the format of questions and comments works very well, and makes the book very user-friendly. This book will help you fight the good fight, finish the race, and keep the faith. Highly recommended.

> Peter Adam, Vicar Emeritus, St Jude's Church,
> Carlton, Victoria, Australia

This wonderful book distills Paul's second letter to Timothy into 36 simple, searching and strategic questions for all who are seeking to preach the Word. Written with clarity and honesty, *The Ministry Medical* is practical and personal, reflective and refreshing. It is a magnificent resource and reminder for all in pastoral ministry and I highly recommend it.

> David Short, Rector of St John's, Vancouver, Canada
> and member of the Council of the Gospel Coalition

...here is God's check-up for any minister of the gospel today. These 36 brilliantly concise chapters call us back to the essential priorities of truly Christian ministry. This will be a book to take down from the shelf again and again, to pray through and to share with colleagues and lay leaders.

> Alasdair Paine, Vicar of St Andrew the Great, Cambridge
> and Trustee of Keswick Ministries

Jonathan Griffiths serves as tutor on the Cornhill Training Course. He previously served as assistant minister at Christ Church, WestbourneWimbledon, London.

ISBN 978-1-78191-232-4

Christian Focus Publications

Our mission statement –

STAYING FAITHFUL
In dependence upon God we seek to impact the world through literature faithful to His infallible Word, the Bible. Our aim is to ensure that the Lord Jesus Christ is presented as the only hope to obtain forgiveness of sin, live a useful life and look forward to heaven with Him.

Our Books are published in four imprints:

CHRISTIAN FOCUS
popular works including biographies, commentaries, basic doctrine and Christian living.

CHRISTIAN HERITAGE
books representing some of the best material from the rich heritage of the church.

MENTOR
books written at a level suitable for Bible College and seminary students, pastors, and other serious readers. The imprint includes commentaries, doctrinal studies, examination of current issues and church history.

CF4·K
children's books for quality Bible teaching and for all age groups: Sunday school curriculum, puzzle and activity books; personal and family devotional titles, biographies and inspirational stories – because you are never too young to know Jesus!

Christian Focus Publications Ltd,
Geanies House, Fearn, Ross-shire,
IV20 1TW, Scotland, United Kingdom.
www.christianfocus.com